Breaking THE
Rule OF
Cool

Break

ng THE

Rule OF

Cool

Interviewing and Reading
Women Beat Writers

Nancy M. Grace and
Ronna C. Johnson

University Press of Mississippi
Jackson

Photograph credits: ruth weiss, San Francisco, 1993,
© by William Westwick; Diane di Prima, © Sheppard
Powell; Brenda Frazer, courtesy of Brenda Frazer;
Joanne Kyger, © Donald Guravich; Hettie Jones,
courtesy of Hettie Jones; Joyce Johnson, courtesy of
Joyce Johnson; Ann Charters, 2003, © Nora Charters;
Janine Pommy Vega, 1998, © Pelver; Anne Waldman,
© Kai Sibley

www.upress.state.ms.us

The University Press of Mississippi is a member of the
Association of American University Presses.

12 11 10 09 08 07 06 05 04   4 3 2 1

∞

Library of Congress Cataloging-in-Publication Data

Breaking the rule of cool : interviewing and reading
women beat writers / Nancy M. Grace and
Ronna C. Johnson.
    p. cm.
Includes bibliographical references and index.
    ISBN 1-57806-653-0 (alk. paper) — ISBN 1-57806-
654-9 (pbk. : alk. paper)
    1. American literature—20th century—History and
criticism. 2. Beat generation. 3. Women and
literature—United States—History—20th century.
4. American literature—Women authors—History
and criticism. 5. Authors, American—20th century—
Interviews. 6. Women authors, American—Interviews.
I. Grace, Nancy McCampbell. II. Johnson, Ronna.
PS228.B6B74 2004

810.9'9287'09045—dc22   2003021200

British Library Cataloging-in-Publication Data
available

To Marianne, Marcia,
Carolyn, and Deb

To Stella and Pamela, Barbara,
Sandy and Eve, Katya, and
Deborah and Alice–sisters

Contents

Preface and Acknowledgments

Beat women writers have often found themselves positioned as women but not read as writers. Indeed, the Beat movement is notable for the considerable number of women writers who were part of the scene, but dismissed or overlooked, even as they wrote both privately and publicly. To recognize Beat women's lives as writers, *Breaking the Rule of Cool: Interviewing and Reading Women Beat Writers* presents literary criticism in tandem with the first collection of interviews with the women writers themselves. The book's combination of critical and historical methods and texts redresses the long eclipse of women Beats by studying both the writings and the writers in a single volume to provide a comprehensive introduction. The study shows that Beat's masculinist, Emersonian insistence on individual truth paradoxically included feminism in its reach, nurturing, if unevenly and inconsistently, female dissidents and artists—too often unseen exemplars of the Beat movement.

To make women Beat writers visible, this study engages in a paradoxical task of defining a category of Beat writing when, in a fundamental way, it is the nature of Beat writing and its dissident aesthetics to refuse labels and prefer contingency, just as did many of the writers, who engaged with other schools or writing scenes, such as the New York school, Black Mountain, or San Francisco Renaissance, simultaneous to their participation in the Beat movement. Several of the women writers reject the Beat category or resist their investiture as Beat writers, an understandable diffidence about a movement whose male adherents often perfunctorily ignored the women's writing and excluded them as viable literary innovators on the basis of their sex. Moreover, it is quintessentially beat for its female exemplars to refuse identification with the movement and generation; it's uncool to desire allegiance. And resistance is bound to occur in bringing into the academy such anti-academic writers as the Beats. Nevertheless, it is the function of literary historians and critics to make sense of literature's evolutions and developments by recognizing and defining schools, movements, and writers' aesthetic tendencies. And particularly in the recovery of overlooked and negated writers, grouping the Beat movement's female practitioners effects their visibility as artists and makes their literary expressions legible while in turn modifying the category, as women writers challenge received notions of Beat writing and aesthetics with, for instance, their works' incorporation of domestic life. If openness is a Beat movement signature, then reconsidering the category and expanding it to include its elided women writers is itself fundamentally a beat move.

Breaking the Rule of Cool, expanding on our earlier work on the three generations of women Beat writers, features nine of the best known ones from the Beat movement's inception to the present. The first Beat generation is represented by ruth weiss; the second by Diane di Prima, Joyce Johnson, Hettie Jones, Ann Charters, Joanne Kyger, Brenda Frazer (Bonnie Bremser); and the third by Janine Pommy Vega and Anne Waldman. The women's contributions to Beat literature and culture, and their relation as Beats to second-wave feminism are articulated in two sections of the book. The first,

"Mapping Women Writers of the Beat Generation," written by Ronna C. Johnson, elucidates literary and aesthetic processes by which the women deepened the refusals of Beat generation discourses, dissenting from the dissenters to make their own beat claim on Beat writing. The essay theorizes the women writers' contributions to the Beat movement, addressing their refusal to be silenced by assumptions about their fitness as subjects and authors of Beat writing, and about their literary strategies; it explores how women Beats broke the rule of Cool that confined their sex to the status of the silent bohemian "chick." The essay also assesses the women's use of the memoir genre to instantiate themselves as beat subjects, focusing on the way they brought the domestic or everyday to bear, in tandem with a brash feminism, on this famous brand of rebel writing. Johnson incorporates discussions of the nine featured writers as well as other significant Beat writers such as Elise Cowen, Lenore Kandel, Sheri Martinelli, and Helen Adam.

The second section of *Breaking the Rule of Cool* presents recent interviews with the nine featured writers. Six of the interviews were conducted by Nancy M. Grace and two by Johnson and Grace. The first parts of the Hettie Jones and Joyce Johnson interviews were first published in *Artful Dodge* 36/37, 1999, and are printed here in slightly shorter form. The interview with Diane di Prima was conducted by poet Tony Moffeit, and originally intended for the *Taos Review*; a substantial portion of that interview is published here for the first time. The interviews are preceded by Grace's essay, "Interviewing Women Beat Writers," which outlines the interviewers' goals for the interviews, the process undertaken to shape the interviews for publication, and major findings from the interviews. This essay demonstrates that the women Beat writers' artistic constructions of female Beat bohemia are related to the narratives of self they generated in the interviews. It elucidates the way their amalgamations of confession and history in their constructions of the female Beat writer's literary and social subjectivity produced complex narratives of the Beat generation. Each of the nine interviews is introduced by a headnote combining biographical data and critical discussion of the author's major artistic accomplishments, thus providing information about writers who are not all well known and about a body of literature that in some cases is out of print or not readily available. The juxtaposition of literary criticism with (auto) biography also illustrates the way that criticism can develop out of, in opposition to, and in harmony with a writer's self-account.

Breaking the Rule of Cool owes a debt for its existence as a book to the insightful interventions of Jennie Skerl who, as a reader for our first book, recognized what we did not: that the critical discussions and interviews that comprise this book could and should stand alone. We also owe a great debt to the women writers themselves, who permitted the interviews and trusted that we would make their lives and work the objects of respectful inquiry and study. Thanks are extended as well to our editor, Seetha Srinivasan, who recognized the value of the work and whose vision helped shape this volume. We are grateful to Maria Damon for her inspired and meticulous critique of our work; and to Susannah Driver-Barstow for her fine, judicious copyediting and acumen. We also acknowledge the generous support of the College of Wooster, which through its Henry Luce III Fund for Distinguished Scholarship provided funds for research and technical support. In particular, we thank our transcribers—Charlotte Wahl, Dale Catteau, and Kathie Clyde—for their patience, precision, and good humor. We are also grateful for Roger Collier's expert assistance with graphic design.

Ronna C. Johnson thanks her summer community in Provincetown, Massachusetts—Allene and Nancy Thibeault, Liza Marinello, Maggie Cassella. Also, colleagues at Tufts University, including Francie

Chew, Alan Lebowitz, and Jonathan Wilson. She is grateful to Maria Damon for her invaluable suggestions for deepening the "Mapping" essay; to Sandra A. Zagarell, who helped invent its method; and to Tim Hunt, for lending it his immense knowledge of Beat generation writing and his critical intelligence. She reserves most thanks for Girard Nakagawa-Mabe, paragon of cool, who makes home, wherever we are, the best place to think and write.

Nancy M. Grace thanks her College of Wooster students who provided enthusiastic and meticulous research support: Hallie Shapiro, Melissa Wagner, Kathryn Youther, Mary Nienaber-Foster, Emily Schadler, and Timothy Drouhard. Also her Wooster colleagues who have furnished stellar examples of scholarship and friendship: Carolyn Durham, Deb Shostak, John Gabriele, and Joanne Frye. Much of this work could not have been done without the love and support of Marianne Bowden, her sister, and Marcia Holbrook, long-time friend. Thanks are due as well to Hella Freud Bernays, who showed her what an interview could be. And to Tom Milligan, her husband, who is always there with a gentle reminder to "follow your bliss."

Breaking THE Rule OF Cool

You know I thought I've got work to do too sometimes. In fact I probably have just as fucking much work to do as you do. A piece of wood fell out of the fire and I poked it back in with my toe.

I am sick I said to the woodpile of doing dishes. I am just as lazy as you. Maybe lazier. The toe of my shoe was scorched from the fire and I rubbed it where the suede was gone.

Just because I happen to be a chick I thought.

. . . And what a god damned concession it was for me to bother to tell you that I was bugged at all I said to the back of his neck. I didn't say it out loud.

I got up and went into the kitchen to do the dishes. And shit I thought I probably won't bother again. But I'll get bugged and not bother to tell you and after a while everything will be awful and I'll never say anything because it's so fucking uncool to talk about it. And that I thought will be that and what a shame.

—DIANE DI PRIMA, from "The Quarrel" (1961)

Mapping Women Writers of the Beat Generation

—Ronna C. Johnson

I

ANATOMIZING THE BEAT GENERATION

> I think the point is, the men didn't push the women literally or celebrate
> them. . . . But then, among the group of people we knew at the time, who
> were the [women] writers of such power as Kerouac or Burroughs? Were
> there any? I don't think so.
>   Were we responsible for the lack of outstanding genius in the women
> we knew? Did we put them down or repress them? I don't think so. . . . [1]
>
> —ALLEN GINSBERG, *The Sunday Camera Magazine*

Feminist critics who have conducted the recovery of overlooked or
elided women writers in twentieth-century literature have identified
wide-ranging forms the neglect of these writers has taken, and
women Beats have been part of this literary landscape of omission
and exclusion.[2] Recognizing women Beat writers is significant for the
many reasons that fuel feminist recovery projects, but also for reasons unique to this group. First, women Beat writers have been in the

unusual and provocative situation of being the agents of their own recovery, writing themselves into Beat and postwar literary history through a spate of memoirs that records their claims to Beat culture, writing, and ethics. The writers' advancement of their own recovery is a self-reflexive phenomenon, a protofeminist act of subjectivity which connects twentieth-century first- and second-wave feminism. Second, women Beat writers produced a larger and more coherent body of work than is readily apparent. Much of this literature is out of print and difficult to find: for example, Joyce Johnson's *Come and Join the Dance* (1962), published under the name Joyce Glassman, or Brenda Frazer's *Troia: Mexican Memoirs* (1969), published under the name Bonnie Bremser. Equally seminal and also out of print are Lenore Kandel's *The Love Book* (1966), Janine Pommy Vega's *Poems to Fernando* (1968), and ruth weiss's *DESERT JOURNAL* (1977). The important manuscript of Elise Cowen's poems assembled from writings found at her death in 1962 was not prepared for publication by the poet and has not yet been published. The collection circulates through private connections and serendipity; it even remains unclear who holds the title to the work. Other women Beats' writing was suppressed by the writer, such as early poetry by Hettie Jones, and has been lost from the record; some work issued by lost small presses is unrecoverable. And, until recently, the few bibliographies of works by women Beat writers have been incomplete or inaccurate. Thus, to study women Beat writers has meant to track dispersed, uncollected, and sometimes unpublished sources, a body of work that in this disarray does not readily present itself as a coherent field of writing.

Finally, women Beat writers unsettle the categories of Beat writing and culture. They entered the Beat movement and deployed beat[3] on their own terms, instrumentally augmenting and in other ways modifying signature discourses and tropes from the more familiar lines pursued by the male exemplars. Thus, a revision of Beat history is required to comprehend the movement's full field in light of the variations wrung by its subaltern women. As a marginalized group within an always already marginalized bohemia, women Beat writers are a literary cohort colonized by the Beat generation's iconic public image. Yet the enormous, undervalued productivity of this underground of female artists suggests that the hipster code of silence, the women's fidelity to family, and even their entrapment in stereotype provided cover for them to develop despite prejudices against female literary expression.

The literature produced by the canonical male Beat writers has always assumed the presence of women Beats by the refusal to recognize them. They have not been absent, but elided, and their denied presence has left immutable traces in Beat discourse and literature— the silent "girls" in black—that remain to be excavated. That is, women Beats have been fundamental to and inextricable from the literary and cultural discourses, communities, and narratives which male Beat writers fronted, but they have been Beat constituents by the paradox of their manifest elision. This status is captured in Lucien Carr's dismissive nicknames for the poet Elise Cowen, "Ellipse" and "Eclipse" (Johnson, *Minor Characters* 130), which convey the cipher's ineradicable (in)visibility and provide a trope for the contradiction that Beat women's status exposes. The marginalization of women undermines the Beat generation's myths of rebellion, its cherished self-image as "dragonslayers of hypocrisy,"[4] contradicting its claims to antihegemonic status. Recognizing women Beat writers and restoring their writing to the movement confirm the hypothesis that phenomena that have been denied a history are nevertheless constitutive of the discourses that efface them. In Foucauldian terms, this means that a Beat discourse could not be produced or perceived as a unitary body without the disqualified and discontinuous knowledges in the disavowed texts by women Beats.

The gender premises effectively defining the Beat writer as male and the woman Beat as cipher are evident in the construction of the literary community that was instrumental to the advance and coherence of the Beat movement. That homogeneous community, predominantly white and male, was inimical to women's artistic emergence. Speciously blaming women for their own negation and eclipse, Allen Ginsberg assumed that a woman writer really worth developing would have been nurtured in the group. As he has suggested, the "strong woman writer who could hold her own" (Peabody 1) should have been able to shoulder her way into the group, which Joyce Johnson depicted as an inhospitable "boy gang" (*Minor Characters* 83). Her notion of the closed "boy gang" fits the way male Beat writers defined themselves and have been identified by virtue of individuals' lasting association in a loose but palpable confederacy in postwar arts communities on both coasts. This association has been mapped in journals and anthologies, such as the canon-making *New American Poetry* (1960), edited by Donald M. Allen, which aimed to define an "almost completely uncharted field" (xiv). Organizing the anthology by the movements and schools so important to launching the new American writers, Allen identified much overlap among Black Mountain, San Francisco, Beat, and New York school poets and poetics. But regardless of the uncharted way and the often obscure writing, the prohibition against women writers was tightly observed in the anthology. Of its forty-three entries only four were women: Helen Adam, Madeline Gleason, Barbara Guest, and Denise Levertov; hardly, in Johnson's idea, a "*girl gang*" (*Minor Characters* 85). Indeed, women writers contemporaneous with Levertov et alia who remained linked to Beat, such as ruth weiss, suffered from its indifference and neglect, suggesting the material value of the men's tribal ethics of mutual support, which, for instance, nurtured and helped to publish the minor poets Peter Orlovsky and Carl Solomon, but not Elise Cowen.

But if it seemed to Ginsberg that there were no women writers of "such power as Kerouac or Burroughs" (Peabody 1), it is because such women were unimaginable given Beat's gendered discourses and discursive practices of exclusion. Women Beat writers were marginalized by the men's premises of female silence (Kerouac, "Origins" 362), centerlessness (Holmes, *Go* xvii), and essentialized darkness. Gary Snyder was puzzled by women poets: while he could understand "what is involved in the psychology of male poets," he did not "know *what* applies in the psychology of female poets," like Freud who could not tell what women wanted and theorized them as the dark continent. Snyder appropriated woman's ineffable "dark side" to serve male poets, assigning it to ministering to "the line of magic that produces poetry" that men write; and, in his view, since a woman innately embodies the "negative side," only if "of her own nature, [she] has a dark side" herself might she "also be creative" (Geneson 80). Ginsberg's certainty that women Beats' neglect resulted from their own insufficiency and Snyder's mystifying essentializing of female energy ("The womb is the gate to the tomb" [Geneson 81]) typify the movement's cavalier, literal erasure of its women writers, miring Beat in an immaturity of "lifestyle" stereotype, iconographic cliché, and hipster sensation.

Complicating the women writers' recognition is the considerable divergence in their proximities to Beat bohemia and their practices of Beat aesthetics. Consider the deviations among ruth weiss and her performance-based spontaneous jazz poetics; Joyce Johnson and her "cool" literary discourse for disruptive "hot" energies (Ronna C. Johnson, " 'And then she went' " 84–85); Diane di Prima and her Digger politics of revolutionary, mystical, vernacular poetics; and Janine Pommy Vega and her abject romantic devotion in *Poems to Fernando*. Yet despite these differences, most engage in formal innovation and experimentation, and even in its diversity, their writing is marked by shared concerns. It tends to the personal and confessional, recounting lived experiences and passions. It tends to hybridize and modify traditional forms and genres, rewriting myths and traditional histories. It tends to challenge and interrogate assumptions about women, gender, and relations between the sexes, and asserts a corrected vision. All women Beat writers express a rebellious, antiestablishment critique of women's assigned place and value in patriarchy, and this gendered emphasis is the radical distinction by which Beat literature is amended by its female practitioners. Their writing exemplifies Rita Felski's (admittedly broad) definition of feminist literature: "all those texts that reveal a critical awareness of women's subordinate position and of gender as a problematic category, however this is expressed" (14).

Three generations of women Beat writers are apparent, a structure which clarifies the longevity of the movement and the continuity of its influences.[5] The list of women writers comprising Beat's three generations in this discussion is not exhaustive. Making a canon of women Beat writers has been a vexed matter because, although the canon can be fixed by historical parameters, its makeup is contingent on the vision of the canon maker.[6] The three generations of women Beat writers correspond to the well-known male writers' first and second generations, and stretch beyond into a third. First-generation Beat writers male and female were born in the 1910s and 1920s. Among Beat writing's progenitors are Madeline Gleason (1903–1979), Helen Adam (1909–1992), Sheri Martinelli (1918–1996), ruth weiss (1928–), and Carol Bergé (1928–). These writers were contemporaneous with Jack Kerouac (1922–1969), Ginsberg (1926–1997) and William S. Burroughs (1914–1997), and, like them, part of the generation whose lives encompassed the traumas of World War II. As artists they worked to revise or escape academic and traditional literary models, such as Adam's manipulations of the ballad form; as

Beat bohemians, they developed innovative literary expressions to fit their post-Hiroshima, post-Auschwitz cold war era, as in weiss's jazz-based street modernisms; as protofeminists they struggled to shape female literary subjectivity, as in Martinelli's manifesto denouncing patriarchy.

Literature of the nascent Beat movement displayed pivotal connections to and departures from experimental modernisms, as well as correlations to and critiques of literary theories promoted by Black Mountain and New Critical schools. Moreover, Beat writing emerged contemporaneously and overlapped with several underground literary schools and movements. In 1957—the pivotal Beat generation year in which *On the Road* was published—Adam started The Maidens, an eccentric, insular San Francisco poetry and performance troop antecedent to and contiguous with the San Francisco Renaissance and the Beat movement; Gleason as well as Eve Triem, James Broughton, Robert Duncan, and Jess participated in this arts coterie, which fostered experimentation, collaboration, and the mixing of genres. In summer 1957, the Spicer-Duncan Sunday afternoons devoted to "lyrically conscious" poetry reached an apex that included John Wieners, George Stanley, James Broughton, Snyder, and Joanne Kyger; there were "mergings and overlaps" in this group of new San Francisco poets with established Beat writers (Ellingham and Killian 106–7). Around this time, Jane Bowles (1917–1973) and Denise Levertov (1923–1997) exemplified the characteristic stylistic liminality of early Beat writing, even as their work ultimately diverged from it, with Bowles inventing a still underestimated esoteric narrative modernism, and Levertov a formalist poetics amalgamating the sacred, the everyday, and the political. Although aesthetic and cultural discontinuities with the Beat movement account for their ultimate disaffiliations from it, Bowles and Levertov are nevertheless visible in accounts of its advent. They illustrate the speculative interaction of women writers with the Beat movement and, by the ways in which their works depart from Beat writing's confessional spontaneity, they clarify the character and function of its distinctive poetics.

Progenitive women writers such as Adam, weiss, and Martinelli remained in the Beat movement or on the marginal turf of the literary avant-garde. Poet, ghost-tale writer, and dramatist Helen Adam enjoyed cult status among Beat and San Francisco Renaissance writers for her embodiment and poeticizing of the weird and the uncanny. Adam's appropriation and reconfiguration of the traditional ballad form challenges the genre to formal as well as substantive modification; then, too, Adam's ballad-style rhymed poems tartly spell an end to women's subjugation to patriarchal tyranny. "Apartment on Twin Peaks" wickedly skewers the banalities of marriage: "I remember, when the moon shines clear / How I'd whisper in my husband's ear / Like a dentist saying 'Open wider' / 'Don't you want to be a good provider?'" (Knight 13–14). Alternatively, the elegiac "Margaretta's Rime," depicting a caged prostitute, prefigures the trapped wife of Andrea Dworkin's theory of intercourse for women under male dominance. The poet assumes the persona and perspective of an Amsterdam prostitute displaying herself (a "spangled garter my only clothing") in the city's red light district windows, a "tourist trifle / For sale in this famous town" (Knight 14). Its tribute to the woman's sacrifice ("the dead heart in my breast") is feminist, rather than witchy. Just so, Adam's verses precede second-wave feminist consciousness, but not vengeful awareness of gender's burdens for women.

There was apparently little overlap or cross-fertilization between first- and second-generation women Beat writers. But one instance of generational recognition and transfer occurred in 1955, when Diane di Prima encountered Sheri Martinelli while visiting Ezra Pound at St. Elizabeth's Hospital in Washington, D.C.; during her sojourn, di Prima, the fledgling poet, stayed with Martinelli, the famed bohemian (di Prima, *Pieces* 198). Pound's acolyte and maybe his mistress, Martinelli was a model, painter, and writer who commanded a hipster style so iconic that she was represented as its prototype in William Gaddis's first novel, *The Recognitions* (1955), and in Anatole Broyard's posthumous memoir of Greenwich Village in the 1950s, *When Kafka Was the Rage* (1993). Martinelli wrote herself into Beat literary history with "Duties of a Lady Female," a simultaneously protofeminist and antifeminist prose poem she composed for Pound that described aspirations of and obstacles for adventurous bohemian women. Playing on stereotypes of female duplicity, the parodic verses attack yet also inscribe anti-woman impulses, reinstating patriarchal dicta of female competitiveness for and subservience to men, the "duties" that reduce women to "lady females." While the form and style of "Duties of a Lady Female," which first appeared in 1959 in the third issue of Martinelli's *Anagogic & Paideumic Review*, are reminiscent of "Howl," its gender focus and satire anticipate second-generation women Beat writers. Therefore, di Prima was the ideal audience for Martinelli's manifesto, just as 1966 was the ideal moment of feminist incipience for her republication of it in the *Floating Bear* newsletter (no. 32, 411–13) (Moore 31–36).

The largest and most cohesive cohort of women Beat writers occurred in the movement's second generation. Directly influenced by seminal works of Kerouac, Ginsberg, and Burroughs, the second Beat generation consisted of such male writers as Philip Whalen (1923–2002), Lew Welch (1926–1971), Ted Joans (1928–2003), Snyder (1930–), Gregory Corso (1930–2000), Michael McClure (1932–), and LeRoi Jones/Amiri Baraka (1934–). The women writers in this second generation, born in the 1930s, and so a decade or more younger than first generation Beats, faced male Beat obliviousness to and/or prejudices against their capacities as writers and rebels. Writers of this generation include Joanna McClure (1930–), Lenore Kandel (1932–), Elise Cowen (1933–1962), Diane di Prima (1934–), Hettie Jones (1934–), Joanne Kyger (1934–), Joyce Johnson (1935–), Ann Charters (1935–), and Brenda Frazer (Bonnie Bremser; 1939–). These writers produced a distinctive body of Beat literature—as, for example, that of di Prima, Kyger, and Johnson—or important individual pieces that advanced Beat aesthetics, such as works by Cowen, Kandel, and Frazer. This generation also boasts a singular Beat exemplar, the scholar Charters, who wrote important literary histories—notably her groundbreaking 1973 biography of Kerouac, with which she began building a canon of Beat writing—and assembled several influential anthologies that have given coherence to Beat as a movement in the secondary literature.

Charters's critical work to explore and demarcate a Beat canon has been distinguished by standards that she has subjected to incessant revision over the thirty years since she published *Kerouac: A Biography*, continually opening the Beat movement for review and expanding her assessments to include greater numbers of women writers. She was the first to institutionalize women writers in the Beat canon when she edited *The Beats: Literary Bohemians in Postwar America* (1983) and included seven women, some of whom were notable for obscure work, such as Frazer and Kandel. This foundational research provided the first reliable scholarly study of women Beat writers, as well as legitimated their artistic departures from the techniques used by male Beat writers, who were also beneficiaries of Charters's research. By virtue of her position as a female intellectual in academe, as well as her position as a bohemian intellectual among Beat writers and, given the Beat generation's skepticism of academia and of women, Charters is an anomaly. But she marks out an exceptional way for outrider thinking and writing to go: her beat move is seditious, through and into the literary and academic establishment.

The work of second-generation women Beat writers is marked by a radical critique of traditional literary genres and forms that have been based on women's subordination, such as the reformulation of the road tale effected by Johnson and Frazer, or the revision of classical myth undertaken by Kyger and di Prima, or Charters's application of credentialed academic discourses and methodologies to the study of outrider writers. Women Beats' critique, which amends literary forms, narrative patterns, and gendered assumptions, is emblematic of the writers' position in the vanguard of the second-wave women's movement. That the Beat movement claims a disproportionately large number of female practitioners among contemporaneous literary schools suggests that Beat culture was nevertheless somehow hospitable to women in the artistic and cultural avant-garde, even if it did not promote women's agency in an intentional, protofeminist sense. While the Beat generation engaged in and perpetrated the sexism of postwar culture, women Beats rejected the 1950s "feminine mystique," a significant move toward the emergence of the second-wave women's movement. However, Betty Friedan, no fan of "bearded, undisciplined beatnikery"(285), saw Beat not as a movement intervening in mainstream American ideologies of conformity and gender conservatism, but as another product of American culture's iniquitous sexism: she saw "retreat into the beat vacuum" as the defeat of a fifties woman by patriarchal culture (74). While not all women Beats read *The Feminine Mystique* when it was published in 1963, they disproved Friedan's skepticism, for they saw and rejected the repressive gender codes she documented, and their dissent against the female conformity expected in the fifties helped to seed second-wave feminism (Meyerowitz; Brienes).

Second-generation women Beats are protofeminist writers, artists whose anticipations of sixties feminism clarify the liminal interval in the twentieth century between first- and second-wave women's movements. Notably escaping the brunt of the Depression and World War II, this generation, considerably younger than most of the men, maintained a maverick independence from their Beat literary models. Second-generation women Beats benefited from advantages of the postwar era, material contingencies that allowed white bohemian women enough social freedom and access to institutions of power to contravene gender repressions. Nearly all second-generation women Beats matriculated in and attended (although often dropped out of) college; in this they partook of a privilege enjoyed by Beat men, the entitlement to scorn and reject establishment institutions that is instrumental to the formation of Beat movement aesthetics.[7] Women's postwar access to secondary education was a pivotal determinant in the emergence of women Beat writers, since it made available to them the status requisite for embracing the Beat generation's Thoreauvian nonconformity and noncompliance, its penchant for downward mobility, to say nothing of its signature sexual freedom. As the women's works attest, sexual freedom—the capacity to take at will lovers both male and female—is at the core of Beat female subjectivity, as well as Beat women's writing, although it was not as great as that in the subsequent era of the sexual revolution.

But the sexual revolution could not have been demanded and achieved without the attainment of the sexual frontier conquered by experimental Beat bohemian women, as exemplified by Joyce Johnson's renegade development as novelist. In 1962, when Johnson was twenty-six, out of college, and publishing her first novel, *Come and Join the Dance*, the first Beat generation novel by and about a woman, Kerouac was forty and *On the Road* was already legendary; Ginsberg was thirty-six and famous for *Howl*; and Burroughs was forty-eight and well beyond *Naked Lunch*. Although Johnson had planned and begun *Come and Join the Dance* before meeting Kerouac and before *On the Road*'s advent, she was writing her novel when the male Beats were exerting formidable influence in avant-garde art circles (*Minor Characters* 74–77). Yet, as in her portrayal of women in bohemia, Johnson refused to suspend her own aesthetic and philosophical influences, directions, and innovations to follow theirs (Grace, "Women of the Beat Generation" 112–14). Her departures from Beat generation and "classic" canonical models mark Johnson's beat move: her contribution to Beat writing was to foreground and heroize female bohemians in innovative narrative form, a move consistent with women Beats' anticipation of the sexual revolution (Ronna C. Johnson, "'And then she went'").

A corollary group of women writers also typifies conditions constraining and defining the experiences of women who wrote and lived in the second generation of the Beat movement: Brigid Murnaghan (1930–), Margaret Randall (1936–), Rochelle Owens (1936–), Diane Wakoski (1937–), and Barbara Moraff (1940–). Owens, Moraff, and Wakoski, as well as Carol Bergé, constituted the poetic body in the oddly titled book *Four Young Lady Poets* (1962), published by Totem Press and Corinth Books and edited by LeRoi Jones and Eli Wilentz. Grouping the poets as women expresses, as the book's condescending title suggests, a contradiction that the presence of women writers in the Beat movement seemed to engender: an inclusion of women writers—the diminutive "young lady poets"—that is achieved by segregating them in their own venue, a move reminiscent of the separate-but-equal doctrine found to be unconstitutional in 1954 in *Brown v. Board of Education*. Such segregation exemplifies the faux egalitarianism effecting the eclipse of women Beat writers. The women writers of the second Beat generation were usually not so obviously sidelined as those in the first, but they were nevertheless discounted through presumptions of their inferiority, such as those effecting their ghettoization in a subculture as "young ladies" among men, "ellipses" among poets.

The transition from Beat to hippie counterculture in the 1960s was encompassed by Beat's second and third generations. While the civil rights movement had a direct influence on counterculture activism, the Beats provided the hippie community with a dissenting style of conduct (Gitlin). Lenore Kandel focused these energies in expressions of women's sexual desire; her psychedelicized poetics served revolutionary notice that the silent Beat "chick" had evolved into the hippie adept of "holy erotica" (Knight 281). Kandel's first broadsides were distinctively of the Beat generation; somber street elegies such as "First They Slaughtered the Angels" and "Junk/Angel" bear the distinctive chanting rhythms and hip street smarts, the anti-authority contentiousness, associated with the male Beats. Kandel brought her Beat perspectives and poetics to the Haight-Ashbury hippie counterculture and merged the two in *The Love Book*, which celebrates the sixties Love Generation through an Eastern-mysticism-inflected, LSD-influenced, psychedelicized poetics of sex and love (Ronna C. Johnson, "Lenore Kandel's *The Love Book*"). Moreover, repeating the primal Beat scene of the seizure of *Howl and Other Poems* in San Francisco in 1956 on grounds of obscenity, *The Love Book* was confiscated and subjected to trial in the same city a decade later. Its legal imbroglios and free-sex, mystical lyrics punctuated the hippie emergence just as "Howl" had announced the Beat ten years before.

However, in Kandel, the Beat generation's continuing challenge to mainstream repressions was effected through female poetic agency, evincing women Beats' prominence with the rise of the women's movement. At the Human Be-In of January 1967, Kandel was the only female speaker to address the historic Gathering of the Tribes; while Timothy Leary advised "turn on, tune in, drop out" and Ginsberg chanted for peace, she read the banned verses of *The Love Book*

(Perry), whose erotic lyrics exalt the sexual revolution from the position of the female lover in the cosmic act of love. The poems daringly textualize the sexual pleasure of the liberated, uninhibited hippie woman, delineating a love aesthetic that, both celebrated and banned, attests to women's fraught place in the era between 1960 and 1970, after the Pill came in and before feminism took off. An icon of bold, free-speaking femininity, Kandel marked the intersection of Beat and Haight-Ashbury countercultures, in the mid-sixties moment of their simultaneity, on the cusp of the women's movement just then gathering momentum in New York and San Francisco in the wake of *The Feminine Mystique*.

The third generation of the Beat movement was born during the Second World War, endured the fifties, and came of age in the sixties. While the second generation of women Beat writers anticipates the second-wave women's movement of the late 1960s and early 1970s, the third generation clarifies the Beat movement's continuity with the hippie counterculture and progressive activist movements, and realizes its feminist inclinations. In contrast to the first and second Beat generations, third-generation Beat writers, evincing greater equality between the sexes, are a mixed group, and can be said to include Ed Sanders (1939–), Bob Dylan (1941–), Jerry Garcia (1942–1995), Lou Reed (1944–), Patti Smith (1946–), Lester Bangs (1948–1982), and Laurie Anderson (1950–). Two other women writers who are self-evidently of the Beat movement, Janine Pommy Vega (1942–) and Anne Waldman (1945–) worked, lived, and formed a degree of spiritual or political common cause with male Beat writers. Contemporaneous with the emergence of second-wave feminism, the writing of the third generation takes women's freedom and autonomy as necessities, but represents and speaks from the midst of the feminist struggle, rather than beyond or after it. Pommy Vega and

Waldman identify with sixties countercultures; their early poetics express aesthetics and idioms distinctive to their Vietnam War era. Yet they looked to living Beat generation writers for influence and inspiration.

Both Pommy Vega and Waldman were included in Beat bohemia and literary circles from the start. They arose not despite of but from within established literary schools and communities, Beat as well as contiguous cultural and literary affiliates in New York and California. Pommy Vega was mentored by Cowen, Herbert Huncke, Orlovsky, and Ginsberg; her first collection, *Poems to Fernando*, was published in the City Lights Pocket Poet Series (no. 22, 1968). Waldman was mentored by Ginsberg, whom she was flattered to say regarded her as his "spiritual wife" (Waldman and Schelling 39), but also by a host of other writers in and around the New York Lower East Side Beat scene, including Ted Berrigan, Ron Padgett, and Ed Sanders, as well as New York school poet Frank O'Hara. Self-publishing her first book, *Giant Night*, in 1968 in the New York–based small press Angel Hair Books, which she founded with Lewis Warsh, Waldman exemplified the do-it-yourself ethos of Beat publishing. Part of late Beat's bohemian circles, Waldman and Pommy Vega are consciously feminist and countercultural writers. They have looked to maternal or female deities for spiritual guidance and inspiration (Pommy Vega, *Tracking* 10) and to women writers for models (Charters, "Anne Waldman" 530–31). Reflecting a fusion of Beat and hippie ethics and aesthetics, both have been practicing Buddhists, adventurers in drug culture experiments, advocates for environmental safety and ecological conservation, proponents for nuclear disarmament and opponents of nuclear energy, and writers involved in shamanistic praxis, New Left–New Age political activism, and poetry teaching. Their work departs from and augments Beat poetics, infusing it with their sixties generation's attitudes and styles, and bringing it to a further level of vision and utterance quite as

decisively as the Beat movement's first-generation originators transformed modernist existential alienation with postmodern play.

II

THE ART OF WRITING IN BETWEEN

> [I]n spite of a persistent fiction, we never write on a blank page, but always
> one that has already been written on.
> —MICHEL DE CERTEAU, *The Practice of Everyday Life*

All three generations of women Beat writers are innovators and practitioners of the experimental techniques that distinguish Beat writing, and understandings of the movement are undermined without
taking their work into account. The integration of writing by women
into topographies of Beat literature defamiliarizes its masculinist
discourses, exposes gendered assumptions about the feminine, and
deconstructs its literary representations of women, showing ways in
which male-authored Beat literature deliberately and inaccurately
restricted women to "everyday practices," and the way the women
writers parlayed these gendered restrictions into a Beat art of their
own, playing out a strategy that Michel de Certeau has named "an art
of being in between."

Women Beat writers have deployed elision and invisibility to serve
their art, by this use subverting from within the literary and cultural
discourses that colonize them. The paradox of women Beats' erased
presence is crystallized in Joanne Kyger's poem "Poison Oak for
Allen." Evidently referring to Ginsberg, the poem captures the peculiar omissions and excisions in the historical record that typify Beat's
negation of its women writers. Discursively ordered on the poet's
absence, the poem makes use of the material that Beat literature has

assigned her; its witty coherence contradicts male Beat myths of female silence and centerlessness, foregrounding the ineradicable invisibility of the poet's status as a gendered object:

> *Here I am reading about your trip to India again,*
> *with Gary Snyder and Peter Orlovsky. Period.*
> *Who took the picture of you three*
>
> *With smart Himalayan backdrop*
> *The bear?*
>
>

September 2, 1996

>
>

(Kyger, *Again* 102)

Kyger refers here to her 1962 trip to India with the aforementioned poets, commemorated in her newly republished journals, *Strange Big Moon: The Japan and India Journals: 1960–1964*. Slighting Beat's gate-keepers via the title's implied curse, the poet torments the oblivious Ginsberg for his continued disregard of her presence and, it is implied, her literary significance. The poem as a Beat text avenges the poet's exclusion by inscribing her inclusion in her complaint, smartly embodying, *pace* Linda Hutcheon, the postmodern double subvert/install maneuver that characterizes much writing by women Beats, whose works appropriate and transform Beat poetics and ethics to inscribe their own subjectivity. For, at once subverting male-authored traditions about women and their lives, and installing women's expressions of female agency and consciousness, it is literature that shows what's there when male hegemony is pushed aside.

The writings of women Beats contest both stereotypes of white women in the 1950s—that they were devoted to hearth and husband—and those of female bohemians—that they were women silent in black. Subjectivity was not an outcome intended for women, who, by both mainstream and Beat notions of gender, were regarded as ineligible for it by virtue of their presumed—and naturalized—inferiority, their essentialized condition as objects—"wife," "chick," "Ellipse." Their works represent women asserting autonomy from fifties gender roles, as well as from the Beat generation's male-defined requirements and dominion, by appropriating, transforming, or correcting Beat discourses to inscribe their own subjectivity, as in the Kyger poem. Women Beat writers functioned in, produced, and expressed Beat ideas in literary and cultural discourses that registered their conformance to Beat codes and norms—the very ones that served to efface them—while using those forms in pursuit of ends extraneous to the dominant Beat ethos. Women Beat writers dissented from gender assumptions of Beat and mainstream cultures; making their own use of the Beat aesthetics and culture by which they were colonized, they developed a subaltern's recourse, an art of being in between.

On Writing "Beat" and Entering the Beat Movement

Women Beat writers working to inscribe female agency confronted and maneuvered the uncertainty and diversity of the term "beat," whose plurality as multi-valenced signifier and trope enhanced opportunities for developing versions of Beat culture and literature that did not enjoin women's eclipse. A contingent signifier that was also, as Kerouac noted, elaborated into a discourse or set of manners ("Origins" 363), "beat" was not coherent and unified, and did not emerge from a process shaping it for hegemonic purposes by the movement. Terms used to explain "beat" are so diverse that the enterprise has yielded a collection of sometimes contradictory fragments, signifiers ever exchanging for other signifiers in a Baudrillardean disequilibrium that has been opportune for those on the Beat movement's margins, such as its women writers. There is Kerouac's range of "beat's" meanings, from "down and out" to "sympathetic" to "beatitude" ("Origins" 363–64); John Clellon Holmes's "spiritual quest" ("Philosophy" 118); Herbert Huncke's strung-out futility and anxiety (Schafer 9); Norman Mailer's "impoten[ce] in the world of action" (478) and jazz as orgasm (482); and LeRoi Jones's "reaction against" ("Beat Generation" 472). Although nearly all these concepts of and synonyms for "beat" are apparently gender neutral, they, as well as the discourses made from them, had the effect of maintaining women's objectification and marginalization.

Women Beat writers did not weigh in on the meaning of "beat" during the period of its salience. They were dismissed in favor of the sensational, sometimes salacious "everyday" narratives they could contribute to Beat literature—tales of madness and suicide, unregulated sexuality, reproductive roulette, domestic servitude. The roles they performed—wife, mother, lover, muse—obscured them as artists; nevertheless, women entered the Beat movement, and even if they did not elaborate on it explicitly, their writing contains, engages, and modifies "beat." Choosing aspects or fragments of "beat" that fit their material realities and political commitments, women Beat writers exploited it to their own purposes while appearing to follow the Beat code of Cool. They revised the roles Beat culture assigned them to articulate alter-visions of the feminine, deploying what de Certeau terms "make-shift creativity"—what is left to those who are colonized by a dominant discourse—to compose a Beat "antidiscipline" (xiv). Women Beats, taking opportunities afforded by its fragmented character, produced "beat" as an alternative culture, aesthetic, rhetoric, system of representation and iconography, and politics. This alternative praxis—a subversion from within—exemplifies the power of the subordinated to achieve agency by "metaphoriz[ing] the dominant order" (de Certeau 32). By making "beat" function in another register, women Beat writers constructed themselves as subjects in a complicated move in which they implemented the discourses that assimilated them while still remaining outside, eclipsed.

In the many literary experiments women Beat writers have undertaken, the domestic or the everyday provides the material and the context of the entry into and transformation of "beat," and, consequently, Beat literature. The postwar establishment as well as bohemian gender codes consigned women Beats to the domestic realm, which the Beat generation had rejected as oppressive of male freedom and conflated with the abhorrent cold war culture, as in *On the Road* or the film *Pull My Daisy*, texts premised on flight from a confinement signified by women and home. Rebellious women Beats appropriated the domestic space defined against them by bohemian and hipster life and used it as a rhetoric and set of representations for their liberation through vehicles usually reserved for men, such as sexual freedom and travel on the road. Because the women's writing contends with such antidomestic perspectives of the Beat generation, and because it is linked to the sphere of women's purdah, its inclusion in the field of the Beat movement is a radical intervention. The women writers defamiliarized assumptions imposed on them according to their gender by using those assumptions to establish styles and convictions alien to the colonization they could not escape (de Certeau 32); to express an upstart female subjectivity. In their literary use of the domestic, they seemed to obey Beat codes of Cool and views about gender, and simultaneously reconfigured "beat" to accommodate their alter-vision.

For instance, the heroine of Joyce Johnson's novel *Come and Join the Dance* is represented as a silent hipster "chick" suffering from beat anomie, acquiescent to male sexual desire and admiration, and an apparently docile follower of male adventurism—an ideal Beat generation woman. Yet the novel depicts her resistance to forces of her assimilation—from her college's pointless rules to her study of the literary canon to her submission to lovers—while giving her the Beat road and leaving hipster men mired in the clutter of domestic life, reversing the gender roles Beat culture subscribed to. That is, the novel instantiates rules, customs, and convictions of the Beat generation for women, but critiques them by reversing the status of the sexes, even while preserving the binary, hierarchic structure of the gender system. Johnson's protagonist retains her marginality in the novel's bohemia, but that social outpost is subverted to achieve her discursive significance and literary vitality—figured as the privileging of her female gaze (Ronna C. Johnson, " 'And then she went' "). These strategies divert to female advantage adverse significations of "beat" while remaining immersed in them, a complex doubling back on the Beat discourse that typifies the work of its women writers.

The poems left behind by the legendary hipster Elise Cowen at her death in 1962 inscribe an alternative "beat," or an antidiscipline of Beat aesthetic practice that defamiliarizes representations imposed on her by the dominant Beat order. Her surviving work, which her censorious parents had sought to destroy, effects her poetic agency even while enacting her assigned place on the Beat margin. Speaking female disaffiliation and alienation, the poems are dark, terse, surreal meditations on death, madness, despair, with a cold war existentialism, a paranoid intensity, that aligns them with Ginsberg's early prophetic utterances. The work conveys an indelible sense of being damaged and yet distinguished by madness, but in verses cool in tone and affect, a sharp contrast to Ginsberg's effusive complaint. Cowen as Beat poet speaks in the voice of the silent "girls" in black, articulating the paradox of women Beats' speechlessness. The poem "Did I Go Mad . . ." (Knight 163) names the beat malady "Waiting / To death," a waiting to die and a dying from the waiting that is being alive. The existential fatigue, the cryptic angst, the gray mood of the poem, all model "cool" hipster languor, but Cowen also amends that discourse and image with the speaker's convoluted lament: "On my brain are welts from / the moving that never moves / On my brain there are welts / from the endless stillness" (Knight 163). The poem represents "beat" as a paradox of immobile movement and interminable quietude; it asserts the poet's refusal of feminine passivity in her embrace of death, the "endless stillness." In this, it produces a hipster antidiscipline of female existential pain and soul.

Cowen achieves more than most depressed cold war hipsters did—she converts the beat paralysis of existential and pathological despair and madness into an opportunity for subjectivity while remaining other within the culture which she assimilated and which assimilated her, diverting it without leaving it. Desire for suicide— the hipster's disease—and its adjunct in the speaker's verse—the movement toward or embrace of death—enact agency where none is usually found, especially for women, diverting the Beat generation's sexist eclipse while embodying it. In this it is relevant to consider the manipulations in the historical record of Joan Vollmer Adams Burroughs who, when she was killed by William S. Burroughs in 1951, left behind little written testimony of her existence. The void in the record enhanced her being rendered a Beat generation legend: a "wife" suicidally desperate in her addiction and passive to Burroughs's perversities with games and guns; thus implicated in her own killing, she has been exploited to exculpate Burroughs from it.[8] In contrast to Joan Burroughs, a casualty of Beat history's silencings, Cowen made a poetic oeuvre of despair and invisibility. She left a record that paradoxically attests to agency while in surrender to nihilistic beat futility; that signifies a hipster subject who is subject to female negation. In reflections that express defiance or resistance, as in LeRoi Jones's idea of beat as a "reaction against" ("Beat Generation" 472), but also resignation, as in Huncke's elegant beat futility, Cowen achieves agency by embracing her nullification by depression, gender, and "cool," in this working with what materials Beat culture assigned her. Using beat to serve her subjectivity, Cowen invaded the normative Beat discourses colonizing her, subversively carving an alternative yet recognizable beat space, metaphorizing the dominant hipster ethos.

Following this tactic of inscribing adaptations of beat, the writings of women Beats show that they performed the socially mandated roles of mother, wife, lover, but with bohemian sexual freedom and through the perspective of hipster existential concerns, and that they brought these redefined roles to bear on their Beat writing. In art as in life, women Beats unfixed their domestic roles from patriarchal stasis and brought them to the more open-ended environments of bohemia, rendering them with notable indifference to conventional prescriptions and with attention instead to materialities of women's lives: di Prima's five children have four different fathers and diverse ethnic and racial heritages; Jones had a mixed-race marriage and biracial children; Frazer resorted to prostitution to support her family and left her daughter to be adopted in Mexico; Johnson was what is now called a single mother; Helen Adam never parted from her sister Pat. In a radical insistence on lived realities that echoes with aesthetics promulgated by male Beats, all but Adam made these domestic arrangements the explicit subject of some portion of their work—and Adam collaborated with Pat on her chef d'oeuvre, the opera *San Francisco's Burning*, composing art within the intimate personal space of their sibling relation. Subjected to the larger Beat paradox of gender inequity, women Beat writers have created their own Beat paradox: their implementation of beat within and by their use of the domestic sphere has instantiated a Beat literary discourse made of materials that male-authored Beat literature has precisely defined itself in reaction against.

Brenda Frazer's *Troia: Mexican Memoirs* (published under her married name, Bonnie Bremser) exploits fissures in Beat discourse to divert "beat" to construct the protagonist's subjectivity, while remaining within Beat culture's norms, which require her subordination; that is, she is instantiated as beat subject and as colonized subaltern at once. *Troia* is made to contain a beat sex narrative that centrally features both maternity and prostitution, but it dissolves the Madonna/whore binary that Beat narratives favor by making the matron equally the whore. As the wife of Beat generation poet Ray Bremser and mother of their baby girl, she is turned out to prostitution by her husband, work which she nevertheless performs as if she were a beat subject. In Frazer's handling, the wife and mother is a sexual subject "enjoying what I am paid for, enjoying it immensely at times" (48). Through the narrator's agency of desire, she achieves subject status, a reversal of the prostitute's usual degradation, which is permitted by the Beat generation's accommodation of sexually adventurous women, the very meaning of the signifier "troia." Yet, even as maternity is an inescapable consequence of Beat's free-sex values in an era of ineffective birth control and illegal abortion, it is antithetical to the Beat ethos. In *Troia* Frazer wrote herself as a protagonist on the road with child, but, unlike di Prima in *Memoirs of a Beatnik*, emphasized ways that maternity is inimical to being Beat for women: it makes women less available for sex, and sex less available to women. *Troia* deploys a beat antidiscipline in its road tale that achieves female subjectivity even while complying with terms of women's objectification: the protagonist, the beat wife and mother who cannot control her bodily impulses either for sex or for fertility is a sexual outlaw who leaves her child to be adopted and becomes an agent of the road. She is the subject-narrator of her (own) Mexican memoir, the "troia"/ prostitute of the title, in this transforming the signifier's social meaning of objectification (whore) to its discursive function as (beat) subject. Women Beat writers' deployment of maternity in concert with rather than severed from female sexuality diverts "beat" to serve female hipsters' agency, subverting Beat culture's norms from within.

As *Troia* illustrates, women Beats transformed their consignment to the domestic, making that realm the place of their agency. In contrast, male Beats abandoned the domestic sphere, reckoning it as a point of departure for the flight from restraint, as depicted in *On the Road*, whose wild narrative movement and male camaraderie are predicated on Sal's divorce, or *Pull My Daisy*, which resolves in the male poets' extrication from the loft ruled by the woman known only as "Milo's wife." Some critics see Beat status signified in the women's collateral or adjunct involvements and roles in Beat generation life (Damon)—as in their production of the vital small press journals *Yugen* and *The Floating Bear* and later *Angel Hair* (Jones and di Prima, and Waldman, respectively); their maintenance of the salon or the pad as domicile and hub of community organization and sustenance (Adam, Jones, Waldman); their bestowal, barter, and performance of sexual favors (Frazer); their tending of children; their employment for money (Johnson); their function as amanuensis (Cowen); their iconographic use as models (Martinelli), managers (Eileen Kaufman), mothers—in addition to the functions of those Maria Damon terms "life-as-art artists" (147) within the Beat movement. But the auxiliary life-acts of those who enable Beat culture are more than merely that, especially when these enabling activities are transformed into fiction, poetry, and nonfiction prose.

By instantiating into literary discourse their domestic or everyday-life practices, women Beat writers refitted Beat literary discourse by negating its antidomestic terms, rendering it the usable context of women's agency rather than of their elision. The everyday practices of consumers are the arts of the oppressed (de Certeau 39) and can be used to transform a dominant order to fit requirements of those subordinated by it. It is not in particular performances of these activities but in the subaltern's consignment to them that everyday practices such as reading, shopping, and cooking (de Certeau 40) are made locus and means of dissident self-assertion. Although male Beats treated women in their circle as adjuncts to their work as writers, the women's conduct of quotidian practices, as in keeping the pad or working to pay the rent, was not performed with the sole goal of enabling the male Beats to live independent art lives. Rendered textually by the subaltern, the conduct of the quotidian is deployed as aesthetic discourse of itself, as the art of women Beats. The everyday activities women Beats represented in their work seem to correspond to the domestic sphere in which they signify, but the activities are in themselves beat arts, a synthesis which has been all along self-evident to some women writers. Among the Beat movement's most understated and elliptical poets, ruth weiss conflates her Beat discourse with the domestic by use of puns and other wordplay. The verses of her 1960 poem "The Brink"—fleet, vernacular, enigmatic, "cool"—simultaneously fuse and disentangle women's sexuality, the domestic sphere, and desire in quick, sharp beat lyrics:

> *the won ton woman*
> *carried the hot dish across town*
> *under her cloak*
> *to keep it hot*
> *instead of flying or sent for*
> *her neighbor she was sick*
>
> *wanton woman*
> *where were you at supper? . . .*

(SINGLE OUT, n.p.)

Female sexuality is conveyed in the double-entendre of the language of food; the "won ton woman" is "wanton." That visual pun trips the distinctions between the registers of nourishment the poem uses, blurring concepts in the everyday language of keeping cooked food and desire hot. The poem exploits women's assigned places, both in the domestic and the sexual ("keep it hot"), to assert a hip subjectivity instantiated in the verse's wit. In weiss's vision, the domestic woman's world of food and cooking blends with the discourses of Beat bohemian arts.

Similarly, in the 1985 poem "Rant," a title suggesting the unbottled rage of the subaltern, di Prima addresses specific conditions—housework, pregnancy, economic need—under which women have labored to produce art. She does not make her poem out of housework, but her poem—expressing an exemplary Beat aesthetic—dismisses boundaries dividing poetry making and daily life-processes: "there is no part of yourself you can separate out / saying, this is memory, this is sensation / this is work I care about, this is how / I make a living" (*Pieces* 159). Rejecting tendencies to separate everyday from existential or artistic pursuits, di Prima articulates a woman-centered poetics in which distinctions among self, labor, and aesthetics are erased. The speaker contends that feminine and manual labor are everyday forms of creative expression; that "woman's work" is beat art, with poetics and techniques engendering consciousness:

> *There is no way you can* not *have a poetics*
> *no matter what you do: plumber, baker, teacher*
> *you do it in the consciousness of making*
> *or not making yr world*
>
> (*Pieces* 160–61)

The rejection of gender, class, and vocational limits about what merits the label "art" and who may be called an artist is a fitting response for the caste of persons who have been by their sex de facto excluded from the categories. The women's everyday activities transferred from the historical/cultural record to the discourses of literary production are themselves poetic discoveries. They are activities represented in literary texts to establish not the subordination but the subjectivity of the female practitioner, who is instantiated by the discursive representation of her actions as agent/narrator. In this simultaneous double function—the representation of the domestic as it is women's domain, and also to effect the inscription of female subjectivity—the life-art practices of women Beats escape the gendered function of service to the strong(er) by serving their own inclinations.

So, too, in her confessional poetry Hettie Jones enacts the self-invention that is the hipster prerogative, clearing a space in the Beat discourse for her bohemian self-representation through the subordinating terms it has left her. Jones points to the cultural drag of 1950s femininity, against which the female Beat poet works to establish the self as hipster subject, in "The Woman in the Green Car." The poem uses the constraints of place, defined by gender, to reject assumptions about postwar suburban maturity and the feminine and overdeterminations of middle-class whiteness for women, the class "death" signified by the destination of Mamaroneck, an affluent Westchester suburb:

> having an argument with him, her boyfriend, he said
> when you grow up you'll go to live in Mamaroneck
> with Marjorie Morningstar
> and she couldn't envision it. When he insisted
> she grew afraid—what did he know?
>
> (Drive 13)

In this recognition of the threat of white middle-class women's suffocating fate, defined in the allusion to Herman Wouk's 1955 novel, *Marjorie Morningstar*, bohemia seems to be a sole and redemptive alternative. Rather than surrender to matronly security on Long

Island, the poet demands to "invent her own life" (13), turning to the improvisational existentialism of Beat bohemia—signified by the speeding green car—for antidote to the conventional feminine roles of housewife or matron in the postwar gender binary. In this representation of female agency, the defiant reject suburbia for bohemia, unlike Marjorie Morningstar, who abandons her bohemian aspirations for the safety of suburban domesticity. Self-invention in the face of unusable cultural conventions and expectations is a male hipster hallmark, which the protofeminist Jones appropriates as her right, altering and augmenting it in claiming the prerogative of self-invention for herself. This appropriation effects a revision or reinvention as women writers find ways to turn Beat aesthetics, discourses, innovations, and assumptions to their advantage; they introduce a way of being of the Beat generation that "obeys other rules and constitutes something like a second level interwoven into the first" (de Certeau 30) even if discordant with it, as for Jones, who deploys the antithesis of hip, the failed bohemian turned middle-class wife Marjorie Morningstar, in order to refuse being her. In such moves, women Beat writers work a new instrumentality into the dominant Beat movement representations and gender assumptions, introducing further heterogeneity into the discourse of "beat."

Beat Women's Memoirs

The women's self-inscription in their memoirs, the repute the memoirs have earned them, and the public's over-interest in biographical aspects of the Beat generation all have given women Beats their own discursive arena, a genre connected to but distinct from the domestic sphere of their eclipse. In transforming "beat" to their own uses in the memoir, women writers have metaphorized Beat discourses; they have written parallel to standard Beat forms and ideas, displacing signification to a register that allows for their subjectivity. Because of its essentially hybrid construction as both fictive and documentary discourse, the memoir is an apt genre for accommodating this meta-phorizing process. In the Beat generation memoir women writers have been able to crystallize and transform extra-literary prohibitions against women to invent an alternative, woman-centered discourse of Beat generation dissent. This is not as obvious a transformation of "beat" as would be direct reform and rehabilitation, as in writing Beat with corrections for sexism. Rather, in their memoirs, so numer-ous as to constitute a subgenre of Beat literature, women Beat writers revise Beat using strategies that do not appear to alter the normative Beat culture by which they as women are colonized. That is, using a genre that is an amalgam of generic forms, Beat's female memoirists (re)tell Beat generation life in a narrative discourse in which they are the memoirs' Beat subjects and yet still women colonized by the norms of Beat culture. The memoir allows them to write their Beat tales in the discursive interstices between the genres it encompasses, and in between the women's discursive positions as both subject and subaltern, to achieve a retrospective, transgressive reconstruction in which they can be figured as subjects.

Beat memoir includes but is not confined to these texts by women writers:[9] Brenda Frazer's *Troia: Mexican Memoirs* (1969), Diane di Prima's *Memoirs of a Beatnik* (1969), Joyce Johnson's *Minor Characters: The Romantic Odyssey of a Woman in the Beat Generation* (1983), Hettie Jones's *How I Became Hettie Jones* (1990), Carolyn Cassady's *Off the Road: My Years with Cassady, Kerouac, and Ginsberg* (1990), and Joan Haverty's *Nobody's Wife* (2001). Janine Pommy Vega's *Tracking the Serpent: Journeys to Four Continents* (1997) amalgamates the female-coded discourse of the memoir with the male-coded road tale in a self-conscious act of literary self-inscription. All the memoirs' female authors save Cassady and Haverty are professional writers and artists; all the texts are in print at this writing save *Troia*.

Women Beat writers' use of the memoir as a Beat literary form calls attention to the way the memoir's self-evidently constructed narratives are not granted the status of the prose fictions produced by the male Beat writers. Indeed, postmodernism's breakdown of literary categories and genres reveals them to be distinctions that are largely a matter of social construction rather than literary consideration. This reclaims the (female) memoirists from middle-brow oblivion, reterritorializing them in the Beat community and literary canon from which they have been elided. Evincing formal contingencies typifying the postmodern, the women's memoirs may be considered to be border texts (Hicks xxx–xxxi): they are sited at and clarify a turning point between genres of fiction (novel, prose narrative, fable) and nonfiction (memoir, history); and between traditional constructions of Beat individuality derived from late modernist emphases and more radical notions of protofeminist subjectivity derived from the postmodern. As border writing and as texts which have an ambiguous status in Beat literature, the women Beat writers' memoirs bear the marks of minor literature (Deleuze and Guattari 50–51): they are deterritorialized texts whose narratives oscillate between invention and change; they are texts exhibiting a displacement of language. This unfixed, contingent status provides women Beat generation memoirists opportunity for rhetorical and generic reform; it is the discursive instability they exploit for narrative assertions of their (beat) subjectivity.

As a minor literature, the Beat generation memoirs are marked by the displacement of their domestic language by the women's instantiation in the hipster milieu. Consider di Prima's double-edged deployments in *Memoirs of a Beatnik*: a chapter about a woman's sex life written to appease the publisher's demand for titillation set next to a chapter recounting her hipster life, the same story corrected for personal and cultural accuracy. Each is distinguished in its subtitle to the shared domestic theme: "A Night by the Fire: What You Would Like to Hear" (106) and "A Night by the Fire: What Actually Happened" (108). While the first chapter exhibits the displacement of domestic discourses by ones of sexual excess, the latter uses domestic discourses to describe the hipster pad as a woman-centered scene; by this double telling the memoir exploits the instability of first-person narration to unfix significations of the domestic. So, too, as texts by Beat women the memoirs evince displacement from discourses of gender circulating in the 1950s, because their Beat-ness contends with establishment norms. Johnson's *Minor Characters* discounts the white middle-class "good girls" attending Barnard to obtain the demeaning M-R-S degree for which college was supposed to prepare them by means of her beat refusal to complete the degree, thus defiantly and disobediently, and sardonically, failing to graduate by one credit in gym. The petty requirements of fifties femininity, of college credits and degrees, are alike displaced by the dissenting narrator's alienation from them and by her aspirations to hipster disengagement from conformist dicta.

Finally, the memoirs reterritorialize the domestic discourses disparaged, banned, or elided in Beat writing by men—that is, they bring domestic discourses back into the Beat movement, through another level of discursive signification interwoven into the first—and thus reconfigure Beat literature to encompass the shadow land of eclipsed women and instantiate them as presence. *How I Became Hettie Jones* constructs a narrative of the female hipster subject based in a specific sense of home and the domestic milieu defined by motherhood and the presence of children. Jones orders her tale of becoming a Beat on a chronological account of the Greenwich Village apartments she and her family occupied during the fifties (Grace, "Snapshots") and the progress of her life from girlhood through marriage, maternity, and divorce. This narrative insistently entwines discourses of the domestic and the hipster, the home and the scene, the interracial bohemian community and the larger civil rights movement, into a metadiscursive account of the protagonist's growth into the hipster subject Hettie Jones, a self configured as woman (the single Hettie Cohen) and as hipster (Cohen married to Jones). This outcome brings the domestic into Beat movement writing; it shows the domestic to be Beat per se. Reterritorializing the women Beats' memoirs as Beat literature recognizes that Beat writing is not merely antidomestic, which much of it is, but that paradoxically it is also focused on and indebted to domestic or everyday arrangements. The women's memoirs justify the conclusion that Beat literature can derive from the domestic, not merely oppose it, which permits a far more nuanced description of Beat generation culture and writing.

Converting "beat" to their own ends in classically Beat generation fashion, women Beat writers embodied domestic femininity even while deploying the rebellious antidomestic Beat discourse, a combination that contradicts itself. As border texts that straddle genres and erode distinctions enforced by gender categories, the memoirs engage with the road narrative, bringing determinants of gender to bear on it. When di Prima was hired to produce a salacious tale of sexual libertinism, *Memoirs of a Beatnik*, an "autobiography" of an odalisque, for the Olympia Press, she was figured as Beat body rather than mind, as woman rather than writer. Yet *Memoirs of a Beatnik* contravenes sexist exploitations of women's sexuality and desire by its point of view in the female narrator's pleasure and the implied narrator's cynical critique of both hipster sexual expectations and square guilt about sex. The memoir further undermines the narrator's confinement to the Beat female body by providing her the resources of hipster men: the picaresque sex narrative concludes on the brink of becoming a road tale by domesticizing that form and by wresting the narrator from the overdeterminations and assumptions of patriarchal sexism with regard to women's bodies.

In the last chapter, "We Set Out," the narration of excited uncertainty at a new departure evokes the earnest narration of *On the Road*, but with the crucial distinction that di Prima's female self/protagonist is pregnant, a spin on the notion of the buddy road tale. This outcome is framed by the narrator's pleas against birth control use and for women to be in a more or less constant state of parturiency; for women's untrammeled enjoyment of free sex. These are radical departures from the traditional road tale of men together without women, never mind children, departures that problematize male Beat pretensions to estrangement and alienation by inscribing a revisionist hybrid protagonist: woman-with-child on the road, a figure that undermines hipster estrangement and alienation by literalizing the buddy tale as perhaps only a woman's story could. Di Prima claims the road as a conduit to her protagonist's subjectivity—where the road normatively has been the site of women's subordination to male agents, as in *On the Road*—but with the pregnant protagonist enacting the road's buddy-tale premise by carrying her "buddy" inside her. This reversal of sexist Beat generation assumptions—using pregnancy as the occasion to take to the road, not grounds for exclusion from it—might be seen as the strategy of "makeshift creativity" used by those colonized as objects. This kind of make-do ingenuity particularly fits with Beat bohemianism, as in the do-it-yourself way di Prima makes literary use of materials assigned her as a woman—her body, her female desires for pregnancy—to prove her credentials as hipster, despite the fact that such materials of the feminine have been deemed antithetical to the hipster subject.

In using the memoir to metaphorize Beat literary narratives, women Beat writers have told Beat generation tales to their own ends, and made something else of them, diverting without leaving the Beat aesthetic register. They have made their narratives articulate their subjectivity while preserving the narrative's integrity as a (proper Beat) woman's tale of darkness, desire, even death. Beat women writers' appropriation of the memoir form to tell stories usually conveyed by Beat prose fiction narratives is elucidated by the notion that the women's use of the memoir is a way to escape censorship. Using the memoir form, which is not the genre privileged by the male Beat writers, allows the women to tell their own Beat tales outside their colonization by Beat literature, without conforming to the norms that compromise or elide them.

CONCLUSION: ACHIEVING THE "'PHALLIC' POSITION"

Women Beat writers reinvent Beat writing's language, method, imagery, and discursive modes by their practice and production in literary texts, an inscription that transforms the writers from objects to subjects. Yet subjectivity for women Beat writers is a compromised achievement in light of the code of Cool and the gendering processes of writing itself. The hipster code, which di Prima identified as "our eternal, tiresome rule of Cool" (*Memoirs* 94), is a set of rules for comportment that mandates terse expression and withheld emotion, and thus defines the hipster while also signifying hipster status. It is a social code with literary ramifications that makes women de facto collaborators with their own oppression, because the essence of cool is the appearance of passivity, indifference, and lack of emotion (Holmes, *Go* 209–11). For women, such passivity is always already syntonic with discourses of the traditional feminine; thus, women playing it cool were doubly playing it as "girls," the "dumb"—both silent and unintelligent—"chicks" hipster men took seriously only for sex (McNeil). Alix Kates Shulman noted the inhibiting dictates of the 1950s hipster's code: "According to the strict code of Cool by which we lived, only weakness moved anyone to extend a relationship beyond the initial passion of the moment. Once a passion peaked, you were supposed to let it go like a poem that had found its form" (105). With emotional "weakness" conflated with the feminine in postwar gender discourses, the code of Cool, which suppresses feeling and expression, censors and prohibits the feminine in both sexes, thereby immunizing hipster men against charges of effeminacy deployed to control male behavior in the postwar era (Ehrenreich). Thus, to act like a hipster is, for both sexes, to act like a "man."

Indeed, rather than effecting the feminization of American culture, as Ann Douglas has argued (xiv), the Beat ethos effected a sweeping masculinization of both sexes to a canonical standard of emotion gendered male in its discursive expressions, the withholding—of feeling, of reaction—that is lionized in high modernist male writers, such as Hemingway. This standard, a literary template for the code of Cool, when enacted by female adherents, such as the mannish vamp Brett Ashley in *The Sun Also Rises*, makes men of women. This outcome, a transformation of the gender binary by means of its collapse into a unitary conformity with masculinity, suggests in turn consequences for the female Beat writer that may compromise her deployment of beat to her own ends of subjectivity. Julia Kristeva has noted a problematic for women who write, that what she calls the " 'phallic' position" that obtains "in a culture where the speaking subjects are conceived of as masters of their speech" (165) might compromise the female writer by masculinizing her. Kyger limns this aspect of the woman Beat writer's impossible condition, her quest to be a person and a poet that gets stalled in gender, in a vision of the way gender compromises female poetic ambition. In *The Tapestry and the Web* (1965), the poet imagines a self simultaneously inspired and hobbled by the masculine: "she's fleet footed / to be a tree, to be Jack Spicer in a dream / to carry this around all day" (49). In this imago of the woman artist, the female poet of fleet talent is rooted and burdened, inspired but stayed by the poetic authority disseminated by the mentor Spicer, whom it is possible to equal only in the private mind ("in a dream"). The poet's ambition is compromised by her gender, which is figured here as an add-on—what is carried "around all day"—with the implication that the masculine (Spicer) permits or effects disenburdenment and thus literary advancement.

Despite her works that reflect second-wave feminism and that purvey a nearly essentialized feminine ideal, such as "Fast Speaking Woman" (1975), Anne Waldman's late work returns to affirmations of the masculine for the female writer. Three decades after Kyger's lament of female ambition, Waldman speaks of the permission to be an artist also in terms of gender in the 1994 essay "Feminafesto." Her rhetoric addresses the attraction to literary bohemia and the calling of poet as evocations and engagements of the masculine, but—and this distinction resonates with postmodern queer theory—Waldman envisions equal access for women to the calling through the acquisition and the performance of gender drag. She claims the status of men because she possesses capacities attributed to them, with the insinuation that, via her masculine qualities, she deserves to be a poet and "free," a genderdefying seizure of privilege that men note and resent:

And a husband would say with accusation *You are just like all the male poets. Just like Robert Creeley. Traveling the globe, leaving hearth and home, abandoning child, jawing with other poets till wee hours, god knows, how can I trust you?* And how could he? For I wanted this other path, desperately. Poet, outrider, free woman. I could hold my own with the boys, I could "drink like a man!" I could "talk like a man!" (*Vow* 22–23).

Waldman's self-comparison to Creeley suggests, as does Kyger's evocation of Spicer, the standard for women's literary aspiration: to possess what is embodied by and given only to men; to be like men. In this, Waldman evokes the end against which Kristeva cautions, the concern that to write is a gendered calling to which women have access only at the expense of their transformation out of femininity and the feminine. It may be that women are masculinized by achieving what Kristeva calls the irreducible " 'phallic' position" that she fears would taint women who write. However, an uncompromised feminine may well be the cost for women writers who defied and surmounted hurdles of gender in the era before the gains of second-wave feminism were established. While women Beat writers' replication of masculine privilege was often uneasy, the subjectivity the women earned in writing beat did effect an equality in and congruence with male-dominant Beat culture that eroded their conformance with femininity.

It may be that the jettisoning of gender to be a writer will prove to be the Beat generation's radical, feminist boon to constructions of the dissident female artist positioned on the margin of culture and subculture. If the ungendering of this subaltern figure is a Beat movement legacy, and if this legacy is usable and valuable, it will be known as such from women Beat writers, from their struggles and transformations in pursuit of their art.

Interviewing Women Beat Writers

—Nancy M. Grace

One of the functions of giving an interview is to work out a knowledge of the past or, as historian Alice Kessler Harris has written, "to preserve what [we] remember for the future" (Grele 5). In the nine interviews included here, ruth weiss, Diane di Prima, Joyce Johnson, Hettie Jones, Ann Charters, Anne Waldman, Janine Pommy Vega, Brenda Frazer, and Joanne Kyger engage in such reflection. This group has not been extensively interviewed.[1] While Waldman has received some attention, and there are a few published interviews with di Prima and Kyger, the total of extant interviews with the women Beat writers falls far short of the resources available in interviews with Allen Ginsberg, Jack Kerouac, William S. Burroughs, and Gary Snyder, among other male Beats, who since the late fifties have used the interview format to elaborate on the Beat generation and many other issues philosophical, political, and aesthetic. These are the texts that have grounded much of the scholarship on the Beat generation.[2] These are also the texts that have worked in concert with the men's literary productions and the discourse of literary critics, historians, and sociologists to construct much of what we know about the women Beat writers. However, the women have their own narratives that constitute them as members of the Beat movement. The interviews in this volume record these stories, showing how community emerges through the women's narratives about their lives and how the articulation of these stories preserves the speakers as historical agents.

These interviews began as oral history, a spoken account of the past, and they stand in the service of three major goals: (1) to help women Beat writers further their subjectivity in the public record of the Beat movement; (2) to understand how these women perceived American postwar literary and social history; and (3) to reconfigure and expand the Beat canon by inclusion of the women's voices. More specifically, the interviews elicit from the writers impressions of the Beat generation and its literature; articulations of their aesthetic practices and philosophies and influences on their writing; accounts of their emergence and development as writers; reflections on female relationships and community; and other pertinent autobiographical information. Tony Moffeit, commenting on his interview with Diane di Prima, expressed these intentions as a search for "an 'existential' document, one in which the poet's intuition is more important than logic, in which through the force of one's personality and will, statements are made that relate to entering a deeper intensity of living."[3] The interviews reveal the character of the speaking subject as a creator of literature—who is she, why does she write, what sustains her creative life, how does her mind work, what makes her unique or binds her with other writers identified with the Beat movement. We did not intend that the writers would provide the definitive statement about the nature of the Beat movement but rather that they would use their autobiographical memories to present multiple narratives that would illuminate that historical moment.

Each interview is based on a set of questions that we constructed to elicit testimony about women writing in the Beat generation. When possible, we sent the questions to the writer in advance so she could prepare responses. Realizing that the conversational nature of the interview produces a certain amount of superficial (although at times valuable and interesting) material, we hoped to minimize this result by giving the writers sufficient time to develop more substantive responses. The interviews themselves were conducted in person, by telephone, and in one case via e-mail. We then transcribed the interviews, determined which areas needed more development, and conducted follow-up interviews by telephone, e-mail, or letter. Subsequently, the authors read the transcripts to make corrections, additions, and deletions so that the texts here are as accurate as possible, regarding not only the factual data but also the critical discourse that the interviews generated. Finally, we edited the revised transcripts for linguistic and narrative coherence. While remaining true to our goals and the historical foundation of the texts, we sought and constructed narrative lines that readers can trace.

The narrative conventions of the interview promulgate a virtual surface upon which subjectivity becomes a linguistic presence scripted intertextually. The interviews in this collection encompass many forms of discourse that the women drew upon to tell their stories. The most dominant is memoir, by which the women selected, described, and reflected on events from the past. For instance, Joyce Johnson looks back at the publication in 1962 of her first novel, *Come and Join the Dance*, as "the biggest disappointment of [her] life," and di Prima remembers the "subterranean stream of anger" caused by her home life as a child and the channeling of that anger into art and motherhood. Hettie Jones recalls the sheer exhilaration and cultural significance of tossing out her girdle and high heels in the fifties.

Other forms include historical record, exemplified by Joanne Kyger's identification of Lew Welch and Ron Loewinsohn as the poets she read with at the 1965 Berkeley Poetry Conference; she even stopped the interview to check publicity documents from the event to support her statement. Anne Waldman's responses to questions about the significance of Gertrude Stein's experimental prose featured literary analysis. Anecdotes about encounters with famous people frequently appear. ruth weiss tells of being taken on early morning joy rides around San Francisco by Neal Cassady—with Kerouac in tow. Waldman declares that "one of the highlights of [her] life as fast speaking woman" was appearing in 1975 with Bob Dylan's Rolling Thunder Revue tour and performing for the master of rap, Muhammad Ali, who was surrounded by nine body guards, "beautiful guys with their pastel suits." Frazer relies on the confessional mode to explain her motive for writing her memoir, "weepingly trying to make things okay between" herself and Ray Bremser. Testimonials to important relationships also abound: Pommy Vega extols Herbert Huncke's capacious, nonsexist spirit; likewise, Ann Charters praises her husband, Sam, for his nontraditional gender role expectations. Aesthetic philosophies of varying lengths characterize parts of all of the interviews.

The significance of this mélange of genres—in essence, the interview genre itself—is the fact that through these forms the women found their memories and narrated themselves out of historical obscurity into a distinct and vibrant community. This community, constructed by nine separate female voices, diverges dramatically from the tight fraternity of the iconic male Beats. The women's narratives do not tell the tale created in situ of a cohesive unit that traveled together, corresponded with each other, wrote collaboratively, edited each other's work, had sex with each other, and shared intimate discussions of aesthetic practices. Some of these women did not even know each other during the height of the Beat movement, a few not meeting until the 1990s when Brenda Knight published *Women of the Beat Generation*. Moreover, women from all the three Beat life. These contexts serve as leitmotifs of the bohemian worlds in which the women chose to live, or were born into, as was the case with Anne Waldman. weiss, for instance, found bohemia in Chicago's Art Circle and San Francisco's North Beach; Kyger in the village of Bolinas, California; Waldman and Jones at St. Mark's Church on the Lower East Side of New York; Charters in the cottages of Berkeley; and Frazer in Mexico. These spaces signify the women's common identity as young iconoclasts, and within these spheres, they crafted lives that valued the supremacy of the imagination, the humanity of the oppressed, and the pursuit of self-knowledge. In their interviews, they tell of knowing from an early age that they were destined for a life that provided them the space and the support to write and to discover themselves—to put at the center of their lives freedom, intellect, and art rather than economic stability or social acceptance. The raw material of their lives fed, and sometimes became, their art. Their stories, such as di Prima's memories of the artisan craftsmen who populated her childhood neighborhood, often recognize the need to seamlessly blend one's vocation with the routines of daily living, to define art not as privilege or hobby but as vocational necessity.

Their narrative of female Beat bohemia presents them not only as inhabitants and caretakers of preexisting bohemian spaces but also as creators of those spaces, both public and private. They remembered themselves as leaders, as does di Prima when she speaks about the *Floating Bear* newsletter and the Poets Press, both of which she cofounded and both of which supported many avant-garde artists. Similarly, weiss recalls how she came to innovate poetry reading to jazz accompaniment in North Beach, and Waldman presents The Jack Kerouac School of Disembodied Poetics, which she founded with Ginsberg, as a space in which young writers carry on the outrider tradition. Pommy Vega tells of being a teenager in the late fifties and trying to find Beat bohemia by transforming her bedroom in Union not only against the state but also against themselves as women, a theme that has not become part of the bohemian canon. In their interviews, the women repeatedly express their awareness of their Beat subjectivity as double-sided and conflicted. They understand that they were subjects with the power to act—Beat culture's emphasis on renegade behavior and the sovereignty of the artist legitimized the female desire to actualize the self. But the women also recognize that they were subjected to the power of others. The Beat generation's patriarchal core, mirroring that of the mainstream culture, relegated women to secondary positions, often disrespecting their art, intelligence, physical bodies, and the domestic and paid labor they performed to support their families. In particular, the interviews present a narrative of the conflict between the twin desires for independent art production and the production of family life—a binary driving the women, such as Charters, Johnson, Jones, and Frazer, to abandon or suppress the bohemian role of independent artist in order to raise a family.

A critical element of the women's Beat bohemian narrative is the trope of writing as an existential act. When applied to women living under patriarchy, this trope can transform the act of putting words on paper into a dangerous and terrifying gesture negating socially accepted roles as wife, mother, and "good girl"—a consciousness that the women Beat writers sought to defy. Johnson recalls writing *Come and Join the Dance* "with so much uncertainty. I could hardly believe I was actually writing a novel, I was so scared. . . . I was quite aware that I was writing about things that a nice young lady should not write about." Pommy Vega talks about how she cried the first time Ginsberg critiqued her poetry, reflecting women's uncertainty regarding their legitimacy as writers. Frazer's story most dramatically illustrates the catch-22 in which a woman writer could find herself. Her *Troia* manuscript, which originated as spontaneous acts of communication with her husband, was the result of transforming the material of her everyday life into art, a practice fostered by the Beat movement. But it was two men, Ray Bremser and Michael Perkins, who decided that *Troia* should be published, and they assumed control, selecting and arranging the letters as a coherent narrative. The message of Frazer's story is that even if a woman was brave enough to compose a dissident text, her status as the subjugated could diminish her status as free bohemian subject.

It is important to note, however, that the female Beat bohemian narrative emerging from the interviews does not characterize as malicious all the men with whom the women associated. Most of the women writers identify males who were sympathetic to their work. However, their story still asserts that the misogynist qualities of Beat bohemia did not encourage sisterly relationships to foster the women's art, did not mentor women artists into the group, and did not validate the women artists as part of the history of the movement. All of the women interviewed are, to greater and lesser extents, cognizant of their lack of agency within male-dominated Beat bohemia and of their lifelong struggles to achieve subjectivity. In response, their narrative of Beat bohemia emphasizes an archetypal American narrative of individuality and everyday heroism—of being the only woman working as an artist or one of only a few combating entrenched sexism; of being in control of sexually charged situations; of being magnanimously forgiving of the abuses they experienced; of seeing their subjugation as no different from that experienced by certain males in their communities; and of overcoming poverty, loneliness, or divorce. The resultant narrative is a finely balanced composite that maximizes the presence of the women as artists, countering the sexism of the male-dominated communities in which they lived, and demonstrating, quite accurately, that they were players in the development of sixties feminism. This women's narrative legitimizes both Beat bohemia's long-held focus on individual independence and second-wave feminism's recognition of a woman's right to fight for her own subjectivity and to help her female compatriots. The interviews express the women writers' need to recognize Beat bohemia and the women's movement, the two communities that have most publicly legitimized them. In the nine interviews that follow, the women Beat writers radically readjust the iconic Beat generation tale to accommodate the historical liberation of women in the second half of the twentieth century. Their story of the Beat movement is articulated with courage, integrity, and their determination to be recognized as individuals who are indebted to, but more than, their Beat inheritance.

Single Out

—ruth weiss

A bohemian free spirit made peripatetic by the vagaries of history, ruth weiss is a self-proclaimed street and Beat poet. Born in Berlin in 1928, weiss escaped Nazi Germany with her parents in 1938 and immigrated to the United States. For more than a decade, she moved frequently, living in New York City, Switzerland, Chicago, and New Orleans. In 1952, she hitchhiked from Chicago to California, where she became a regular on the North Beach poetry scene, pioneering jazz poetry readings at a club called The Cellar. Her community in the San Francisco Bay area has long included painters, sculptors, filmmakers, and musicians, a blend contributing to her fifty-year production of plays, films, and paintings, which are an amalgamation of modernism and Beat.

Like many of her Beat contemporaries, weiss defines poetic language as a free-flowing force moving outward from the unconscious toward self and others. As a poet who frequently reads with jazz musicians, weiss grounds her poetics in the interplay of contrived form and spontaneous production, both in the act of constructing the text and in public performance. weiss's poetry is often made of haiku-like lyrics (Kerouac is said to have admired her facility with the form) that stream down the page almost faster than the eye can follow.

The subject is frequently compressed in the abstract workings of the collected words, and upper case is used emphatically throughout, rendering the poems esoteric and hermetic. Her masterwork, *DESERT JOURNAL* (1977), alluding to the Biblical forty days and forty nights of prophetic wandering and meditation, typifies this modernist heritage. weiss composed *DESERT JOURNAL* from 1961 to 1968, limiting the text of each of the forty days to five pieces of paper, relying on spontaneity and improvisation to enter the wilderness of the imagination. The multi- and trans-gendered speaker of the poem seeks harmonic transcendence in the surrealistic and mundane, as in T. S. Eliot's *The Four Quartets* and Ginsberg's *Howl*.

To map the speaker's psychic terrain, weiss mixed spontaneity with the linguistic experiments of one of her favorite writers, Gertrude Stein. On the fourth day, the speaker concludes:

> *back broken*
> *broken back*
> *the cat MONK*
> *allows his belly*
> *with cunt-markings*
> *to be stroked*
> *purring to death*
> *BE NOT AFRAID*
> *I AM READY*
> *FOR THAT SEPARATION*
> *THAT IS ONE* (n.p.)

These lines exemplify the way weiss wields doggerel, contemporary slang, neologisms, and word inversions to track the free associations of the moving mind. By day forty, the human voice has become "...shiver & quail / frail tone / strong as longing / bone & marrow / bone to arrow / lighter than light" (n.p.), and the speaker emerges as a unifying female principle propelled by a giant male toward light. The short, clipped lines of the poem cycle encode a self that resists human form, yet whose voice of semantic innovation authors itself as human.

This effect is underscored by weiss's performance of the poem. Reading lines from the preface, "call your number / read your day," she invites the audience to join her in authorship, allowing anonymous voices to initiate the prophetic experience by determining which day will be read first and the order of those to follow. *DESERT JOURNAL,* then, refusing linearity through spontaneous composition, cut-up/ collaborative performance, semi-grammaticality, and surrealism, propels itself backward into modernism and forward into Beat and the postmodern (Grace, "ruth weiss's *DESERT JOURNAL*").

Apart from the esoteric qualities of *DESERT JOURNAL,* much of weiss's poetry foregrounds referential language, particularly to her 1938 escape from the Nazis, as in "full circle," a meditation on the escape, her arrival in the United States, and an episode in 1963 when she and her then-husband Mel Weitsman, a Zen priest, parted ways:

> *the ship WESTERNLAND. From the port of* vliessingen.
> *taking us to* america. *To the land of the west.*
> *to the new world.*
>
> *but i know it is the old world. of copper-sheen skin.*
>
> *i know* new york *is a city. still it is a shock when*
> *i arrive. where is the welcome of painted red skin.*
> *where are the feathers. where are the drums. was*
> *it a book. was it a dream. (full circle* 52)

The memories of a little girl call forth the fallacy of America as "new," inverting Europe and the United States, coloring the poet's past with rootless caricatures etched in personal and cultural memory. The trope foreshadows the rupture of weiss's relationship with her husband and her rescue by a spirit guide, directing her back to North Beach and her vocation as poet.

"full circle" is more elegiac than many of weiss's works, but its conclusion reflects her belief in poetry as a conveyance of hope. As Warren French has noted, weiss's poetry is distinctly upbeat (65). "TRAIN SONG," for instance, in memory of Beat poet Jack Micheline, defies death: "you smile / 'there is always a beginning / but never an end' / see you around" (*A NEW VIEW* 67). "Something Current" typifies her comedic voice: "the hard thing / being a genius / is that one has to spend / so much time / doing nothing" (*SINGLE OUT* n.p.). Her Beat voice resonates more with Diane di Prima's tough wit and Kerouac's immigrant joy than with John Clellon Holmes's troubled alienation or Herbert Huncke's hipster despondency.

weiss's take on Beat is portrayed in her black-and-white sixteen-millimeter film, *THE BRINK* (1961). As screenplay writer and director, she relied on spontaneity and found objects to construct the film. It features a "he" and "she" who journey around San Francisco, moving through love toward completion as human beings. With this theme the film augments the vision of Beat culture, representing a heterogeneous egalitarianism that counters the misogyny of the 1959 Robert Frank/Alfred Leslie film *Pull My Daisy*. weiss also has performed in a number of independent films and written and produced seven plays. Her linguistic wit, her works' commemoration of its Holocaust origins, her jazzy line scrolling down the page, and her fondness for mixed media exploration place weiss at the beginning of the Beat generation, where she was both inventor and practitioner of Beat poetics.

Part One of the following interview was conducted by Nancy Grace via telephone on July 7, 8, and 9, 1999. weiss was at her home in Albion, California. Part Two was conducted by Grace and Hallie Shapiro in

Wooster, Ohio, on April 2, 2002; the poet Janet DeBar was also present. Part Three was conducted by Grace at ruth weiss's home in Albion, California, on August 23, 2002.

Part I

July 7, 8, and 9, 1999

NANCY GRACE: Why don't we start the interview with a foundational question? What does Beat mean to you?

ruth weiss: You know Beat and the beatnik were a kind of put-down in the fifties—it was a joke by the media. But since then it has occurred to me that it is really an alternative. I've come to embrace it now. If somebody had said Beat, I would say no, no, I am not a Beat, you know, I am not Beat. But, you see, it has come to turn around—it has come to mean an alternative approach to life away from the materialism that exploded after World War II.

NG: Has that been a fairly recent transformation in your thinking?

rw: I had no idea Beat was going to make such a wedge into the consciousness that developed through art and politics at that time. At the time, I was not politically involved. Because of my escape from the Nazis, I didn't want to have anything to do with politics. But it came out anyway—from seeing a beautiful road covered with huge advertisements, to trying to stop the death penalty and racism. So Beat for me wasn't like Ferlinghetti and others whose politics were more overt. But it crept through my poetry anyway. Now fifty years later, I am living in the middle of the redwoods, trying to stop the cutting of the oldgrowth.

NG: Do you engage in processes like spontaneous writing that we tend to associate with Beat writing?

rw: First of all, I expand my poetry into whatever medium I use. I paint, I do plays, I've done only one film. If I knew how to use a camera I would have made many films. I have been told I am a visual poet. I am connected to visual artists. I am constantly exploring new ways of expressing poetry. It is always poetry. All my plays are poetry. The same with film, the way I did my film *THE BRINK* [1961]. My reference is jazz. I've always considered myself a jazz poet. In jazz, one goes into it [the performance], and then somewhere between tunes there will be an introduction [of the musicians and song] and, of course, again at the end. The titles come after the fact in a jazz performance, and that is exactly how I did my film.

NG: So you are always in a sense rewriting, like jazz improv?

rw: No, I don't, no. This is what I do. I work on a piece. I put myself at a desk, and I am writing. Say a friend of mine has died and I want to do a poem because two days later there will be a wake, and I am going to read for it, so I focus on this person. Or I do a poem to a piece of art. I focus on that piece of art; I enter it. I will have fifty pieces of paper with one line or two lines, lines repeated—it just covers the room. I know I am wasting a lot of paper—I hope I always have all the paper I need! Then comes the essence. I will maybe work twenty-four hours until the piece is finished. I do not rewrite. Does that make sense? Other times, I will come home, I have been out all night writing in the bar, and one idea starts another idea and then it is a fragment and I just leave it. It is perfect the way it is. I do not rewrite. To be spontaneous, I don't even think. I let the heart, the eyes, the hands just move with it. It comes out that way and trails off sometimes into unfinished sentences, and I leave it that way. That's the way I do spontaneous writing.

NG: So you don't draft at all?

rw: The only time so far as drafting goes is when a book is published. I make sure that the line is exactly the way I want it, but I may change one word here and there. I really like working in the present tense. As I said, I extend my poetry into whatever form, whether it is a novel or a story or a play, so I rewrite. I go through the piece and make sure that it's all in the present tense. I write it like I am there, so then the person who reads it, or hears it from me, is there with me.

NG: In what ways has your work progressed over the years?
rw: I just want to mention one thing, that my work works in a spiral form. A spiral is a very important symbol for me. In other words, it isn't like it goes here to there and from there to here. It goes here and then it goes around and then it goes around, repeating themes through the decades. It isn't progressing in a linear form, but in an open circular form. You see what I am saying? But it really goes around, you know, and hits the same point again in a higher level.

NG: What, or who, were some of the fundamental influences on your writing?
rw: I wrote my first poem at age five in the German language and always knew I was a poet. As for influences, well, not influences, but let's say expansion of consciousness into poetry: Goethe and Schiller. I'll give you more names from different directions. Maria Rainer Rilke, his passionate angel. Edgar Allen Poe, his fixation with death yet expressed with such beauty that even though it dealt with the ugly it turned it into the fantastic. I was already doing my own version of modern poetry. I discovered modern poetry when I lived at a place called the Art Circle in 1949 in Chicago. It was a rooming house for artists at seven dollars a week. There people turned me on to writers like Anaïs Nin, Henry Miller—*The Colossus of Maroussi*, a book of pure light; Isak Dinesen, Djuna Barnes—I love her novel *Nightwood*.

I also read Virginia Woolf's *Orlando* at that time. A large influence on my writing was the films that came out in the sixties. Truffaut. The New Wave from France, *Breathless, Hiroshima Mon Amour*. It's the breaking through language. It wasn't only what they said but how they said it.

N G: Stein was an influence too, wasn't she?

r w: I would definitely say so. People used to make jokes about Stein. Her musical realism made the heart break. Oh, absolutely. I love that woman! "There's no there there." Well, that's a joke too because the phrase continues. She didn't mean that Oakland wasn't there—she was trailing it off into dimensions. Her influence is obvious in my fiftieth birthday poem, "SOMETHING CURRENT," the last poem in *SINGLE OUT*.

N G: Why did you turn to film?

r w: Now first of all I love movies. They were both my inspiration and escape. I would spend hours in the movie house. I knew every movie house where you could go for twenty-five cents if you went at noon and watched three or four movies. Then those wonderful, new foreign films came out around the late fifties and early sixties. Antonioni, Fellini, Truffaut, Bergman. From different countries and languages. Oh, of course, Kurasawa. And then there was a movie theatre called The Vogue that showed these new films. The Vogue still exists; it's in San Francisco. I lived on nothing. I had no way to pay the two-dollar entrance, so I phoned The Vogue to talk to the manager, representing myself as a reviewer. I didn't do reviews, but I wrote poems in response to the films.

N G: How did you come to do your film *THE BRINK*?

r w: I am in San Francisco, and most of my friends were painters and musicians rather than poets. I flitted in and out of all kinds of scenes.

There was Wally Berman.[1] Then there was *Beatitude*, a North Beach poetry rag with its eclectic mix, and so on. Elias Romero, who did light shows.[2] I sort of skipped, hopped here and there a little bit. People called me a hummingbird. Paul Beattie, his wife Dee, and my husband of that time, Mel Weitsman, connected and we lived across the street from each other. One day Paul Beattie, a painter, told me he had just bought a 16-mm camera and asked me to write a script. I had just finished my narrative poem "THE BRINK" [in 1960], so he asked me to turn it into a film script, which I did. I asked friends to be in it. I took them to the places I wanted to film, told them what was to happen there, and they would improvise. I don't know how to use a camera, but I did the editing. My best friend, artist Sutter Marin, played "He" and another painter friend, Lori Lawyer, played "She" in the film. He [Sutter Marin] was my best friend since 1952 when I first hitchhiked to San Francisco. He died of AIDS in 1985. I'm grateful I have a record in this film of him.

I used a lot of my impressions from my wanderings around San Francisco and the Bay area. A lot of spontaneous magic happened with the film. For example, we are in the cafeteria, and there is a scene of the couple who are the main characters, and then you'll see a shot of this old couple. They just happened to be sitting there, just fit into the scene.

NG: So they were found "objects" for the film?

rw: Yes, it was that way. You see this is how I work, with a solid core, like the pit of a peach. In *DESERT JOURNAL*, I gave myself a discipline of five written pages at a time, so I have a circumscribed discipline but within that discipline I allow complete freedom.

---

1. Wallace Berman (1926–1976) was a photographer and painter.
2. Elias Romero was one of the major developers of the psychedelic light shows of the sixties.

NG: That sounds like Kerouac's descriptions of his writing.

rw: You know, he and I had a fantastic connection on multiple levels. That was before I had published anything, and I don't know if he had done something in a previous first novel yet or not, maybe, but *On the Road* wasn't written.

NG: *The Town and the City*, his first novel, was 1950.

rw: Right, I met him two years after that. But I didn't know he had a book out, and then we connected, but there was no physical attraction between us.

NG: Where did you meet?

rw: I don't know exactly. All I know is that I was living in a building called The Hotel Wentley[3] at the corner of Polk and Sutter. I had a room there for twenty-two dollars a month, and I forgot where we met, but he would drop by my place at three or four in the morning carrying his bottle of red wine. We'd start writing haiku to each other, kind of a dialogue, and then at some point he'd pass out. Neal Cassady, as if by clockwork, would show up before dawn, "Okay, let's pick Jack up." About Neal . . . I am sure everybody knows that Neal loved cars and liked to drive fast and was a good driver. I was not much into cars, you know. I didn't know anybody who had a car, and I am from a Europe that didn't have cars. So he would say, "Time to see the sun come up." He would carry Jack downstairs into one of his stolen cars. There's a street in San Francisco called Lombard. Every tourist knows it. It is like a snake, a one-way street. On the other side of the city was the same kind of a street, but a two-way street, and what would Neal do? He would be at the top of the hill, and he would

3. The Hotel Wentley, a shabby hotel, attracted artists and was commemorated in John Wieners's collection titled *The Hotel Wentley Poems*.

go seventy-five miles an hour, which was a lot then, down that hill—width for one car. If ever a car had come from the other way I wouldn't be here to tell you about it. Then he would drive me back to the Wentley, and off they went. I never saw Jack in North Beach.

NG: You say you and Kerouac wrote haiku. What is it about the haiku that attracts you?

rw: Haiku is a fabulous discipline for making each word succinct, meant, cutting out the fat, a perfect exercise for poetry. By cutting out the fat, making it bone. Someone who reviewed my *DESERT JOURNAL* called me the "master of the eraser."

NG: Do you use primarily the seventeen-syllable form?

rw: In one of my plays, *M & M*, one of the characters says, "All translations are phony." Seventeen syllables is the Japanese form of haiku, but I use it most of the time in the English [form] anyway, as do most people who write haiku. As in *DESERT JOURNAL*, I gave myself a certain discipline, and then within that discipline I do free form.

NG: Kerouac's poetry often seems propelled by the sound of the syllable rather than the meaning of the discrete word, which strikes me as relevant to your poetry.

rw: Well, for the thing to really work the meaning and the reverberation of the sound have to hit at the same point. Kerouac was able to hit. A lot of people think they want to perform with jazz, but they haven't the ear to tune into that kind of nuance. It is a matter of nuance rather than syllable. Haven't you ever met people who may have a different philosophy of life than yours and yet you connect? And there are other people with whom you have the same philosophy and the same way of thinking and yet don't connect. The bridge isn't there. As I said before, we had this fantastic connection, to jump in and not verbalize first. Just let yourself fall into this creative vortex.

NG: What about the ways in which your poetry and jazz intersect?
rw: My phrasing and rhythms depend on what I hear. It's a dialogue with the musicians. I never use music as a background. I give the musicians room to come up with riffs of their own. I lower my voice, raise my voice. I may repeat phrases. I may make up sounds. Sometimes people tell me they hear Japanese or African. It just comes to me. I don't know what I am going to do. And that's what is exciting.

NG: Did you work to bebop much?
rw: Bebop was definitely my turn on. I discovered jazz at the Art Circle. I was listening to Lady Day, who was there before bebop. You know Billie Holiday had an incredible way of making the sounds live. The lyrics she sang were all so negative, like "he left me to die"—you know, really heavy blues like "it doesn't matter if you hit me, I will come back." But her voice gave life to the song. And Lester Young, who also came before bebop, but he made the inroad for bebop, took off on riffs. Bird, Monk, Bud Powell. Well, there is Django Rhinehart who was doing it in the twenties . . . gypsy guitar in Paris. In classical music Schoenberg, Shostakovich, Bartok. These were the people I was listening to.

NG: There's a mingling of personal and cultural history that gives your work a lot of power. I see that in *DESERT JOURNAL*.
rw: *DESERT JOURNAL* has an energy that is beyond anything that I ever thought would happen, but to this day I use it as a performance piece. There are forty poems—forty days.[4] When I do a performance, reading solo or with musicians, I say to the audience, "Give me a number from one to forty." And that is the piece I read. I never know

---

4. *DESERT JOURNAL* contains forty poems, titled consecutively "FIRST DAY" through "FORTIETH DAY."

which one I am going to read. That keeps me on my improvised toes, often with surprising responses from the audience, like "How did you know this about me?"

NG: So *DESERT JOURNAL* is always a different poem? That makes the poem more of a circle than a line.

rw: I have never worked with straight lines. "The dot become a line become a circle become a dot"—that's a line from one of the poems in *DESERT JOURNAL*. That is a very strong image in my work: a dot become a line, become a circle.

NG: Do you consider *DESERT JOURNAL* your most significant work?

rw: I do consider it my most profound work up-to-date, published. It went beyond the discipline I had planned for it. Energy keeps building through the years. It is a perfect performance piece. It is living language with a definite focus and shifting patterns like sand in the desert. Do you want to hear the story? There was a poetry contest for a narrative poem to win a thousand dollars—now this is in the sixties. I had just finished "THE BRINK," which is a narrative poem, and I thought I would send it. It didn't win. So I thought I would write a novel. I would write two hundred pages, any nonsense that came to my head, for forty days, write five pages a day, five times forty is two hundred. So I disciplined myself to write five pages in one sitting, and it could be one word on the page, but it had to be five pages—that would be one day. It took seven years. By the time it was finished, it had entered another dimension. That writing took me to the most barren place, the desert. I was born under the sign of Cancer and water is very important to me. So I was entering this inner desert. It named itself *DESERT JOURNAL*. I had never been to an actual desert. I was about three-quarters through the book when I did go to the desert.

NG: Did that trip to the desert change the direction of the book?
rw: No, it just confirmed my reference to it.

NG: Were there any particular individuals who gave you support?
rw: You see most of my support came from friends, and most of my friends were painters and musicians. Two artists that I worked with a lot, whose work I titled for their shows in galleries and museums— they even paid me for those titles. One of them is Sutter Marin. He saw me through a lot of relationships, you know, husbands, lovers. Another one that I worked with was Ernie Nadalini—he always signed his paintings Nadalini. One of the poets to whom I felt connected was Madeline Gleason. We met in the late fifties. We were booked on the same program at a bookstore, and I had just finished this kind of collage poem, and she and her lover Mary Greer were sitting in the first row almost falling off their chairs laughing. When it was Maddy's turn to read, I fell in love with her work. From then on it was a deep, deep friendship. Maddy actually started the first poetry festival in San Francisco in 1947.[5] She passed away in 1979 at the age of seventy-five. The last two years of her life, my partner Paul Blake took care of her.

Now as far as supporters of my work, do you want to know who really supported me in those days? Bartenders in North Beach! They would buy my books. Yes, they bought the books. There was especially one bartender, Deno Petrucchi. He was born and grew up in North Beach. He was tending bars when he was about sixteen and

---

5. In 1947, Madeline Gleason, Robert Duncan, and James Broughton started the Festival of Contemporary Poetry at the Labaudt Gallery.

seventeen, and you know you are supposed to be twenty-one. Deno and I were good friends. I will tell you a story about Deno. One day in the seventies I am walking to the bar where Deno was working at that time. And Deno said, "What are you drinking?" And I said, "I just sold my first book to the San Francisco Main Library and here's my five dollar check—I want a beer." He picked up my check, put the beer in front of me and a five dollar bill and said, "I will never cash this check." He not only bought my books, but he also collected a lot of other poetry and art from our neighborhood. He died in 1994.

NG: That's really grass-roots.

rw: That's how it's always worked for me. I have read in the most unlikely places—in a gay motorcycle bar—anywhere on the street, just anywhere, and it has always been like that.

NG: What about the way you spell your name in all lower case?

rw: People think it is e. e. cummings, but that's not so. My original language is German. Well, in German all nouns are capitalized. This was my own rebellion against law and order. I probably began [that] in the sixties.

NG: What are your thoughts on the resurgence of interest in the Beats?

rw: I certainly found this true in Europe, when I was invited in 1998 to take part in festivals and other performances. There is a parallel between the suppressive political era of the fifties and the right wing movement now. And there is a seriousness in the young people as we are entering 2000. The young people are much more serious than they are given credit for. I have a great deal of respect for them. And this breaking of lines, like multi-media? We were doing a lot of that in the fifties, and now it seems to be happening again. Well, you know how it happens with art. The mainstream picks it up, it becomes homogenized, and then new things pop up. Timing is everything.

Part II

April 2, 2002

rw: How shall we start? Okay, I will tell a story I've never told before. I left home in '49 and started out with the bohemians. Moved into the Art Circle in Chicago. In order to survive, I started modeling in art schools. One time I was modeling, and there was a poster behind me of San Francisco, at which point I thought "Aha." That was 1949. One day one of my friends came to visit and told me to come upstairs to the living room where there was a jam session going on. I was in the middle of writing, I wanted to stay in my poem, and he grabbed the poem and looked at it, and he said, "Oh, they've got to hear this." So he pulled me upstairs, and I started reading, but instead of listening, they just started playing behind me. That's how my whole thing with jazz and poetry started.

Anyway, in 1952 I hitchhiked out to San Francisco, and I went immediately to North Beach, which was my last ride. In about 1955, the whole Beat thing happened. I also encountered a musician I knew from New Orleans. I ran into him in the street, and he said, "Come on over and jam with us." Well, I just used to make up sounds and read some poems, and, you know, every few days or so I would just go over there and jam and sometimes I would just listen. In 1956, three of those musicians opened up a club called The Cellar. One was Jack Minger. The other was Sonny Wayne, he's now Sonny Nelson. The third was Wil Carlson. Jack Minger's wife and I would wait tables.

A little beer and wine club—it was down home, nothing fancy. None of this minimum two drink stuff. Once a week, on Wednesday, I did poetry and jazz. I did this for months, and then I started inviting other poets. I did this for about two years or so. Then one day I needed to leave the city, so I went to Big Sur. Well, it was only after that that some of the other well-known poets, whose names I'm not going to mention because everyone knows them, ended up doing the same thing. Only they were very smart. They recorded them and got records out of it. So nobody knows that I did this, innovate jazz and poetry in San Francisco in 1956 at The Cellar.

I landed with artists like Wally Berman and his group who were into alchemy and the surreal. And then Kenneth Rexroth had a weekly evening thing[6] and I went to a couple of those. I was invited. Helen Adam was there. But I thought it was much too cerebral—a lot of literary preening. But I want to get back to the poetry thing. There were all these spinning balls that kind of touched on each other. They weren't against each other, but they were all spinning in their own groups.

HALLIE SHAPIRO: Is there a particular sense of community that is specific to the Beat culture?

rw: We certainly didn't consider ourselves beatniks. That was a very bad word. Really, an insult. I think it just happened. There's always been creative centers, you know. Artists of all kinds gravitate to certain sections of the world, whether it's Paris or the Village in New York. As far as community, my particular time was in North Beach in San Francisco. When I lived in Chicago, artists were known as bohemians. I guess I gravitated to San Francisco because there would

---

6. weiss is referring to Rexroth's Friday evening salons, attended by writers such as Robert Duncan, Philip Lamantia, Jack Spicer, and others.

be other artists there. When I first got there, I didn't quite find them right away. So, as far as community, well, it comes and goes. Artists have the tendency to need solitude and also to need those wild communications, and it becomes rather incestuous if you don't go out and make other connections, which most artists try and do. I used to like walking in the middle of the night, and meeting people, talking to them in twenty-four-hour coffee shops, where all kinds of magic would happen. We didn't move as a phalanx, you know, that's for sure.

Of course, I always have been a bar person, or since that time. And I would drink, but I drink very slowly. I can have a sip of beer for two hours. But I like going to the bars, sometimes just leaning back observing or listening. So it would be nice to stay in San Francisco. See, one of the things I like most about San Francisco is that it's such a walking city. You didn't have to use public transportation to get to other parts of town. I'd just walk, find a bar, put my foot in and feel the atmosphere. If I felt right, I would sit down, and maybe there would be somebody there I knew or somebody there I wanted to talk to. Maybe I just wanted to write. San Francisco pretends that it never gets cold! But it's a damp and dense city. The places are not warm. So most of the communication is in coffee shops or bars. That's where you go out to meet other people. It also keeps you fluid. You're not stuck with having some people come over and then try to get them out. Or how you visit someone and then you want to leave. The bar's open-ended. In New York, people lived in cold water flats. These weekly things, those were in somebody's house. I actually started a salon kind of situation when I had a seven room apartment in the late fifties—well, when did I get that apartment?—1957. Brew Moore[7] and his wife had split up, and they'd given us, Mel and me, their flat.

---

7. Brew Moore (1924–1973) was a tenor saxophonist.

I started a salon about every two weeks or so. People would meet there and read poetry. After about six months, I got tired of it. You know—we didn't have plastic cups—and I was tired of washing glasses.

HS: Beat literature has been portrayed as heavily male-dominated. What are your thoughts on that?

rw: Somewhere there was an ego thing that was to keep the women out. My luck with some of the names like Kerouac was that I was never anybody's girlfriend, so they treated me a little better than the other women they were involved with. I had very good friends, but they didn't treat their women well. When it came right down to it, we were not invited into the center of things, just the periphery. I mean, there was the Auerhahn Press; Philip Lamantia did his best to try to get me published by it. No, we don't publish any women. Ferlinghetti said the same thing to me. My book, *GALLERY OF WOMEN*, was portraits of women, and in 1959 I approached him to do that. He said no, but eventually it did get published in 1959 by Adler Press in San Francisco. He also said I wasn't political enough. My work was rather subtle, you know. Women were put in the background. Okay, I'll end with this. *Women of the Beat Generation,* which was done by Brenda Knight in 1996, there's a photograph of me in that book reading at the street fair, in 1959, and if you look at it closely with a magnifying glass, you see all these names [on the poster] and they're all male [names], except for Helen Adam, who was a decade older than we were, so she was given more respect. No other women were mentioned. Now, the joke is that most of these men have vanished from the poetry scene. But I also knew a lot of male poets, quite wonderful, who were also not acknowledged because they were not in the center of things. So it wasn't only the women. Some of these men made it a very cliquish situation. Well, no more than anything else. I'm sure academia, I'm sure corporations, I'm sure every place has its own little clique.

Part III

August 23, 2002

NG: Can you talk some about Madeline Gleason? What was it about her poetry that attracted you, and did you read each other's poetry?

rw: Yes, we loved reading to each other. We'd go over and have dinner with her and end up drinking Irish Mist. Yeah, she was a good drinker. Well, okay, one thing we have in common I think is the short words, you know, we have different ways of coming out with them, but she would say these sharp little things—not go on and on—that would just tickle your funny bone. And there was always this impish kind of humor that came out. We'd end up laughing. She did wonderful spot checks about people she'd describe, and you would instantly see them and there would be—well, I don't want to say cartoons because they weren't; they were full bodied—but you would really get the character in a few sketches. She was also a wonderful painter. She did small oils. Very intense night scenes. And she loved the circus. Or there would be a painting of one lone house with one light in the dark. And there was also, well, you know, she was Irish and had that Irish mystic and mystery and believing in the little people and that kind of thing.

NG: So you would read each other's poetry?

rw: To each other, but also aloud. We both believed in the oral tradition, which is continued today, and they call it "spoken word." But in those days, that was not done except in very academic situations. But, you know, what can I say? She had a wit. That's it, the word "wit"! And she loved language, but she wasn't verbose. She was very lyrical. Her major work, they're really intense love poems, and she really had a lot of wit and humor, but there was a lot of depth to her. "Love" was a big word for her. I don't know if she went to Mass or not, but she certainly had a deep religious connection, yes, in the way I do without having a form. And she had a wonderful voice.

NG: Can you describe it?
rw: I can't! In the audio tapes of *Women of the Beat Generation*, I read her poem. When you listen to it, you'll see how different I do my own work than I do hers. I try to enter her kind of rhythms, but I could not simulate her voice, which was very, very rich, wonderful, not loud, not booming, but very penetrating. I will tell you the last time she ever read, she was very, very ill, and it was just a few weeks before she died, and she was living on Bernal Heights. And the bar the Wild Side West had also moved to Bernal Heights. We used to read when the Wild Side was in North Beach. This was in the seventies now that I'm talking about because we'd known each other all these years. But the last reading—so here she's reading. She's very frail, and all these women friends were going to read her poetry. And I said—and I was a little drunk—I said, "Maddy, will you just go and read your own fucking stuff?" And she looked at me and she smiled. She got up, and even though—as frail as she was, you could hear, and of course this was in a bar! You could absolutely feel it—hear the poem—I mean, when she did those poems she wasn't frail.

NG: And you heard Helen Adam too, of course.
rw: I heard Helen Adam. Of course, she did these incantations like a wild witch. Have you ever heard her read? You know, she was in that

Scottish ballad tradition, and they were very spooky, very spooky poems that she did. Gothic I would say. Very gothic. The kids today think they invented gothic! She had this wild, witchy voice—a wild, witchy voice.

NG: At various times, you've identified yourself as a street poet. What's the significance of being a street poet as opposed to someone who came out of another tradition?

rw: It's funny because my language isn't exactly of the street. But I always seem to connect with people. It's a certain reference to moments that are very human and very understood, about the underdog. Someone like Jack Micheline was definitely a street poet, [but] if somebody has read my work they would never think that I was a street poet. But I have done a lot of performances on the street very successfully, with people, and I love doing this. I think it's just a certain reality, you know.

NG: The way you're connecting with your audience in that moment?

rw: Yes, exactly.

NG: So it's not the language?

rw: Well, it is language too. It's also reference points. Like *DESERT JOURNAL*, which is a very complicated thing to read. But when I read it out loud, even if people can barely spell, they always see what I'm saying.

NG: So it's more than just using the vernacular.

rw: Right.

NG: How did your position as a street poet affect your relationships with other poets?

rw: I don't know. Well, I have to tell you several things. One thing about street poets. I have not always read to other poets when I had a reading. When I have audiences, they are so mixed that people can't believe it. I seem to attract the off-beat kind of people. I've read in pizza places, and it's worked, you know? That is one of the things—I like to read in unexpected places. Not places where poetry's usually read. I've walked around the city and connected with places that never had poetry readings. Like where maybe the old pensioners would hang out. I'd talk the owner into letting me do a weekly thing, and I would end up doing it and these people would come. There was a bar in San Francisco in the seventies. It was just a neighborhood bar, and mostly the pensioners, who lived upstairs in the building, came down every night. So I started this poetry reading, and there were never more than about ten, twelve people doing their nightly drinking—and listening. Then one night—I did this for about six months, once a week—there was this rather silent, bent-over-the-bar kind of person sitting there, and he sent me a drink. He didn't even look at me. And I went over to thank him. He was mumbling, and it turned out that he ships out. He said, "I've been looking for an image all my life, and you just gave it to me." A street person, right!?

I've had people who say, "Oh, I don't really like poetry" because of this idea in their heads of what poetry is, and they will connect with me. So I've done most of my connecting this way rather than follow-ing or being part of the inner clique of these regular poetry circles, although I've been in poetry festivals with them.

NG: How did you start hitchhiking? What was that like for a young woman at that time, the early fifties?

rw: I tell you, it was very easy. It had nothing to do with Kerouac or anything. Okay, I was born in Europe, in Berlin, and I came to the States, and in 1946 after I graduated from high school, my parents went to work, with, as Americans, the Army of Occupation. So I was with them, and they sent me to school in Switzerland, all of which I didn't want to do. Well, how did I get around? A lot of European people— I mean, I did it [hitchhiking] in Germany, and of course being an American, the only vehicles were the American ones. They always picked me up, the soldiers! I didn't have any problems. I wore my saddle shoes and jeans, and they knew I was American. Then in Switzerland, I had practically no money. So what did I do? Because I liked to move, I got on the road and put my thumb out. I went to Geneva and I went to Brussels and later on I went with a friend to Paris. We didn't have any money; we hitchhiked. So I came back to the States, and hitchhiking seemed the most natural thing to do. It never occurred to me that it was something unusual. But I'd already been doing it in Europe with no problems.

NG: Was it easy in the States to get rides?
rw: Yeah, oh, yeah. I traveled from New York to New Orleans with a friend. Sometimes by myself. I still have a photograph of a truck driver who picked us up outside of New York, and he insisted on taking a picture with us. He had a camera. Actually, I was again traveling to San Francisco, and we were in Nebraska, Boys Town, and this young guy who had just gotten out of the Army picked us up. I had no problems. Not ever. I did not even think of that and I didn't expect it. I never got hit on. But also having a street sense and being a bar person I sort of have my guards out.

NG: Did you see many women your age hitchhiking in the United States?
rw: No-o-o-o-o. No. No.

NG: Because you rarely hear about any women doing that. Your experiences were very unusual.

rw: And that was long before *On the Road* was written!

NG: What was your best or most unusual ride?
rw: This one out of Omaha, Nebraska. We somehow ended up somewhere near Pike's Peak. And of course we had to go up.

NG: You were with a friend?
rw: Yes. We got to Pike's Peak, and of course we have to go up there. None of us had ever been up there. We get to the top. There weren't any other cars. I mean, today it's probably non-stop! No, there weren't any other cars. It was toward sunset. We got to the top just as the sun was setting. And it was just the most exhilarating! We all went to the top in three different directions and it was like "Ahhhhh!" It was incredible.

NG: What about the ride that dropped you off at North Beach and said, "This is where you belong." How did all that happen?
rw: Now I was alone at that point. You see, my friend and I had a huge fight outside Santa Barbara, and I went on the road alone.

NG: Was your friend male or female?
rw: Male. We were very connected. Anyway, I left the restaurant and put my hand out, and a woman with a young girl stopped. Today, would a woman with a child stop?!? She was taking her girl to school, and she took me fifty miles. Then I got in a car with six soldiers. Can you believe that? On their way to Bakersfield. They dropped me off in Fresno, since one of the soldiers was getting off in Fresno. Maybe he was going to see his family. They were young. There were six of them, can you imagine? It was hot; it was in August. And he paid for a hotel room for me, cheap. We had supper together, and then he left. I got one or two more rides, and the last ride—he was going home to San Francisco, and it wasn't that far. He stopped at his house first, and he

took me upstairs. I guess his wife and kids were gone that day, or were coming home later, and I took a shower, and he fed me something, and then we hopped in the car to go back. Nothing—not ever coming on—no problems! He took me straight to North Beach, right to Broadway and Columbus, and said, "This is where you belong. This is where you belong." And dropped me right off. It was the bohemian section. Because I told him I was a poet.

Pieces of a Song

—Diane di Prima

Beat's most famously woman poet is Diane di Prima. Her dedication to that vocation, combined with a brazen repudiation of prescriptions for female behavior, has rendered her a paragon of artistic independence for many of the women Beat writers. Di Prima was born into a Catholic Italian family in Brooklyn in 1934. Her maternal grandfather was a spirited anarchist who taught her to love literature and to remain passionately independent. In the early fifties she briefly attended Swarthmore College, but left to pursue a life in poetry in New York's Lower East Side. She wrote and performed her own poetry, met Ginsberg and Kerouac, and in 1961 she and LeRoi Jones/Amiri Baraka began *The Floating Bear*, a newsletter that was one of the most influential small press publications of the era. In the same year she co-founded the New York Poets Theatre, and in 1964 she and her then-husband, Alan Marlowe, founded the Poets Press, publishing works by Audre Lorde, Jean Genet, and Herbert Huncke. By the late sixties, di Prima had moved to San Francisco, where she worked with the Diggers, studied Zen and the magical arts, raised five children, taught at New College of California, and continues to write.

Di Prima's poetics has consistently relied upon the felt sense of language, the sanctity of spontaneous creation, and the need to seek

new sources of imaginative stimulation. Her early poetry, represented in *This Kind of Bird Flies Backwards* (1958) and *Dinners and
Nightmares* (1961), showcases these Beat literary interests by drawing
upon the bohemian enclave of Greenwich Village. The poems in these
texts revel in the domestic squalor and luxury that characterize the
emergence of the woman Beat poet. Many unabashedly speak the hipster argot that drew on the black vernacular. Reflective of the movement's romantic and modernist antecedents and its links to the
postmodern, these two collections cross literary borders, collaging love
poems, lists, monologues, conversations, laments, and other forms.
Di Prima's theatrical play with voice and character reveals skepticism
of the idea that women are content with subordination and the con-
viction that women desire and are fit for self-determination, sexual
liberation, and independence.

Di Prima has inimitably addressed the female body as the site upon
which female agency is constructed through pleasure, reproduction,
exploitation, and resistance. Her poetics, and especially her quasi-fic-
tive *Memoirs of a Beatnik*, critique the angel/whore image of woman
promulgated by many male Beat writers as she claims the right to her
own sexual and reproductive powers. However, di Prima's oeuvre
makes it clear that asserting such rights through poetics is not auto-
matically liberating. The repercussions of patriarchy's use of imprisonment, pain, and death are woven throughout her poetry. An
unmarried woman may choose to have a child and serenade it, as in
"Song for Baby-O, Unborn": "Sweetheart / when you break thru /
you'll find / a poet here / not quite what one would choose" (*This Kind*
37), but if she did not want the pregnancy, she faced a grim alternative.
As di Prima wrote in *Recollections of My Life as a Woman*, "[a]bortions
in those days were held to be simply women's business. . . . One of
the unsung, unspoken, ways women risked their lives. . . . I had
always gone to bed with any lover knowing I could become pregnant,

knowing I could die, over the encounter" (230). This untenable position becomes the subject of poetic meditation in "Brass Furnace Going Out: Song, after an Abortion," which through a transcendental voice gives primordial shape to the poet's vision of the lost child:

> *the water was cold the day you slipped into the river*
>
> . . . .
>
> *your face no sooner dissolved than I thought I saw*
> *a kneecap sticking up where the current is the strongest*
> *a turtle*
>> *older than the stars*
> *walked on your bones*
>
> (Charters, *Portable* 365)

While "Brass Furnace" might be misread as an anti-abortion poem, it stands more persuasively as testimony to the poet's belief in the life force and in the woman artist's role as "the door into the world" (di Prima, *Recollections* 230).

Di Prima has remained faithful to this impulse, and later collections, such as *Revolutionary Letters* (1971), *The Calculus of Variation* (1972), and *Pieces of a Song: Selected Poems* (1990), attest to an artistic practice committed to civil and women's rights, Zen Buddhism, and the study of myth and magic. *Loba: Parts 1–16* (1978, 1998), her visionary exploration of woman as wolf goddess, best expresses these interests. Di Prima aligns the poetics of *Loba* with Robert Duncan's concept of composition by field, explaining that the creation of this work in progress "is like taking the ideogrammic method and extending it, so that the poem can include everything; and each 'thing' (image, stanza, song, quote, blob of light) has equal weight in the Field . . . implying, like within an ideogram, the unsaid commonalities, which themselves form other dimensions."[1] In this poetic space, di Prima constructs representations of the goddess, the mother, the artist, and others shapeshifting into an essentialist female community. The poet enunciates her mission in "The Loba Addresses the Goddess/Or the Poet as Priestess Addresses the Loba-Goddess":

> *Is it not in yr service that I wear myself out*
> *running ragged among these hills, driving children*
> *to forgotten movies? In yr service*
> *broom & pen.*

(Loba 134)

The ampersand and the stenographic "yr," vestiges of di Prima's Poundian and Black Mountain heritage, mingle with the sermonic and the vernacular to assert that across time women artists in the service of the literary spirit toil on, a rich and rhizomic community.

Parts One through Three of the following interview were conducted on July 29, 1989, by the poet Tony Moffeit in Boulder, Colorado, while di Prima was teaching at Naropa Institute. Part Four was conducted by Moffeit via e-mail in August 2002.

Part I

July 29, 1989

TONY MOFFEIT: Early on, what were the influences or the forces that drove you creatively?

---

1. This is an excerpt from an informal statement di Prima made to Michael McClure in early September 2002 regarding whether she considered herself a "projective" poet in the Charles Olson vein. "MMcC then asked me to write down what I'd just said, and mail it to him. I did so the very same day." E-mail from di Prima to Nancy Grace, January 31, 2003.

DIANE DI PRIMA: Over time I've come to see that, well, when you're in the middle of it, you don't notice that what you're doing is really very different from anybody else, especially if you're living with a great deal of energy and passion, so when I think of my young years when I was first living alone and writing, and then I decided I wanted a baby, but I didn't want any man around—that was 1957, that was just my life, you know. But, looking back on it, I see a couple of things. One is a lot of energy that triggered it off; aside from a passionate energy, a passionate love of literature, was a big energy of anger.

TM: Anger?

DP: From the home situation, which at that point in my life wasn't even really that accessible to me; neither the anger nor the memories, because I just took at face value what I was told about my home life—how perfect it had been—and so I figured I was just this crazy rebel doing these things, having come from this perfect home. But now looking back as an older woman, I can see that I was triggered a lot by a subterranean stream of anger that I think, considering everything, I used pretty well. I could have used it in a much more destructive way than to write books and have babies. But there was a very strong sense of—and this was true for most of the people I knew who were artists at that time in New York—a strong sense of us against the world. So it was very easy to form extended family communities, that took care of each other. I think we may have all come from the dysfunctionalness of post-Depression and then that crazy Second World War situation, but we all felt like we had to take care of each other. When people ask me now about why there isn't an art community, I think it's partly that difference. I perceive myself as having come semi-blind out of various situations, that is, not seeing them, and being reactive to some point, but then having had the good luck to have the anarchist grandfather I had, who read me Dante when

I was four, and all those kinds of exposures to some kind of European attitude that art is very important.

And not only art. I remember that we honored all the crafts people in our world very much. In other words, the man who came to plaster a wall. Even my father would say (we didn't use sheet rock in those days, we plastered), "It looks easy, but it's a high skill and they used wet plaster to paint the fresco painting." So it was a constant interlocking of art and regular skills for daily life. So there was an awareness of the world that kept it on course, but there was this undercurrent of just anger and the fact that you had to get away from regular society.

TM: And there was a community there to offer support.

DP: No, I think we were the community. We made the community. There was no community. When I hit the Lower East Side in 1953, there were no other people like me. Nobody on the block could figure me out. They thought I must be a whore because women didn't live alone, you know. It was a Polish block. There were Polish blocks, Ukranian blocks, and then slowly, you found a few other people doing the same thing in other areas and you made a community. There was no community there.

TM: Were these writers, musicians, artists?

DP: Dancers, painters, writers mostly. The musicians were a little older and already an established scene, but you didn't really get into the scene, you went to hear the music. The scene was not that open to new, young, white eighteen-year-old kids. But the music was a big support. And there was an older community of painters. But, again, they had their world. You would drop in at some of the places they hung out and talk a little, but in terms of making an extended family, we were doing that ourselves.

TM: A magical era in terms of all the arts. There were some exciting things being done in all the arts in the early to the late fifties.

DP: Yeah. Some of it might have been also that we had been cut off during the war from what the arts were in other places. I remember also bars putting on plays of Sartre. Things like that. So the ideas from Europe and probably the East, although we didn't know it quite yet then, were all starting to come in, and we had previously been quite isolated during the Second World War.

TM: What advice would you have for the writers who are starting out?

DP: Well, I think a few things. One would be to really honor the others in their community who are trying to be artists and to forge your own community, your own family, out of that. Honor that it [art] comes from a place. You know you may want to bring in all of the world, and that's important to bring in all kinds of influences from everywhere, but also respect that you're living in Michigan or whatever and work out of your own ground and with your own people. That's one thing.

And another thing is to really realize that you can't value too highly your own curiosity, inquisitiveness and passion for the arts. And not to let that get blunted by other people's cynicism or casualness. If you lose your inquisitiveness, Pound said this too, you're dead as an artist. You know, you've got to be curious about even art forms that put you off and things you don't like, but beyond the arts—about everything.

Those things: to have that basis of some kind of an extended family, compassion for each other, and honor the intent of the artist, whether or not the work has shown anything yet. You know, that's really important, because how are we going to get to the work otherwise? And a lot of people get nipped in the bud by cynicism and materialism in this culture without having had that chance. And if there's anything in your area that can form a nucleus for this family, like one bookstore with some far-out old guy who really still reads the Dore Dante or whatever, use it, use it, really gravitate to it. Use it because within the fact that it looks like a cultural desert, everywhere there are people with information. And, of course, to really give yourself a lot of room. Give yourself a lot of room to fuck up, to not write, to write again, to make mistakes.

TM: Could we talk about Zen, because I understand you studied and practiced?
DP: I studied Zen for a long time, yeah.

TM: How has it influenced your writing and your life?
DP: Well, yes, I think that Buddhism in general has been. But way back before any of us meditated or practiced Zen or anything really, D.T. Suzuki's books were an influence in the early fifties. And I remember because one of my teachers in the arts was a choreographer named James Waring, and he was close friends with Merce Cunningham and John Cage and so that influence of D.T. was in a direct lineage there. And we were all reading that stuff and it was influencing us in a great number of ways in our work. I would say some of them [those artists] were accepting that every form—it goes back to the notion of organic form—every form is real so you don't have to manipulate your work to get it into shape. Or as Robert Duncan later put it, consciousness itself is shapely. So trusting the basic field of consciousness and not trying— because the writing of the forties and the early fifties was very obsessed with the "well wrought urn." Remember that book by Cleanth Brooks? And all the "let's get this material and jam it into this shape," you know. So it was a big influence on opening the form and opening oneself to one's own consciousness.

And then, in the early sixties, I met Shunryu Suzuki, who became my teacher and started the Zen Center in San Francisco. I studied with Shunryu Suzuki and started to sit zazen around '62, and moved out to San Francisco in '67, and one of the main reasons was to sit at Zen

Center there and study with him. The other main reason was to work with the Diggers and the revolutionary situation that was going on. And Shunryu Suzuki died in '71, so I had about four years, and part of that time I was up in the North country, living in a commune, but most of the time I was right in town and sitting with him every day. And then, after he died, I didn't stay with Zen Center, because organizations per se are not my thing, and there wasn't that feeling of a strong pull to the lineage heir of Suzuki, who was an American man [Richard Baker], but I continued to sit and I would use various teachers who had been at Zen Center at that time: Katagiri Roshi, who taught in Minneapolis, and Kobun Chino Roshi.

TM: At Naropa?
DP: Yeah. I would just see them occasionally and I would sort of have an interview with them to check my practice, and a lot of the years I sat regularly, some of the years I didn't. And then, around '83, I decided I'd gone as far as I could go on the instructions that I'd gotten from Shunryu Suzuki and since I'd been here at Naropa all those years and had made good acquaintance with Trungpa Rinpoche and also felt that I needed a practice that included more magical elements, 'cause I was working a lot in Western magic, I asked to become his student in '83. So I've been studying Tibetan Buddhism in recent years and doing some of those practices. Just begun the Vajrayana practice. So it's been an interesting journey. It's been really, really, really strong.

Part II

July 29, 1989

TM: What were some of your early influences in terms of poetry?
DP: I'd have to say that the first big influence in poetry was Keats. When I was about twelve, I discovered philosophy and I started

to plough my way through all the philosophers and then through the grown-ups' novels. And then in the middle of one of Somerset Maugham's novels, whatever was in the Brooklyn Public Library, I found this quote from Keats—And I thought, whoever this guy is I'd better find him. And that led me over to the poetry section. I just read everything by Keats and then I got completely involved in the Romantics, but at that point in my life I'd say the main influence of that sort, we're talking about age thirteen or fourteen, was Keats's letters on poetry. And then around fourteen, I realized seriously that I had to commit myself to being a writer. It was really very, I would say, a traumatic moment; I was very sad. I realized from my teenage point of view that I was going to have to give up a lot of stuff to do this. I don't know how I knew that, but I knew it. So then I decided that what I would do is just write every day. I just had these school composition books with the black and white covers, and everyday I'd write something and—then, when I went away to college, the only use the college was to me really was they had a bookstore.

I went to Swarthmore for a year and a half and they had all these modern poets. In college, I found Auden on the shelf there in the bookstore, and then I found Pound. And everybody had a charge account at the bookstore, in those days. I left college after a year, a year and a half, because it wasn't suiting my desire to write. And just before I left I hit the bookstore and I charged—oh, you know, *The Cantos, Spirit of Romance, Make It New*, and cummings, and Eliot, of course. But the main big thing that happened to me was I left college when I was eighteen; I'd started at sixteen, and I went home to a little apartment on the Lower East Side, and I began to read everything Pound suggested in *The ABC of Reading*, which meant I found a Homeric Greek grammar. I read a little bit—I never got good at it—but I read a little Greek. I was able to sound it out and hear it. A little Dante, you know. Languages became an obsession. And by '55 I was writing to Pound and I went to visit him for two weeks at St. Elizabeth's [Hospital in Washington, D.C.]. He was staying with his close friend, Sheri Martinelli, the painter, kind of you could say his mistress, but he was in the hospital and she wasn't.

TM: Was he in fairly good condition?

DP: He was very coherent and talking a lot. I guess it was a few years later that he stopped talking. He talked a lot about his memories of New York, things he thought that we should do—I was with a friend—he thought that I should manage somehow single-handedly to get Pro Musica Antiqua on to national television. I was living on seventy dollars a month at that time, and I had saved up fifty-five dollars to come and see him. You know, twenty-five dollars was the bus fare and the other thirty dollars was to live on. Pound and I had many, many good days and good stories and just a feeling of being accepted as a serious artist. Which is what I found among almost all the great artists. If you say that's what you're up to—and you've probably found this too—they take you seriously and take you in on that level as a peer, and it's very inspiring, especially when you're young.

TM: This is probably a good time to talk about *Loba*. Generally, how the work has evolved, where you are with it, how you came to write it. When did it begin?

DP: In 1971, I was on the road and that first poem, "Ave," stands outside of the main poem. It's like an introduction, though I didn't know it then. Then a few months later, early '72, for me things like that—the large works—often they are something that come to you rather than [something] that you've figured out and crafted. Because of that sense of accepting consciousness, of seeing consciousness itself as being shapely. But I was teaching in a high school in Watsonville [California], with another teacher, a Cuban American from San Francisco. He was doing the bilingual part. And all of a sudden, I started to hear these lines. I mean that's not so unusual for me to hear a few lines, and if I write them down they'll lead into a whole poem, but it's usually a one-page poem or something like that. And so I sort of dropped back and let Elias finish teaching that class and I just wrote down what I got, which is that first little section: "If he did not come apart in her hands. . . ." And the first few sections, two or three, came in like that. And then I realized that I was on to something that wanted to be written, so I started.

I had a babysitter coming in three times a week in the morning at that point, and I set that time aside for this one work. And what it began to be was—I would often [make] collages with wolves or coyotes or wild animals and so bring the energy in until the writing started each of these mornings. The first part of the book, Part One, which ends with that "Loba Dances" poem—I thought that was the whole poem. It seemed like a finished product. And my husband at that time who was a poet, Grant Fisher, said, "You know, I think that the poem's not finished." And then sometime later it started up again, again with just being heard and then written. "The day lay like a pearl in her lap," I wrote in a car while somebody else was chattering at me a hundred miles an hour. And then it went on and for the first few years it was the main thing I was writing. Not a lot of other poems happened at the same time. That was the main thing—all the energy went into that one poem. And the material kept expanding and went from personal into stuff from Gnosticism and from other sources and so on, they just kept pouring into it. So that when we published in '78, the 200 pages that are there—that was a lot of it. Since then, I think there have been about another 100 or 120 pages. People say, well, how do you know if a poem's part of *Loba*? You just know. Certain things just feel like they're part of *Loba*.

TM: Have you completed it?
DP: No. No. It's an ongoing work. What's happened, I think, is a shift, it's like a different stage of the journey. You could say it's more

abstract, but I don't think that's quite it. It's not so much the life of the physical, emotional woman, like in the early parts—the child-bearing and all that. It's more like the life of the soul. And I had a dream one time that said if I lived long enough, I'd get into the part of *Loba* that was the life of the spirit. This is a different phase of the poem, definitely. It has a whole series of hymns to Tahuti, the Egyptian god of writing, in terms of him as a secret lover of Isis, and a lot of stuff like that. I'm putting in a bunch of translations I did of hymns to Kali that Ramprasad, the nineteenth-century saint, wrote.

TM: Many times you've been called the major female poet to emerge from the Beats. Was there an important message that the Beats gave the world?

DP: You know, it's hard to think about oneself as a piece of a move-ment, because you're yourself. The movement stays the movement and you keep changing. I think the Beat movement was terribly important in its time and still is important for young people now. I think that part of the message that the young people keep picking up on is the importance of really being yourself, and staying with your feelings, that your feelings are worthy of writing about, worthy of that consideration. You know, how much of Jack [Kerouac's] writing is from one little street corner, spinning off into the wonders and strangeness of existence itself.

And I think that especially it still stands, to a large extent, as some kind of monument or bulwark that you can honor all that stuff inside you as opposed to just so-called realistic writing that just says "this street corner had a brown house on it." And that sense of adven-ture that goes with that, that whole *On the Road* sense. But I do think that, in general, that sense that the world is open to you. You can get on a steamer and go to Costa Rica. And that what happens to you on those adventures and what your sense and feeling of it all is, is what you can write about, is the matter of the writing. And that's really important. One of the things for me, simply, when I started writing, was the joy of the street language. I still use it. I love it in *Loba* to be able to go into some very poetic place and then drop into street jargon and drop out again.

TM: And you do it successfully. It's not an easy thing to do.

DP: Yeah. It's kind of by ear that you do it. So then the other thing that the Beats—that time—had that was very important for me was the whole sense of time and timing and syncopation that we got out of jazz. And for me, that was always at the bottom of my work. When I was just titling my new selected poems and the title I wanted was *Pieces of a Song*—that's what I finally got—it was like referring to the jazz piece, "Pieces of a Dream." But it was also like, hey, these are the pieces I managed to write down of a song that's much bigger, but the other parts, I was doing something else, I didn't catch, you know. So that jazz sense. The sense of both melody line and syncopation as in something like, say, the early seventies. Rollins. It was always there. And with Monk. I remember Monk in the fifties. So that stuff, and the sense of adventure. That the world is really there as an adventure and you can bring that excitement to it. I think those things are important still.

TM: Are there, of those writers, any with whom you feel a special kinship?

DP: From the Beat gang? I think that there were a few of us that were latecomers to that, we were the babies. One of them was John Wieners. And he is the guy who can really take the most banal cliché and make it shine, just by his sound and his ear. I feel a lot of kinship with him. And I don't know whether you include these in the Beats, but my buddies are also Michael McClure and Philip Whalen. And I don't think there's probably been a greater poetic genius in the second half of this century in some ways than Gregory Corso, although only some of it gets to paper. But when it does, I mean, it's flaming. It's amazing. He puts his heroes, Baudelaire and Shelley, to shame sometimes, but that's sheer genius and it's not necessarily work. There's a big difference and the musicians know that. There's a lot of genius that doesn't get into the work.[2]

And, of course, you know, Allen [Ginsberg's] always been a staunch good friend and we've always had a lot to learn from each other and talk about, and when I was young I learned a lot. When his *Howl* came out I had already written my first book of poetry, *This Kind of Bird Flies Backward*, which was all in street language. And I'd been told that there was nobody in the world who would publish it, and actually *Howl* being published made it more possible for these other things to happen. My second book was *Dinners and Nightmares*, another slang book. Allen and Jack and I looked at it together one night before it came out. So there was a kind of closeness. In terms of direct influence, though, I'd say that Robert Duncan and Charles Olson were it, and are still, and early on, for technique and for learning my sound and my line, nobody like Creeley.

TM: In the introduction to her anthology, *Early Ripening: American Women's Poetry Now*, Marge Piercy lists you as one of the giants of American poets. Do you have a sense of being a giant among modern women poets?

DP: If you're a working artist, you constantly have the sense of what you haven't managed to achieve yet. What you haven't done, right? And then, over the years for the first time, I really got a sense—not of me—but of the giantness of the thrust of art in the twentieth century. This feeling I get like I was riding, surfing some kind of incredible

---

2. John Wieners (1934–2001), Philip Whalen (1923–2002), Gregory Corso (1930–2000).

wave. That we really didn't have any sense of where it was going. That feels great. I feel confident of the work of my contemporaries and me. But I can't say mine is it. Do you see what I'm saying? It's a whole. In one way it's like we're all working on one piece. And that's not trying to be fake humble.

The other thing I want to tell you here I've told to a few classes. There have been billions of us making art and in some way we have been the leavening or the thing that made human life possible when it was full of death or plague or war, which it always was. In all the pain of life—art was a kind of leavening. And being part of this gang of maybe billions, but certainly many millions of anonymous artists— being a part of that work crew in some way is a bigger honor than any reward that our single work brings us in terms of what we can have or make. Also it makes it much easier to live in a world of literary competition and endless critical articles and analyses of the poem because, hey, that's like this foam on the top [and] we're sort of the sea surge underneath.

Part III

July 29, 1989

TM: Are there popular culture figures we haven't talked about? Are there musicians, dancers, actors who have that same sense of exploration, adventure?
DP: Yeah. I mean I would go with my bag lunch and see the same Cocteau movie all day long. You'd pay once and just stay there. Yeah. Where, you know, all those European elements that we'd been cut off from by the war, late Surrealism and so on, were all there. You'd see *Blood of a Poet* six times, eight times. But one of the huge terms of

popular media we haven't talked about at all is song. We have song-writers, some of whom made it and stayed there like Dylan, and some of whom occasionally reached that perfection and then fell off into something else, like, say, Donovan. I've always been aware of the art form of the song. Without the blues I don't think we would have had the permission to make that jump into song again at all, you know. Talk about influences on my early life: women blues singers.

TM: Oh yes. I remember that list in *Loba*—
DP: Yeah. Sarah Cox is in there, Chippie Hill, Trixie Smith, and you know there weren't a lot of records out then, but I had a couple of anthologies that I played, blues anthologies. And I played them over and over—women's blues—and they were a big part of my sense of my own strength too. Yeah, yeah, yeah. And also for us as women, that sense of absolute self-reliance, you know. Whatever came down, you could do it on your own.

TM: You touched briefly on Surrealism. Are you conscious of that particular influence?
DP: Oh, I think it's been there from way back in the fifties. Maybe, maybe more closely related in the first place to the Dadaists than the Surrealists, it might be, you know. That sense of like non-random randomness, you know, in my early stuff. In the early sixties, I did a whole book called *The Calculus of Variation*. What I actually was doing was just following, looking at the wall and letting the images arise and following any image only as far as it went, not trying to make sense out of it, not trying to complete the sentence and going on to whatever next image arose. At first, I could only work twenty minutes at a time on this. It was prose and I used an electric typewriter and went very fast. That kind of automatic writing. Then eventually I reached the point where I could stay with that kind of process for two

or two and a half hours. Which is a meditative process, really, it's like another form of meditation. Not making anything out of the stuff, but just letting the images happen.

Part IV

August 2002

TM: Has your vision of yourself as an artist changed over the years or has it remained the same?

DP: In many ways, the vision is surprisingly still the same. Added to the original vision of the artist is that sense that one wants to be of use: to ease the burden of an almost totally dark world by keeping the spark of the imagination alive and glowing. As for the "rewards," which are even more pitiful and ridiculous now than they were then—that remains the same: it's easy not to want them. And to stay with the fact that one does the work for its own sake. All else becomes confusing and abstract. Without that strong compass, I would get trapped in trends and theories: try to please others, hence repeat or undo the work that's been given me. As for the life, it has been more samurai than hermit. No regrets, but the times called and still call for a certain amount of action. Nowhere in my wildest dreams would I have expected to find myself connected to so many by mail, phone, postcard, poem, e-mail. But I could, myself, wish for more time alone. Music and candlelight and quill pens like I had at fifteen.

TM: The issues of action and isolation, commitment and yet time alone. Samurai. Hermit. How do you balance the warrior with the hermit? Toughness with compassion? How do you achieve focus in the midst of the chaos?

DP: I think that actually "warrior vs. hermit" is a developmental process. There's a time for action. At least for me there was first a time for aesthetic action—theatres, presses, the *Floating Bear* newsletter. It tapered off slowly: I still had Poets Press for a while after, and then followed it with Eidolon Editions. At the same time, though I left the New York Poets Theatre behind by 1965, I did pick up that thread and produce one more of my plays, *Whale Honey*, a full-length piece. So there was a kind of tapering off of the public arts persona: publisher, producer, actress. Both the press and the theatre had a tapering off period.

This period of arts activism, if I may call it that, overlapped with the beginnings of political activism. I was thrown into that role willy-nilly by *The Floating Bear* bust in 1961,[3] and then of course two years later I was arrested, along with Jonas Mekas, for showing Jean Genet's film *Chant d'Amour* at the New York Poets Theatre. I had always expected it, having been to anarchist rallies as a tyke, but the fifties weren't right for my kind of activism. Later in the sixties, it was actually possible, or so it felt, to work for some of the ideals I'd been raised with—my grandfather was an anarchist and a friend of Emma Goldman—but had never acted on except in isolated instances. By the late sixties, I moved to California partly to work with the Diggers, delivering free food, writing and performing *Revolutionary Letters* on the streets—they also went out to over 200 underground newspapers via the Liberation News Service—doing free readings at the Straight Theatre on Haight Street.

There was a period of time when this kind of work was useful, and then it wasn't. I found that I needed to reassess: I am not a person who joins organizations, nor do I like to be a leader but to work with and among peers. Over the years since the early seventies, I've done what came to hand to do in the way of benefits, getting food, medical

3. In 1961, LeRoi Jones and Diane di Prima as editors of the *Floating Bear* newsletter were arrested for sending what the authorities called obscene material through the mail.

goods to where they were needed, but have never again found myself in the midst of a communal movement in the same way. Nor do I miss it. As I said, I think for me the "warrior" work was and is part of a developmental process.

From 1970, I've taught poetry in various places, and that's a kind of "warrior" path, if you do it the way I like to. Right now, most of my livelihood comes from two private classes I give each year. They are nine-month commitments for my students, and we cover a lot of ground: artistic, spiritual, and in some sense political.

All this time I have always kept "hermit" time for myself. Buddhism has helped. There are meditation retreats, both private and group retreats, and study periods, and besides that I've always had one or two places I'd go to write and/or study. Going on the road is also a retreat of sorts, if you don't get too caught up in the life of the place you find yourself in. A motel room makes a perfect monastic space. At this point in my life—I am sixty-eight—I'd prefer to have my time for painting, writing, and meditation. I don't feel any pull to be out in the world, but I do have to teach, and I almost never refuse to read or speak at benefits when I can be of use. By now, though, I know that my most important work in the world—political and spiritual— is my writing, especially *Loba*, and the autobiography.

TM: And how do you maintain your focus in the midst of all this?
DP: Oh, focus in chaos: that's what meditation practice is all about, isn't it? Bringing awareness/focus to all situations and times. There's always chaos inside and out, and at the same time we aim at keeping some bare attention going throughout. And chaos is blest. It's the ground out of which it all grows.

TM: Can you discuss some of these ideas as they translate to the different forms in which you work: poetry, fiction, autobiography?

DP: I would have to say that for me developmentally, poetry came first, and comes last, and is the one continuous thread of possibility in the work. Which is not to say that all poetry comes in the same way, or has the same aim. For instance, the *Revolutionary Letters* were for the most part consciously written, constructed for a particular purpose. They started off as street theater, guerilla theater if you will, on the streets of New York City and later, San Francisco. This was contrary to how most of my work was coming by that time. Mostly it was "received."

But I'd best start at the beginning: early poetry, more or less consciously written—high school years, and later, through my first two books, *This Kind of Bird Flies Backward* and *Dinners and Nightmares*. So 'til about 1960. What I mean by that is that I wrote, perhaps, it's hard to remember back that far, from an idea as much as heard, in my mind, rhythms or words, and I shaped it with much rewriting in order to search out and define the sound of street speech in New York City right after the Korean War. By the time I'm writing the poems to LeRoi Jones that are in *The New Handbook of Heaven* [1960–61], I have given myself over to "the moving mind" as Phil Whalen called it, and am more or less accepting dictation, and doing very little revision at all. Only when I dropped the ball, when my attention broke, did I find it necessary to revise a little. Minimally. This is my main way of writing poetry to this day, though of course I do whatever else I feel like. This change partly grew out of the early work—I had gone as far as I could with deliberate revision—and partly out of learning from Jack Kerouac to go back to the original draft when the work goes dead from revision, and working with James Waring, taking his choreography classes, which presented a lot of Cage's ideas.

I am "receiving" the text in *The New Handbook of Heaven* and *The Calculus of Variation* [1961–64], which by the way is on the line between poetry and prose, written in prose paragraphs, but an ecstatic text and a faulty one. By the time I had finished it, I decided not to revise it as I had once planned, and realized I was no longer interested in the polished piece, writing as artifact. In that sense prose can be and is as visionary as poetry, if *The Calculus* is prose. And yes, auto-biography, too, can be visionary, sometimes quite literally so—at least I aimed for that in *Recollections [of My Life as a Woman]*.

Fiction is another matter, and I have written some fiction—stories and an unfinished novel, *Not Quite Buffalo Stew*—which have that visionary quality. On the other hand, *Memoirs of a Beatnik*—which I explain in the "Afterword" was written as a potboiler—is a mix of reportage, the flavor of the early fifties, and fiction. But as for what prose can do, it can do anything you as the writer can do with it. And it is often, though not always, "received" as poetry is. Different in how you return to the visions, how you sustain the energy and thrust of the work.

However, and this is where I was going with this, pointing to the developmental process, having accepted that most of my poetry was and will be "received," I was also free to write deliberately for various reasons and occasions, which is what I was saying about *Revolutionary Letters*; and also to write for play or the fun of it, fun with the language, the old forms, as well as with random techniques: dice, cut-up, which are some of the things I find myself doing just for the joy of it. And the "received" poems can come as image or heard words or a rhythm in my head or in the pulse/body. Or sometimes suggested by music. So poetry becomes a vast field in which I play, or pray, or make edifices for various motives or for the joy of it.

As for poetry becoming a spiritual autobiography, I would say that in one way this is inevitable, and in another sense it doesn't work that way at all. That is, for me if I set out to map my spiritual autobiography through poems, I would be bored; be boring—as are most academic poets—because self-conscious; and probably only be doing the kind of poem I already knew how to do. However, the scope of the work

over the years of a life, the sweep of it, is inevitably a spiritual autobiography, but not for the poet necessarily to see or mold. That's for
some others to figure later. I think that poetry plays over us, like a magic
lantern over a screen and we record what we can. What others may later
see as "spiritual autobiography" is just that the screen becomes larger
and more subtle; it "sees" or "shows" more.

TM: What about your current and future work and how they relate
to the ideas you have discussed?
DP: I am sixty-eight and fully cognizant that at this point I may live
twenty minutes, twenty days or twenty years. At present, I am not
looking ahead or back too much. There is a great deal of my work
from the past fifty years which has not seen the light of day, and I'd
like to get it better organized, and/or published in some cases. In any
case, I'd like to leave it in some kind of shape for others to do something with, if they wish.

There are many unpublished potential books of poems from the
fifties and sixties; all the magickal [sic] or "trance" workings from the
late seventies and early eighties; a book of my plays, *ZipCode*. There's
another autobiographical book, the first, written in 1965 in the form
of a year-long letter to Freddie Herko after his suicide. This book,
together with about 400 black and white photos, has been about half
laid out for many years for my own press to publish but is now way
too big a work for me to engage in. What I have in my sights at the
moment, however, is the second volume of my autobiography, which
has the working title *The Grail Is a Green Stone*. This would pick up
from when I left New York City in 1965 and would be mostly concerned with spiritual and political experiments and quests. I'd also
like to complete Book III of *Loba*, about which I haven't very much of
a clue, although about thirty pages of poems already exist. All I know
is what I was "told"—that Book I dealt with the physical/sexual life of

woman; and Book II dealt with the soul; and that Book III, if I lived to write it, would trace the journey of the Spirit. I'm not at all sure what that means.

Meanwhile, I love my private teaching work, especially working with the same young persons for four or five years and seeing them catch fire. And I'm showing my paintings, practicing Tibetan Buddhist meditation, and catching the poems that fly in the window and stay for a moment. My life is very rich. I am looking to spend a bit of time traveling: there's so much of the world I haven't seen. But if that doesn't happen, so be it! I remind myself that some of my most loved poets never left England. Or wherever they started. The best travel has always been in the realm of the imagination.

Artista

—Brenda (Bonnie) Frazer

Bonnie Frazer has lived along a border of American mainstream culture, dropping out for writing and hipster adventure and dropping in for work and family life several times over. Similarly, her work has probed a fault line of American writing, the point at which confession borders salacious entertainment. Frazer was born in Washington, D.C., in 1939—the end of the Depression. Her father worked for the Department of Labor. After studying briefly at Sweet Briar College, in 1959 she met Beat poet Ray Bremser and married him three weeks later. In 1961 she, Bremser, and their baby daughter, Rachel, fled to Mexico to evade New Jersey prison authorities pursuing Bremser for parole violation. A year later, Frazer, who had given up her child for adoption in Mexico and resorted to prostitution to survive, produced *Troia: Mexican Memoirs* (under the name Bonnie Bremser) as an epistolary entertainment for Ray while he was again in prison in New Jersey. Bremser, along with the book's editor, Michael Perkins, arranged the letters into a narrative, and *Troia* was published at Bremser's insistence in 1969. It came out in Great Britain under the title *For Love of Ray* in 1971. Frazer eventually left both Bremser and the Beat counterculture, obtained a master's degree in soil science, and worked for the U.S. Department of Agriculture as a soil surveyor to support herself and her children. Frazer is now retired and lives in Michigan, where she has returned to writing, expanding her memoir of life in the Beat movement. *Troia* is Frazer's major published work, an exemplar that advances the movement's signature aesthetic while integrating female sexuality, consciousness, and desire, as well as a woman's maternality and artistic ambition, into the Beat literary and cultural domain.

Writing *Troia* was an act of high romanticism for Frazer, a last recourse for the isolated and despairing artist who had returned to the United States. The work follows Beat aesthetics of immersion in memory and imagination enhanced by sensory deformation. This exemplifies Frazer's intention to use language to connect, to escape, and to transform, ambitions that evolved from her emulation of Kerouac's methods for composing poetry and prose. Frazer's poetics also evince certain political impulses of the Beat avant-garde, especially the belief that writing must be freed from market pressures and the writer should pursue fame and profit through art. To that end, the narrative refuses the memoir's usual conciliatory overtures to readers and in strident voice rejects accommodation or compromise to assert an untrammeled subjectivity. Deprecating the reader as a voyeuristic "thrill seeker," the narrator assumes a hostile posture: "I intend to clear the atmosphere at least for my own breathing. That's how much I care for your morals—clear enough? Get off my back—I will moan and groan in misery no more" (5). The narrator jettisons the guilt and shame that moralists may demand for her sexual promiscuity, open prostitution, and relinquishment of her child, all behaviors violating long-held patriarchal constraints on women's lives and conduct. In this, *Troia* echoes the most uncompromising manifestos of second-wave feminism, such as The S.C.U.M. Manifesto of 1967, WITCH of 1968, or THE FEMINISTS v. THE MARRIAGE LICENSE of 1969.

Troia complicates the male-centered Beat road tale with domestic determinants and exposes the way marriage impedes not the male road but female equality of subjectivity and sexual self-determination. *Troia* instantiates into Beat discourses a mobile female protagonist whose picaresque adventures in existential and sexual hazard are modified from the male model by the presence of her baby: "The bus ride to Mexico City . . . I am constantly with the baby on my lap, broken hearted at every spell of crying, the frustration of not being a very good mother really—trying to groove, trying to groove under the circumstances—and in spite of it" (9). Frazer's language conveys the burdens of the road for bohemian women who are mothers; motherhood is a highly likely consequence of a life of free sex, and thus is to be expected when women take to the road. Yet, more than being a domestic modification of the road tale, *Troia* is a narrative-on-demand that elaborates the ways in which the sexual double standard undermines female agency and liberation on the road. Frazer quotes into the tale Bremser's letter to her in which he commissions the narrative he requires, and which he will employ for his titillation: " . . . tell me some sexual items . . . draw up a plan, a plot, a sequence! . . . Make your flesh delirious for me, but unperformed without me!" (75). Frazer's very narrative expression is constructed for patriarchal delectation. She is obliged to report rather than merely represent how she is rendered not writer, but Beat body, tumescent and unfulfilled. In this, Frazer's text reveals how its terms of production qualify her narrative, which paradoxically serves as her bid for recognition as Beat writer as well as the negation of it.

A protofeminist text connecting the protagonist to other Beat women through its sexual politics, *Troia* inscribes a semiotics of female sexual liberation that exposes the overdetermined failure of that bid. Unlike in any male road narrative, for Frazer the road's sexual opportunities degenerate from metaphoric to literal prostitution. "Troia" means sexual adventurer, and the narrative explicitly asks what sexual adventuring can mean for women in patriarchy—under laws of male again. I've been through so many different sorts of experiences, career experience, and I've had two careers since then, one as a dairy farmer and then one as a soil tester/soil surveyor [soil scientist] with the U.S. Department of Agriculture. A lot of that spontaneity and being in the midst of a literary movement is gone for me now. I'm isolated. So I've started learning how to write just like everybody else does at this point. I even attempted to go back and take English courses because I wanted to understand what I was doing. Whereas before when I wrote *Mexican Memoirs*, I'd just sit down, smoke a joint, sit at a typewriter, and go. Put it in a pile and that was that. That was the process.

NG: What was the impetus for writing *Mexican Memoirs*?

BF: *Mexican Memoirs* was not conceived as a book. It was composed in a series of two-page writings that were sent to Ray, who was in jail, on a weekly basis. By claiming it was business correspondence we sidestepped the one-page-a-week rule on correspondence. It was an effort to communicate with Ray over the difficult experiences in Mexico. We never talked much before and then the limitations of jail made communication more urgent. In many ways, especially remembering times when [our daughter] Rachel was still with us and Ray was free, that writing was an escape to a better time.

NG: You were in the midst of an incredible literary scene when you wrote the memoir. What was it like for you to be with all these people who were doing ground-breaking work?

BF: Well, it started off—my relationship with Ray that is—with a poetry reading and Gregory Corso, Allen Ginsberg, Peter Orlovsky, Ray [Bremser 1934–1998], Cecil Taylor, LeRoi Jones, and A. B. Spellman [were there] in D.C. [in 1959]. So poetry was the social scene as well. Ray and I had our romance, and three weeks later we were married. Then I went to live in New York, that was what life was—neither one of us had a job, Ray was reading at coffee shops, and then we just circulated.

That's all we did. But we weren't like Janine [Pommy Vega]; she was with Orlovsky and Ginsberg in a live-in situation. It wasn't that way for us. We were a married couple and had our own life. Ray was in this poetic process all the time, so my total focus was on Ray. I was watching him write. I learned his opinions. I looked at the books he looked at. We were inspired by the same things. We experienced all the things that he wrote about together. So in a sense that was my literary education.

NG: Who were you reading at the time?

BF: Well, I'd read Kerouac when I was still in college, when *On the Road* came out [in 1957]. I think maybe I read *The Subterraneans* shortly after that—it was probably available also. And Ray had been the librarian at the jail, and he was able to order everything that he wanted, so he was really well read. He read a lot of Rilke and Ginsberg. He knew all the poets. And I was just following along. He told me about Rimbaud and he told me about Baudelaire, so that was the way I learned. The funny thing is that I stopped reading in that period of time. I read Ray's poetry. I typed Ray's poetry. But as far as keeping up with things, having a literary perspective or being well read or anything like that, I totally abandoned that. Except for that reading in D.C., it was almost exclusively Ray that I heard read after that. I didn't hear Ginsberg read after that, not in that couple of years when we were on the Village scene. Ray and I were happily married only about six months before he was arrested for parole violation. Then began the series of unfortunate events that sent us to Mexico. At that point, we were just Village poets, just hanging out. Don Allen was just coming out with his anthology then, and Ray had two poems in that. He was very much respected by Don Allen, so he had a reputation as a poet at that point. The fact that the subsequent events interfered with all that wiped it away. But in that period of time he had a lot of potential as a poet. He was looking forward to not just reading in coffee shops.

NG: When you look back at *Mexican Memoirs*, are there ways in which you see all those influences manifesting themselves in that work? Not that you were modeling Kerouac exclusively, but—
BF: No, I was.

NG: You were thinking about that?
BF: Yes. It was copying, but it's different from sitting down and copybook copying. It's more like what you hear changes the way you think and the way you speak, and so that's what it was like. Even now, the way he [Kerouac] fits words together—the sweetness of it, the way things expand when you look at it. If I try to keep those things in mind, if I try to keep the transcendent quality in mind when I'm writing, which I have a really hard time doing now, but then I was able to do it. I was able to say, well, if it doesn't do that for me then I got to try harder so it does.

NG: You were really pushing to achieve that.
BF: Yes, yes. Well, I had Ray on the other end always reading what I wrote every day too. It kind of had to measure up. I guess I really owe a lot of credit to Kerouac. If I sound like Kerouac it's because I tried to. I read him while I was writing, just like I listened to Bessie Smith. I think it is in *Dr. Sax* that he talks about a way of concentrating, visualizing; though he didn't use those terms which are now so common. I obeyed him. And I still do think of him as a wonder of the literary world. He had the knack of the long sentence, which is carried by emotional weight fueled by transcendent flashes of realization. I don't have those strong references now, even though my study of literature is much more complete. The closest I come now is Genet, and then I can get excited, or Melville, but I can't even aspire because the immediate experience is different.

NG: What it is about Genet and Melville that you're using?

BF: Genet is so original and so unselfconscious. The thing that inspires me most about Genet is that he'd just sit down and write, write, write in a notebook, and send it off. Huncke used to do the same thing. It's got to come from inside. Maybe it's the sadness of Genet, the sadness that flowers into something proud, the way he molded jail experiences, the way he turned it into a lovely homosexual fantasy. I wish I could do that. And as far as Melville, Melville is just so large-moving emotionally, and that's what I think about that period of time with [Ray and me]—that there was so much emotional content, that everything was on an emotional plane. Melville can describe that.

I've been catching up. Now it's my opportunity to be well read. All the stuff that was on the college book lists that I didn't read when I was sneaking out all the sexual literature in the library. Now I'm going back and reading it. But back then with Ray, we studied things, but we studied them in terms of what they did to us from moment to moment. There was a lot of partying, a lot of new awareness, mind levels raising, with the drugs and so on. The literary experiences, the music experiences, all were enhanced, so we would learn and experience and just maybe we'd sing along with Slam Stewart or something. But we'd also mouth the words to Kerouac, sort of internalize it.

We always had a phonograph. I'd say that fifty percent of our time was spent just sitting listening to records. Coltrane, modern jazz. I learned all of the musicians. I knew all of their names, all of their styles. I could sing along with them; I could anticipate when the riffs were going to be in the changes. This was what we did.

NG: Have you thought much about how jazz had an impact on your writing?

BF: Music is the big thing. Coltrane, Monk, Ray Charles, Bessie Smith. Others document it all, but I wish I could bring more to it. It cannot be over-emphasized. We adored Coltrane with almost the same fervor that I adored Ray. Can't explain it, love and poetry and music transcended everyday ordinary relationships for us. And Ray was a jazz poet, and so he thought of the typewriter keyboard as an instrument. Maybe he wasn't quite so specific about that as some of the other poets were, like maybe McClure, who was getting really graphic about the way things came out on the page. I know that just before I started writing *Mexican Memoirs*, I'd been back working with the U.S. government as a clerk/typist, and I was typing bills of lading for the General Services Administration. "Shwack! Shwack!" piles of things! So when I was then ready to be mechanically agile, when I started writing *Troia*, I would listen to music at the same time and it would just blend together.

NG: Do you still write with music?

BF: Oh boy. I hardly ever turn the radio on any more. I'm a silence person now. Extremely so. Sometimes I do hear some music that I find exciting. I wish I had a collection of the old music. I'll tell you what happened when John Coltrane died. It was in 1967. It was an ending for a lot of us. I couldn't believe in the records any more. Even the records didn't survive as artifacts. Didn't have it any more. A lot of the excitement was gone.

NG: Do you notice a difference now in your writing since you've become a "silence" person?

BF: I do. My writing now is—well I don't want to put myself down because I'm just getting comfortable with some of the things I'm writing—but everything that I've written so far on this *Beat Chronicles* manuscript is like notes. I mean it's all just flat. It has no emotional connect. It's empty. But I knew that I was forcing myself and I'd sit down and write. I was able to be disciplined, and that's a connection with the way I used to write too, because I was very disciplined when

I wrote *Mexican Memoirs* every day. Get up, had my little ritual routine, and write my two pages in the morning. And then the rest of the day I spent all of the time reconstructing in my mind, going over things, and feeling things evolve about what I would write the next day. I was a recluse then. So I was able to say, "All I have to do is sit down and write two pages a day and that'll be that."

NG: You were living it, re-living it, recreating it every day. Your reasons for writing now are different, aren't they?

BF: I have a lot of reasons for writing. I want the full story to be available, and also there's something about a jail experience for the people who are in there—it's never-ending, even after you've served your time. You don't ever really get a clean slate. You never get absolved of what happened. If by chance it was a misunderstanding, the misunderstanding never ends either. So I thought maybe I could gain some absolution by writing about it. But then there's another reason for writing too. I adored Ray, and I was very young and naïve, and I had a hard time seeing things realistically. Now I have to balance the good with the bad. Because even though I do still care for Ray, I wouldn't live with him. I wouldn't now go through any of the things that he goes through. I wouldn't want to spend probably more than half an hour with him, but I still have the same tenderness.

NG: For your writing now, do you look at letters or photographs? How do the materials one uses serve as catalysts for memory? Do you go back to visit places?

BF: All of those things I do now. When I wrote *Mexican Memoirs*, it was all of this focus and concentration. Of course that [experience had occurred] only a year previously, and it was all emotionally connected. It was like I could sit there and write about something. I would be with Ray in that time, reconstruct that time. Now I do all the writerly things. I keep journals. I painstakingly keep two or three different kinds of journals. And write down dreams. Then what I have done lately, which I've never done before in my life, is go back through and screen through all of my journals for specific content. So I do find passages in my journal that have some of that movement that I want, or jog memories, or sometimes I pick things up, or sometimes I just, like right now, what I'm doing, is just . . . just waiting, waiting, waiting for it . . . waiting for an understanding so I can finish this off.

NG: In *Mexican Memoirs*, you wrote about painting and drawing. Do you still paint? Is that part of the writing process?
BF: I'm a trend person, and that one [ended]. But I think about it sometimes, and I love painters. At one point, you know in that period of time when I was writing *Mexican Memoirs*, I also read *Dear Theo*, and as I first started the manuscript, I saw the Van Gogh show at the Phillips Gallery in Washington, and I had just this huge emotional response, the writing—everything—was going to be okay. You know, as I'm talking to you I get a sense that I need something to feed me, to be creative, to have the energy. It's necessary for creativity. In the old days, the searching through drugs was there too. In a way, there's a lot of rehabilitation to do around that, to not think that I have to have some artificial stimulus in order to write. To be yourself, even if you're—well, what do they say?—crazy wisdom sort of thing.

Maybe there was an advantage to the fact that we [women of the Beat generation] didn't hang together all the time, the way the guys did, [the way they] would travel from coast-to-coast together in a car or something like that. Maybe we had some advantage—the isolation that all of us experienced as women. Maybe in some ways it was formative in that we were able to retain some characteristics.

NG: That strikes me as a characteristic of some Beats. What does the term "beat" mean to you?

BF: "Beat" is like Huncke said, a carnie term. It's a leftover from the thirties and forties Depression years, of the wandering vagrant. That Kerouac romanticized it was wonderful because it was the tone of the time, an offspring of anarchy and bohemianism that went before, all of which I studied before I'd ever met Ray. The social antagonism of being seen as beatniks, or even as hippies, is a little skewed because we were in a lower division of the counterculture, criminally affiliated with the streetwise aspect of things. So I always resist that discussion. It seems out of place. I loved the way Allen would talk about ordinary people as "angels" and bum cigarettes just to talk to common folk on the street. It was somehow an attitude like that.

NG: In your memoir, some of the sexual events seem similar to di Prima's in *Memoirs of a Beatnik*. She admits she fabricated much of that. Did you?

BF: No. Nothing made up. [But] she's an inspiration to me. When I've called her, she has this answering machine and it says, "I'm in isolation now; I'm writing. You can leave a message now and I'll get back to you in a month or so." It's great. Okay, that's the way you do it.

NG: On the surface, your memoir and hers do seem similar. But you have that incredible introduction that just hits the reader in the face.

BF: That's my editor, Michael Perkins. He put it together. I have notes. I have no idea where those sections were in the original manuscript. He picked and chose among the pieces. You touch on something there that I think is interesting. As writers we'd all like to be able to be storytellers, to create, to fictionalize. That is my dream. Couldn't I just write about something besides me? That's the epitome of creativity to me, for a writer to be able to come up with that artificial stuff that you're talking about. But that wasn't the way I was taught how to write, and it happened that I had to tell the truth. My life at that point required for me to identify what the truth was for me in all of that mess that I experienced over that year. To communicate to Ray—I think I tried to say this—to try and get our relationship back on a level after I'd had so many of these sexual experiences and many of which had been required of me by the situation and by him. There's so much emotional pain there that I needed to get at it the only way I thought. This was therapy for me. This was before I would allow the need of a therapist. I was trying to sort things out for myself. So the truth was essential to me then. Proper memory, and if I rhapsodized a little bit that was just because I had all this poetic background to tell me that transcending was what you wanted to achieve in writing. Kerouac was doing that at the time; everybody was doing it. Marijuana was taking us to other levels. You needed to be moving to other levels all the time.

NG: So the truth was always at the center for you as you wrote *Mexican Memoirs?*

BF: Trying to get at the truth, and if there was some humor in it, if it was amusing to Ray, if it was sexually titillating, then that too. But my purpose was to improve the relationship between Ray and me. And I had sent Ray to jail before then too. I had this huge burden of guilt because I'd told him that I couldn't live that way anymore. I couldn't live the desperate life anymore. I'd asked him to turn himself in, straighten out all this unfortunate misunderstanding. So then he was in jail. In some ways I was forced to deal with my solitude then, just as Ray was. At some point I started making a few decisions on my own. When to stop using drugs for instance. It was difficult because there was so much pain. I found that I could focus out of the pain by writing. When Ray was in jail I began to have some support in terms of legal responsibility. Ray was seen as a hero, a victim of a faulty system.

He was that, and in my campaign to get him out of jail I received support. Painters gave me paintings to sell. The Living Theater gave us money for lawyers. Ray was more of a cause than a literary figure then. Elaine DeKooning did a series of sketches of me and read my manuscript. She sent me a telegraph saying I was a genius. People would come into my little place and look at the writing in piles and enjoy reading it. But through that time when I wrote, a period of one year, I was as much in isolation as if my little apartment were a cell. I just wanted to be left alone. I was just sort of weepingly trying to make things okay between us. That's what I was writing for.

I think it was in *Dear Theo* that Van Gogh absolved himself of this creative stance of being, and I think the book actually said, "I'm not a writer. This is not a book. Put all of that aside." So that left it open for my writing to be just a daily exercise that I did. Then somebody took it and formed it into a book. Ray kind of turned it over, and I hardened myself to it because there was so much vulnerability for me, but I do know that I wrote two pages a day for the better part of a year, so it's probably 400 to 500 small pages.

NG: It's a strikingly powerful introduction.

BF: I like the introduction too. It's the only part that I really have had any experience at reading. I think I'm going to take courage and start reading some of the more prurient parts of it. The past two years, I've said you can anthologize this, you can anthologize that, but I've kept it to the neutral passages.

NG: The voice in the introduction is loud and angry. You condemn the reader but also invite that reader on a wild ride. So the reader moves into the story with trepidation.

BF: There was an opportunity there for me to stand on my own feet, actually, when I was writing. It was extremely painful not only because

Ray was missing, but also I had just stopped using heroin at that point, and much of the anger and energy in it [*Troia: Mexican Memoirs*] probably comes from my biological or physiological make-up at that point. But I had an apartment. I had a space of my own, which I had almost never had in my life. When we were in Mexico, it was always hotel rooms or people's houses. No privacy. [But when I started writing], I had that [privacy], and I was making some decisions for myself. Yes, I had made Ray go back to jail, and that made me feel guilty. But still, I was pushing towards beginning to have things my way, instead of just letting things carry me along. So it was a liberating experience for me. And like I say, nobody really expected me to turn up writing there, to quit my job. So it was a thrill for me in a way to stand on my own feet.

See, when I was in my twenties, I'd rejected the idea of having a career. I didn't want to have anything to do with the things that involved—wardrobes, work ethic. I didn't want to have anything to do with those normalities. In that, I deprived myself of the things that initiative can do for you, the idea that you have a purpose, that you can do something. So the writing gave me something to do, and I had a purpose, and that sort of obsessive sense of what a purpose did for me before now led to this work. I had Ray captive on the inside in jail. He wasn't doing any of the bad stuff that he'd been doing before, you know. He was there. And I always knew where to reach him. I didn't have to wait for him to come home at night. So I was really having this experience of being myself in my own space, which I hadn't done before. I think that's a woman's pattern—a breaking out pattern.

NG: That's interesting that you had to remove the identity of writer in order to do it.

BF: Yes, it is. Well, I had this self-consciousness that said when I had to put "I" on the page, "I did this or I did that," it flustered me. You talk about taboos, that was like a taboo for me. So I never did that. I don't know how many times I used the "I" pronoun in the book, but every time I had the urge to, I quelled that urge. There's something about memoirs that can be so boring and so trivial. There's a fear there that you're going to offend somebody by writing about yourself, by being the overblown ego. So you always want to trim and pare back, so that's what we did. I don't do that very well anymore.

NG: You wrote in *Mexican Memoirs* that you had become Mexican, that you had become black. You mentioned that your daughter Rachel was white and that everyone was fascinated with her skin color. How did your concept of race affect identity in *Mexican Memoirs*?

BF: You don't really know what your make-up is that way, in dealing with differences, until you've lived some place where you're the minority, and then you start to think, "Maybe I could say everybody that had darker skin seems against me." I could be paranoid about my whiteness. Maybe some of that came out, I don't know. I think what I was doing there is like when I was talking about Melville and *Pierre, or the Ambiguities*, and the black and white, the dark woman and the blond woman. What I was doing was identifying, in a way, my psychology, my make-up, and I think I wrote someplace in the memoir that I dyed my hair blond for a period of time, and then I dyed it black. The black hair came after the separation from Rachel. Much of that may have been just sort of a despair, sort of a feeling. It was almost as though the people in Mexico are so open to their poverty, or so open to the oppression of being down-trodden or something like that. That's what I was identifying with, that darkness in myself as, okay, now the worst has happened to me, yet these people can accept me. And being a prostitute in Mexico, I was accepted—the sequence in Veracruz where the police chief, the woman, the *procuradura policía* there, she was procuring women for the john. But she was a well-accepted member of the community, and she respected me as a woman even though we were doing this demeaning thing for women. So there's something there that's almost an acceptance of conditions and still able to not be crushed by it. At that time I was taking a lot of benzedrine and it was affecting my nerves. When I left Rachel with Jovita and then came back and they had this smoke-filled room and were doing the rituals—that was a different kind of blackness. That was my paranoia against black magic.

So I don't know if it really relates to what we experienced in the sixties as a kind of brotherhood of black and white. We lived in a community where there was a lot of mixing, even racial mixing, Hettie and LeRoi, and Elvin Jones and his wife were a mixed marriage. But what we had more of was a togetherness with the jazz musicians, the people that were down and out, the junkies and all of that lot, and a lot of that was black culture at that time. So we felt like we were very liberal. Now whether we truly were or not, I don't know, but it was an ideology at that time to be very liberal. But it's more of being a woman and being a minority myself. So I'm always having to question my values on racial issues. But it was a big issue in the fifties and sixties. It was the social issue that I wanted something to happen about. And it was happening, not because of me, but it was happening because of what other people were doing.

NG: Did you know LeRoi and Hettie very well?
BF: They were some of the first people that I met when we were in New York together. Ray and I went over there one time, maybe after I'd known him for a month. One of the issues of *Yugen* had just come out with one of Ray's poems in it. They had a kind of party—I think they were always having parties then—and there were all poets there, like Barbara Moraff was there, the sort of subgroup of the Beat generation. They [Hettie and LeRoi] were the mother and father of the literary scene at that time. They were making things happen in an

organized way that wasn't happening otherwise. Maybe not on a Don Allen level, or maybe not on an academic level, but on the little magazine scene, they were putting it together like nobody else was. And they were married, they had kids, they were living a normal life. They were very hip, and yet they were paying the bills, which was incomprehensible to me. How could you do both at once?

NG: You were talking about the civil rights movement—the sense of people coming together and the way LeRoi Jones decided to separate from Hettie, from the white world.

BF: That was painful for me. He had stopped me on the street one time and I told him I'd quit my job so I could write, and he said, "How will you live?" As if it were a bad idea. That was kind of a negative experience. Ray was in jail then. The next time I saw LeRoi on the street, he ignored me. And I've never talked to him since. Not by choice, but I just never encountered him since then. But that was the beginning of that exclusiveness of black militancy. Maybe that's what the [race] riots [of the sixties] were about, I don't know. But a lot of the openness that had been so comfortable for me before then had closed down and I felt so bad about that. I understood. But it was very confusing to lose. It was almost like this is a price we have to pay, but it didn't feel good.

NG: During those times, was Allen Ginsberg an important person for you?

BF: Allen's importance to me began when he came back from India [in 1963]. Before then I'd seen him as kind of a nuisance. We had some run-ins with him. We stayed in his apartment at one point and—housekeeping, no, I didn't do it, and things got pretty messy. When he came back, he was upset. That sort of branded us from then on. He had the relationship with Ray, the correspondence when Ray was in jail, and that was how they got to know each other. At that point, I never really had a friendship with Allen until he came back from India—I think maybe Ray was arrested at that time, maybe he was in the Tombs in New York City—and Allen gave me encouragement and I experienced his kindness. That was probably the first time that I saw him as a kind person, that something had evolved in him when he came back from India. He had this image, this wonderful image, of the satchel and the notebooks, this writerly thing, and he could carry a satchel like a woman did. It was so beautiful. It was so different. And I just admired him so much. He had this sweetness. From then on, I wasn't so much afraid of him as I had been before. I had my scary moments with Allen, though, because he was very patriarchal.

I didn't really have the connections that Ray had. I'd just benefit from them now and then if I, as Ray's wife, sought people out. Let's see, I read a poem one time, in '62 or so. Allen was there and told me that I read it well. It was a drug-oriented poem. Allen would never totally commit himself to a drug scene. He'd use drugs, but it was different. He had his life, I think, in control.

Later on Allen became a big figure for me and recently Allen's been the one who says to me, "You are a writer." When *Troia* was being circulated, I would meet people, they would think of me as a writer. After that, I didn't think of myself as a writer anymore. I was trying hard to be a normal person with a paycheck, raise my kids properly, all this stuff. Then Ann Charters published her anthology of Beat writing [*The Portable Beat Reader* 1992], and had the reading for the coming-out of the anthology; she wanted me to read, and I didn't respond.[1] Allen said, "Well, why didn't you read?" and I said, "Well, I didn't have anything to read," and he said, "You don't have to. Read somebody else. Read Kerouac." But you need to have confidence to do those things. Of course,

---

1. *The Portable Beat Reader* includes an excerpt from *Troia: Mexican Memoirs* in which Frazer writes about traveling through Mexico on a bus with her baby daughter Rachel (465–71).

Allen was this way with everybody, telling us to get involved, communicate, and be organized about your writing. It's sort of like brush your teeth in the morning. That's the way Allen was. He'd tell you how to live as a writer. And that's important, you know. But he would drop these things now and then and say, "You know, it's time for you to get together a book and have a book." He said this a couple of years ago on New Year's. It's like, wow, that's a New Year's resolution. And sure enough, that's when I decided that I would retire from my job [as a soil scientist] and take up writing and be serious about it. So he was very supportive, very supportive. He was that way for everybody. Everybody that he came in contact with, I believe, felt that support and encouragement from him, a real creative thing.

NG: What about the place of female friendships? You address that to some extent in *Mexican Memoirs*. You acknowledge the idea of a woman having female friends, which Beat literature seldom does.

BF: I can't recall that I did. In terms of real friendships, I didn't have any friends until probably within the space of the past ten to fifteen years. A friendly relation, I had no comprehension of. It was either all or nothing. When I was writing *Troia*, I was always very shy. But I didn't talk. I'd say that I was pretty close to being autistic up until I wrote *Troia*. I didn't talk. I was so . . . shy . . . what do you call it . . . inferiority complex, all that. So the relationships I had—they were about touching—they were physical relationships—the sexuality, and I don't think I'm alone in this. I've heard other women say the same thing, that the relationships began with touching. The lovemaking was really central, rather than getting to know somebody over the years and then marrying him. Maybe that's what the sexual revolution did for us, I don't know, but a lot of my self-expressiveness was this physical thing, this comfort zone between two people. I really relied on that. But then that became isolating. To pursue something that intensely was isolating. I probably didn't have any opportunities for female friendships until Ray was in jail and I had this place of my own and I had this thing that I was doing. I didn't have any real friends. Well, this is my own particular odyssey. I never had the support of family and friends until just recently. Now I'm rich in that.

NG: There is a section in *Mexican Memoirs* where you discuss a woman named Jovita, and you juxtapose your relationship with her to relationships with males.

BF: Yes, she was very loyal. Yes, I was moved by that. But it wasn't a friendship where I would sit down and talk to her. She was doing things for me that I needed done. She was anticipating my needs, that sort of thing, kind of like a mother would. Since I lacked my family too, there would have been in places a desire to set up kind of sister relationships. I don't mean to just condemn myself, but many, many other women just focused on men in that period of time. It was almost as though— no, I don't want to say that it was competitive because that was the teenage kind of thing—it was just because it was so intensely personal. There's also this ambiguity about my sexuality. I noticed in later years that I identified a lot with homosexuals. I felt drawn to homosexuals—male homosexuals. I just never straightened that out about friends at all. Sort of like an apartment. I never had an apartment until that point when I wrote *Mexican Memoirs*, and yet it was liberating when I was writing because being able to express myself just brought me to that point where I could think about people.

NG: Were you aware of the radical nature of *Mexican Memoirs*, publishing one's story as a prostitute and the sexuality that was graphically expressed in there?

BF: I'll tell you what—and I don't know if I'll ever come up to it again—but I thought that I was doing a revolutionary thing with that.

I felt righteous about being a prostitute. I felt like what I was doing was more honest than free love. I was . . . I was conscious of that. I thought it was something that needed to be done. I thought prostitutes needed a spokesperson. Given that we were righteous about everything. I had to work hard to drop the anger and a consciousness of the anger and the exclusion, the separateness, the alienation, all of that was a part of that time. I don't know if people experienced it as intensely as we did, being criminals, but it was there. It was an awareness.

NG: Where are you now as a writer? Is that an identity that you still carry with you after all these years?
BF: I never thought of myself as a writer until people started paying attention, or until Ray got my book published and then years later got me a reading at St. Mark's Church. And I did want to be responsible to my kids, which in some ways caused me to turn my back on the past, and my writing career kind of carried on without me for some time. I was, and still am, in awe of people like di Prima or even small time poets just making the scene at readings or in little mags, who can carry on their lives and be called writers. I was never like that, never had the opportunity for professionalism. Never possessed a body of work, except for *Troia: Mexican Memoirs*, which I abandoned in a sense. Allen always told me that I didn't have to be stuck with *Troia*'s image, that my life since then is actually more interesting. Only it's too big to write about yet.

Places to Go

—*Joanne Kyger*

Joanne Kyger's immersion in the cultural climate in which the San Francisco Renaissance converged with the Beat movement aligns her historically with many other writers discussed in this study. But her impress on the poetry scenes and poetics with which she is identified—an ironic wryness, understated, pacific, and tensile—suggests the California character of her work. Born in 1934 in Vallejo, California, Kyger studied at the University of California at Santa Barbara. She has developed a poetics of personal expression mediated through classical forms, obscure local allusions, and cryptic, dark irony; her later work expresses an Eastern aesthetic reflecting her serious, long-term Buddhist practice.

Kyger was in her early twenties when in 1958 she presented her first important poem in San Francisco, "The Maze," which brought her notice in the Sunday poetry meetings led by Robert Duncan and Jack Spicer, under whose intimidating tutelage she made her debut into the literary avant-garde. Kyger had other literary connections in the San Francisco scene, however, including friendships with John Wieners, Philip Whalen, Allen Ginsberg, and Lew Welch. Married for four years to Gary Snyder, Kyger lived in Japan with him and together they traveled to India to meet Ginsberg and Peter Orlovsky, to make the pilgrimage Kyger recounts in *The Japan and India Journals 1960–1964* (1981). While San Francisco Renaissance and Beat generation literary circles were the sites of Kyger's emergence, neither her poetics—an independent, personal poetry often responding to canon or myth—nor her subsequent influences and interests—Buddhism, psychedelics, American Indian lore, practices of New Age communities—remain with the fifties. They look to the sixties counterculture and beyond to the New Age.

Kyger's poetry manifests an interest in the burdens imposed and the perspectives permitted by gender and the feminine, as in her revision of Penelope's story in "The Odyssey Poems" (*Tapestry* 53–61). However, her gendered emphasis is more understated than the pronouncements of di Prima, or the insistences of Johnson, or the decrees of Martinelli. She takes an oblique way through women's experiences and perspectives and tells it slant in the Dickensonian tradition. This cool distance is exemplified in the 1960 poem "waiting again" (*Tapestry* 33), in which the speaker insists on her remove: "I am no picker from the sea of its riches / I watch the weaving—the woman who sits at her loom / What was her name? the goddess I mean / —not that mortal one." Kyger aligns herself as poet with mortal and divine weavers, a stance of waiting detachment from event.

Kyger augmented her fascination with Penelope and other Homeric subjects in *The Tapestry and the Web* (1965) with observations in other cultural registers that witness women's lives. Such witness ranges from the personal to the cultural (as in the peyote trip captured in "vision of heaven & hell," [*Tapestry* 36]) to the art historical, the latter an adjunct to her focus on myth and theogony. Turning to contemporary culture, the poem "My Sister Evelyne" (*Tapestry* 39) sketches the imprisonment of white, middle-class women of the 1950s, dependent on wily arts for survival:

> *Louise is her middle name*
> *a foul tongued determination*
>   *brought material rewards for her*
> *an extra piece of meat, TV dinners served*
>   *in the dark, expensive shoes.*
>   *perfect teeth*

Pacified with the signifiers of bourgeois comfort, "material rewards" darkened in a blue television-screen light are depicted as pathetic substitutes for life, and the sister, Louise, as entombed in her own shrewishness. The other side of that captivity, the dangers faced by women who abandon themselves to patriarchal protection, is written on the face of the maiden in the poem "Tapestry" (*Tapestry* 40), dated "4.62." In this poem based on a detail from a European tapestry, the figure of a "coquettish" maiden in "sideways" turn with "uncombed" hair and "raised up" hand is unexpectedly brought into focus in the arresting conclusion: "You can tell / Puffeyes and the broken turned nose. / Searching / for bigger & better things." The battered face, the valiant optimism, the ominous implication of transparency ("You can tell") anticipate the more widespread attention that will be paid to such realities as a result of the coming women's movement.

Kyger's *Japan and India Journals* is a remarkable text that participates in the Beat movement literary practice of self-disclosure and confession, the publication of letters, journals, and other private papers both as adjuncts to and as art *tout court*. The record of the neophyte poet's passages through time, cultures, marriage, and consciousness seduces with witty charisma. Her entries inscribe a literary history of American writers on the expatriate road in the East. This journey is definitively the seeking of the sixties, and Kyger places herself directly in this vaunted time and place. Diffidence and discrimination ("Rereading Kerouac's *Subterraneans*. I keep putting him down until I start reading him then I can't" [71], or Ginsberg's "big hangup is that he wants quick enlightenment, he won't sit or train for it" [191]) are matched by an open excitement of discovery: "Olson's Projective Verse hits me like a wallop" (60). Charting the domestic life and the writing life with equanimity, Kyger's journals attest to the fraught emergence of women writers in Beat and associated movements.

Some women writers have been ambivalent about being identified with the Beat movement. Kyger captures the anger at being dismissed and overlooked in Beat history, as in "Poison Oak for Allen" (1996), simultaneous with the skepticism of and resistance to being categorized as a Beat writer, as in "A Brisk Wind is Blowing / Thoughts to Philip on the Phone" (1999). The poet's dialogue with Whalen disdains literary categories too often invented by critics or the media rather than by writers and inscribes a poet's refusal of any literary affiliation other than self-possession—which is, in a meta-irony, after all a characteristically Beat stance:

> *The New York Times says I'm a Language Poet*
> *Are you?*
> *Of course not.*
>
> *Are you a Beat Poet?*
> *No, I'm my own Poet*
>
> *George Stanley says you're an Oregon Poet*
> *Ha ha*
>
> *Do you understand what deconstruction is?*
> *No*

Well if you don't, I won't keep trying
May 14, 1999

(*Again* 156)

Kyger expresses a contingency about Beat that destabilizes the category and that signifies the postmodernism Beat has been seen to anticipate. This deft doubleness and complicated simplicity evocative of the koan, the paradoxes of Beat history and poetry, typify Kyger's Beat moves.

The Tapestry and the Web, Places to Go (1970), *The Wonderful Focus of You* (1979), *The Japan and India Journals 1960–64* (reissued as *Strange Big Moon* in 2000), and *Phenomenological* (1989) are among Kyger's better known works. The anthology *As Ever: Selected Poems* (2002) contains much of her early out-of-print work.

This interview was conducted by Nancy Grace on August 22, 2002, at the home of Joanne Kyger in Bolinas, California.

NANCY GRACE: When did you first realize that you were, or wanted to be, a poet?

JOANNE KYGER: My first poem was published when I was four, in a little kindergarten publication. I think it had an impression on me because my mother was impressed. I don't think I really thought about being a poet until, let's see, I was in college, twenty years old, when life was all so emotional. I didn't have that concentration, or focus, to be able to write, say, a story or prose, although I did try and wrote a feature column for the college paper. I studied with Hugh Kenner when I was at UCSB [University of California—Santa Barbara]. I had him for freshman English, but he obviously wasn't just a freshman lecturer. I realized that there were students from Germany who were coming to study Pound with him. In '57, I first came to San Francisco. The "Howl" trial was going on then. You know, North

Beach was just a very small place. I was living nearby, and they had this bar called The Place, and it didn't take me long to make connections.

NG: Your nickname from that time was Miss Kids, wasn't it? How'd that come about?

JK: George Papermaster, who worked the stockroom at Brentano's at the City of Paris where I worked in 1957–58 used to call everyone "kids." I started doing the same, and when I met John Wieners and Joe Dunn at The Place, they started calling me Miss Kids.

NG: You were writing at the time?

JK: I was writing at the time, but I hadn't quite formed a voice yet. But I never figured writing poetry could be a life's work. There were very few people I knew then who made a livelihood from writing at that point, unless you did something horrible and went into the academy! That was antithetical to everything that the New American Poetry was all about.

NG: So, then, how did you make a living?

JK: I'd worked as a secretary in a bookstore. You know, I had these secretarial skills so I could always find work.

NG: But when did you really realize that you were a poet?

JK: I don't think I ever had that idea. I remember John Wieners once saying, "If you're a poet, you're married to poetry." Well, I wasn't married to it! I remember traveling with Gary [Snyder] once, and he was trying to make decisions about how to identify himself on his passport, and we decided that putting "writer" down was always better than putting a "poet" down because, you know, "poet" stuck out so much. Still I don't tell people that I'm a poet because it brings out all those images of greeting cards or whatever. That's what I think of myself: I'm a writer, I can write in lots of different ways.

NG: Have your practices of writing poetry changed since those early years?
JK: Writing was to find out what the writing was about, or what a poem was, or when was it finished. So, I'd say that it hasn't changed too much. I think you're always thinking about trying to get away from repeating yourself, writing the same poem. Notebook writing and reading supply a lot of insight on what you're trying to do. And poetry readings, public readings, where you're selecting and seeing what's good.

NG: So then do you go back and revise?
JK: I try not to. I do very little. It either works or it doesn't.

NG: What about the importance of Duncan and Spicer to your development as a poet?
JK: They were my first teachers. The thing about Duncan and Spicer was that they didn't encourage people to publish a lot. There was no race to publish. There weren't a lot of places to publish in either. There was *Beatitude*, but that was more along the lines of the street Beat poetry. There was *Poetry Chicago*. And then there were the small books that White Rabbit Press put out. But the sense was that there should be no anxiety or push to print. I think that had a lot to do with the fact that the magazines that were publishing at that point, like *The Sewanee Review*, *The Kenyon Review*, and some of the more establishment East coast publications—they weren't interested in the New American Poetry. There was a whole new series of publications that came out, like *Big Table*, *Chicago Review*, *Evergreen Review*, and *Yugen*. Small presses started up, like Auerhahn, White Rabbit, and Coyote Press, that published some of these new writers. There was Jack Spicer's *J* mimeograph

magazine. That's where I was first published. And that seemed like enough [laughs]. So I didn't have any big anxiety about publishing, but if everybody else was going to get printed, well, I wanted to be printed too, but I also had to have something that I thought was okay.

NG: And how did you know when it was okay to print?

JK: Well, that was the big question, of course. Finally, ultimately, it's yourself that decides. But you show it to people. And that's when Philip Whalen was very encouraging to me. Those four years when I was in Japan, he was very supportive of work that I sent over for him to look at. Eventually, you just learn to trust your own voice. There isn't anybody else who's going to tell you. I remember Ginsberg having a difficult time. I don't know how many poets he really liked. He liked the idea of there being this brotherhood of poets, but . . . I guess he liked Gary's. He could hear Gary's poetry. Philip's he couldn't "get" too well. It was too much of Philip's own mind. And I don't think he quite knew what to make of mine at times, so he wasn't a good teacher in that way. And I don't think he was trying to be a good teacher. So eventually, you just get used to your own judgment.

NG: What's your sense of being labeled San Francisco Renaissance or Beat or whatever other labels critics have placed upon you and your poetry? How does that work for you as a writer?

JK: It's useful for people in an academic way to have a label, to get a handle on it. I resisted the Beat label during the time I was associated with the Beat writers because they never considered me a Beat writer. I didn't consider myself a Beat writer. And they never said, "Oh, you're one of us," ever! So at this late date, I just don't need it. Plus the Beat writers were looked on with a certain amount of scorn by Duncan and Spicer. They [the Beats] were out there beating their own drum. The biggest names were Ginsberg and Kerouac—they had the media celebrity status, at least Kerouac did. Then Snyder, Whalen, McClure, Corso. We can see that historically. But Beat was considered an East coast phenomenon. San Francisco had already had its own renaissance . . . from Berkeley. It was already there, which is why the so-called Beat thing had a place to flower or to re-energize itself in the San Francisco scene. So it was the media that made it the movement it was.

NG: How do you distinguish your poetry from what was called Beat at the time?

JK: I don't think I thought about Beat poetry. I thought about the individuals who were writing at the time. Certainly Gary was different from Allen, from McClure. And there was a generic Beat poetry, which was what the extended Bob Kaufman school of street poetry ended up by being, which had a certain flavor of its own.

NG: What was it like for you as a woman poet in this group, especially with Duncan and Spicer?

JK: Well, beside the fact that most of them were gay, which had its restrictive directions, I very much enjoyed being a woman in that circle. I mean, sexuality was out of the way at that point. So there wasn't any confusion. We could just be friends. And, I don't think—you know, that question is asked a lot, and I don't think there was the same kind of feminist identity in the middle fifties that people have now. I think it's something that has evolved. At that point, it wasn't yet of interest. Most women that I went to school with in Santa Barbara were not interested in what I was interested in.

NG: Well, what were they interested in?

JK: Oh, I don't know, they were interested in sororities. Maybe it was just the school that I went to. I was more interested in sources and thinking about things in a deeper way. I'd started out in philosophy, and Buddhism was of interest to me, and consciousness. What goes on in your mind—where does it come from? what are you supposed to do with your life? and things like that. Identity. And I didn't find too many women, or men, at that point, let's put it that way, who were interested in those questions. So I was already off the mainstream in some way.

NG: Was it more relationships with individuals, Philip Whalen, for example, and others who supported your development as a poet?
JK: Well, I was part of a group that I corresponded with from 1960–64. And when I came back from Japan in '64 there were still parts of it in North Beach: Stan Persky and Robin Blaser and Larry Fagin, and George Stanley, Richard Duerden, Spicer. And Persky's *Open Space* magazine came out, and that went on every month for a year, and that was very helpful in publishing all the new work that I and everyone else was doing then. There was still a San Francisco-based voice that considered itself part of the San Francisco Renaissance—like David Meltzer and Lawrence Ferlinghetti, who were still there.

NG: So this was a comfortable environment for you? Some of the other women poets and writers that we've talked to have certainly not had any kind of supportive community. But it sounds as if you really did.
JK: I think I did. Yes. For example, when I came back from Japan, Don Allen wanted to publish my first book. So, let's say that there was always a small group of my peers to read my work; there was always an audience for what I did.

NG: In terms of the community were there other women writers that you saw, maybe even from a distance?
JK: Diane Wakoski. She came to a meeting once, and Jack Spicer said something, and she cried, and I thought, oh, she's just not strong enough to put up with these people! You couldn't be thin-skinned!

Ruth Witt-Diamant was running the Poetry Center then, and she was a woman who was very open. Denise Levertov was writing, but she already knew who she was as a writer; and she wasn't around. Dora Fitzgerald [Dora Dull] was part of our small group, but she wasn't really a writer; she was married to the poet Harold Dull. Then she ran away and had her own adventures. And also in San Francisco, there was ruth weiss, but she was more of a jazz poet, and already had her own way etched out. So there was, no, I didn't know any women who were contemporary writers. Diane di Prima was on the other coast, and I wasn't quite sure about how I felt about her early work. It was a little too confessional. I remember reading Sylvia Plath's "Daddy" in '66 and thinking that that was a very strong poem. I met Anne Waldman in New York in '66, and I realized that there were other women writers who were practicing and genuinely devoted to their writing.

I came back out here [California] in '69 so essentially this community has played a large part in my life. In the early days in the seventies there were a lot of young poets who moved out here and they had children, and it became a real community. Like Tom and Angelica Clark, Lewis and Phoebe MacAdams, the Berksons, the Saroyans, the Thorpes. The women of Bolinas were very strong and very independent and thought they could raise their own children. I remember going to some of the first women's groups that I'd ever been to out here, which were very exciting, very grounded. So I think my sense of the women's movement really happened here in this community.

NG: You write about women in *The Tapestry and the Web.* How did that book come about? You were reading Joseph Campbell at the time? **JK:** I'd read Joseph Campbell earlier when I was at UCSB. So I became aware of this whole other way of looking at literature and movements. I saw that *The Hero with a Thousand Faces* is built on this story that Joseph Campbell weaves all the way through it—you know, the young hero and his journey. So I think that's when I understood that it was possible to have this narrative, this old narrative that could go through your life that was common to all humans. And you saw your own life in terms of that. It also took me out of the dangers of any confessional writing—why did I always hate that?

NG: Why *did* you hate confessional writing?
JK: It was so limiting. I never wanted to be called a poetess because it seemed that it was just concerned with your particular female identity, whereas I thought the identity of a writer was much bigger than that. And that's part of it, that you should be able to tell, or go into, these other dimensions and characters and not get hooked on your own personal identity. And so I think that belief allowed me see the legitimacy of Homer and this larger story of the *Odyssey* that I could use as a structure or a reference. So mostly those poems in *The Tapestry and the Web* are the ones that just hung around, passed the test of being there.

NG: Those poems have such an array of voices, certainly the humor, wonderful, biting. I love the way you play with the common vernacular.
JK: I really wanted to be able to do that, and to see the line move, to keep that effect of making a picture, a weaving, a tapestry.

NG: Were you intentionally, then, rewriting or parodying the Odysseus myth through a feminist construction?
JK: I didn't think of rewriting or parodying *The Odyssey*, but more of entering the story and seeing what applied to me, my life, seeing what fit.

NG: You read from *The Tapestry and the Web* at the 1965 Berkeley Poetry Conference, right? With Lenore Kandel?
JK: No, I didn't read with her. She read at a "Special Reading." I read on Saturday, July 24, with Lew Welch and Ron Loewinsohn. Ron Loewinsohn said Lenore Kandel was the "Tokyo Rose of Poetry" after

he heard her read at the Berkeley Poetry Conference [July 12–24, 1965]. Her poetry was so pointedly sexual, kind of astounding but abundantly of the time. There was a very heightened atmosphere there, very heady, both in Berkeley and in San Francisco.

NG: Were you keeping a journal at that time? Were you doing the daily journal writing?
JK: *The Japan and India Journals* were written from '60 to '64 and published. But yes, I kept extensive journals during '65, '66, '67, and on. I have some other earlier notebooks and journals, but because of the fact that I was in one place and it was a foreign country, the Japan journal took on more dimensions. Also Gary kept a daily book, and that gave me an example of someone who was involved in that practice. I kept these journals in these little binders, and then Gary had them bound for me in these three volumes. So they already looked like books. So when the time came, people were saying, "Everybody's published their India journals. What about yours?!"[1] And my Indian journal, the section on India, was a journal written on the spot—worried about the drip-dry dress and the rupees—but I gave all three volumes to Tom Clark to read, who was living here in Bolinas, and he said, well, what about just doing the whole thing? And Michael Wolfe, of Tombouctou Press, who started his press here, said he would do it. Then I had to think about how I was going to feel in terms of making this private material public. And I didn't sit down and retype it all the way through; I couldn't quite handle that. Some of it was in handwriting, and some of it was typed in these three bound volumes. So the typesetter set it from the original.

And then I realized that, okay, this private writing is going to become public, and maybe other women in the world are going to read it and say this is okay, this is normal, this is what can happen

---

1. See Gary Snyder, *Earth House Hold*. New York: New Directions, 1957; and Allen Ginsberg, *Indian Journal. March 1962–May 1963*. San Francisco, CA: Dave Haselwood Books and City Lights Books, 1970.

to one. I also realized that this was what Ginsberg was doing: taking down the wall between the private and the public. Once you did that, you were out in the open.

NG: How did that fit with your ambivalent feelings about confessional poetry? Did you perceive *The Japan and India Journals* as having confessional qualities in it?

JK: Not too many. Mostly because it was a working/writing book. It has a lot of dreams in it. In the beginning, it is more of a "what am I doing in this marriage?" kind of thing, but mostly I felt it held up in how it looked at the world. So it wasn't a diary kind of book that goes on and on about "I can't stand this one moment longer!" A certain amount of that can be useful for yourself, but it's a very "stuck" way to keep on writing. I occasionally give journal writing classes, and I just try to show what a wide variety of directions you can take.

NG: Did you edit the *Journals* much?

JK: No. I edited a few things out, but I didn't rewrite anything because once I did that the whole thing would collapse. So I said, "This is how it is. This is what I wrote and how I wrote it." That's why the form of the *Journals* is so idiosyncratic. Everyone who read it liked it a lot. There weren't a lot of reviews. I showed it to him [Gary Snyder] before I published it. I sent it to him, and wondered if his sense of privacy was going to be offended by it. His reply is in the introduction.[2] But I realized I had a perfect right to publish it. At that point I think it probably was very healthy; I took on another dimension as a writer.

---

2. In the introduction to the first edition of *The Japan and India Journals: 1960–1964*, Kyger wrote that Gary Snyder had sent her a postcard about publishing the *Journals*: "It sometimes seems like a chronicle of food and drink—were we really that sociable? I guess so. I see people much less frequently these past years." (*Strange Big Moon*, xii).

NG: Could you talk a little about your friend Nemi Frost? You mention her several times in the *Journals*.

JK: Nemi Frost was a self-taught painter, probably most influenced by Aubrey Beardsley. Her sister Annie also lived in San Francisco, and I got her old apartment over La Rocca's on Columbus when I moved there from Santa Barbara at the beginning of 1957. Nemi, who was bored with Santa Barbara by that time, moved up to San Francisco and found her own place and niche. She had a great sense of humor and became friends with many of the North Beach poets, like Jack Spicer, who dedicated a poem to her. She had a show of her paintings at the Coffee Gallery in '58, and still paints and exhibits her work.

NG: At one point, you write in the *Journals* that reading Kerouac made you feel good. What it was in his texts that made you feel that way?

JK: I was reading a letter, a long letter that he'd [Kerouac] sent to Gary. I think it was the fact that he was able to be spontaneous, that he was an incredibly accurate typist, and that he was so completely honest. If you've looked at the two volumes of his letters that have come out, you can see that he's a person who could write the truth about himself. He has a huge practice of looking through his dream life as self-analysis. I think it's his honesty that just really impressed me so much, that there was so little superficial cover-up.

NG: You write about Ginsberg and Orlovsky, when Ginsberg was with the Dalai Lama and seemed so eager to get quick enlightenment.

JK: Oh, yes, well, it was my way of getting back at him a little bit. It was the truth. There's nothing I wrote that I wouldn't stand behind. Allen was so completely absorbed in his own career and life and direction. And promotion of his friends.

NG: What was the impetus for going to Japan and India?

JK: Well, the impetus for going to Japan was to study Zen and to be with Gary and see what was happening in terms of historical Buddhism and see its history. Somehow I thought that Japan was—it was all in the air then—some kind of answer. Ginsberg was also planning a trip to India, and I thought it would be great to go. We met up in Delhi after Gary and I had been traveling for three months. I did most of the research for that trip, and at that point you could get all these great travel books from the India Tourist's Bureau, so we kind of figured out this trek—and we were gone for six months. It was great, wonderful!

NG: And the *Journals*, then, recount your life there as a narrative. You have said that your poetry presents your idea of life as a narrative.

JK: Well, life is made up of stories. And it is all autobiographical narrative. In the last few years, I've been trying to figure out where the narrative is going.

NG: I've heard your poetry described as woman-centered.

JK: Well, I think of voice as taking on a lot of personas and personalities, but you can only go so far with that because you are writing out of yourself. But I think of self as more than a distinct female voice or male voice. Do I believe in such a thing as a distinct female voice or mode of writing? Yes, I guess I could believe in it. But it would be a duality, part of a duality. But I think it's always a danger to set a male/female dichotomy or duality; the self is more than the sum of the parts.

NG: Well, Virginia Woolf does make the argument that you can see a particular female perspective on the world.

JK: Sure. I don't think that's something that I think about right now. I don't know what I think about—I think about the current U.S. administration [George W. Bush]. It drives me up a wall. It's been on my mind so much—I don't quite know what they're going to do next.

NG: Has your poetry then become more political?

JK: Oh, yes, certainly within the last year. How could you avoid that? Everybody keeps waiting for the younger generation to do something. When are they going to go out and demonstrate like they did in the sixties?

NG: I know what you mean, but to return to your thoughts on writing, how do you perceive the page and the movement of your lines? How do you develop your sense of the page as space and the poetic line?

JK: Well, I was always interested in how, from the beginning, you get your voice on the page. What is the line? So Charles Olson's "Projective Verse" is something that I've paid a lot of attention to. It has a lot to do with building a picture or tapestry through these linear movements of the line on the page and trying to make a tension of lines so when it [the line] breaks there's a certain energy that keeps you moving; that holds the end of the line and picks up on the next—the kinetics of what a line movement on the page is. How you can put your inflection down, learning how to chart the breath on the page. But it mostly has to do with a physical visceral process. Your breath stops and starts again as you move from the left to the right. Words centered in the middle of the page have a certain energy focus. It has to do with breathing. It has to do with timing and inflection and the combination of the two. It's not just a visual arrangement of the two. You know, for me, poets that just line up along the left hand margin have just gotten completely stuck. Why bother to even break the line? Why not just have a run-on Jamesian-Kerouacian paragraph? You look at some poetry books, and all you see are those little blocks of words on the page. It seems pre-packaged. Where's the vitality in that form?

NG: When you write, do you think about the performance of the poem, reading it to an audience?

JK: I don't know if I think about it, but I'm aware of the fact that a voice is going out there. Probably not as much as Anne [Waldman], who uses her voice much more—she knows the particular thrust of her voice, so she probably works towards that. And Bobbie [Louise Hawkins], who could read a telephone book and break your heart! That's just the beautiful breath breathing.

NG: It's interesting to consider how the poet moves from the creation on the page, to the performance of those lines in front of a live audience. How do you move from that one space into that other?
JK: Well, you've already charted your voice on the page, so you follow what your page says.

NG: So you're not improvising to any great extent?
JK: No. If circumstances are fortuitous, you can. Your timing has to do with how you put it on the page, and if it doesn't work then either you change it or let it go. But I would say that all poetry needs to be read out loud to give it a sound dimension. I think you need to read it physically out loud. Ideally, if you have placed it on the page right, anybody can read that poem and still get that same conversational, rhythmic, jazz sort of tone of voice that you intend. Ideally, that's what you're doing: charting the voice on the page so that it can be picked up by anybody.

NG: So it's not then intended as a visual document?
JK: Not as an end in itself, like concrete poetry.

NG: Many slam poets and spoken word poets resist publishing because they believe the poetry isn't meant to be on the page; it exists in the moment that it's performed.
JK: It's certainly a way of getting it off the page. Spoken word and performance poetry seem to be really carrying that particular energy.

I don't see it in book form much. Poetry always needs to get off the page. It needs air. So I think that's very healthy. But I also think poetry needs the other dimension too. I noticed that slam poetry, or rap poetry, uses that iambic line or other repetitive beats to keep it moving, and probably reading it on the page might be overly predictable.

NG: I've heard you say that you consider your poetry "California poetry." What do you mean by that?

JK: Well, it's because I live here, so if I were living some place else, I'd reflect that too. The fact that I lived in a landscape and in a place is something that the voice of the poetry reflects. So that's just to say you go beyond your inner walls because you're located in a physical place. So poetry is that intersection of yourself and the landscape and the weather and all that produces—community, voice, what's going on. And since I live in California, my poetry is reflective of what North Coast, Pacific Rim, ocean culture is about. It's seasonally defined, it's more laid back, it's not so aggressive; it's, you know, a different rhythm from the East coast.

NG: What about your Buddhist practice—how does it function in your poetic practice?

JK: Buddhism is something that is hopefully unselfconscious. There were other sorts of religious questing going on, such a heady . . . Zen Buddhism is the practice of sitting meditation, and so is writing. Writing is a practice—it's something that you do every day without thinking about it, whether it's good or bad, and it's just something that you do—you *do* writing. I think I use Buddhist terms a lot and vocabulary but hopefully not in any opaque way.

NG: Why was that spiritual quest important for you early on?

JK: A spiritual quest. I don't know if I'd call it a spiritual quest, but I think it was important for women. What is religion? I didn't even know what it was! I didn't know what the self was! I didn't know anything. And in Japan, at first seeing all these dark Buddhas—was that part of religion? Did you have to be a Christian or a Buddhist? It's not either/or. I think of myself as being interested in religion, being involved in religion all the time and seeing all the different forms of it. Having spent time in Mexico and seeing Guadalupe of Mexico there, and how people react inside the churches with this devotion. I'm always overcome by other people's devotion—because it seems to be this reference point where all this yearning and hope can rest and ask and petition. Certainly in that way of just asking, something happens, is revealed. So just to see religion in its basic bhakti[3] practice of devotion is always amazing to me. You can feel the strength that comes from it. A part of the life of religion. It's fascinating.

NG: Does that philosophy then connect to the idea of the poet as a prophet, which characterized some Beat poets? Do you subscribe to that belief?

JK: Not for me necessarily. But certainly for someone like Ginsberg who took on one of the largest public voices of a poet in the last half of the century. I think you have to have a dedicated commitment and ability to do that, so of course not every poet can become a prophet.

NG: Can one choose to?

JK: I don't know. What if you're a lousy prophet or you don't tell the truth or you get pissed off!

NG: Are there other poets that you knew or read who you would place in that category as Ginsberg?

---

3. Bhakti is a Hindu term meaning devotion to one god with all of life's activities directed to the god's service.

JK: Maybe Walt Whitman. Certainly that was the model from the century before. Diane di Prima can come out with writing that's very strong—that poem about the imagination, "Rant." Ferlinghetti. Ed Sanders too. There are different kinds of poets. There's the Kenneth Koch kind of poet that is able to take the inanimate and have it talk back, keeping everything alive. There's the ecological poet, like Snyder. Ginsberg used to talk a lot about expanded consciousness: poets expanding their consciousness so that they could talk about all these other dimensions without having to hold onto a separate, or a particular, identity. You could take on a larger cultural or political identity. I think that takes a large heart and dedication. His [Ginsberg's] private life was always open. I don't think many people want to do that.

NG: That can be a huge risk.
JK: Or even beyond risk. I think he [Ginsberg] was genuinely committed to his political investigation. Song writing took over so much in the late sixties, political message songs like Bob Dylan's. We don't expect the individual poet's voice anymore to speak out like it used to in the late sixties and early seventies. Certainly the readings that we used to have out here in San Francisco with [so many] people don't happen anymore.

NG: When you teach young poets, then, do you see them taking on that political role?
JK: Some of them at Naropa and at New College of San Francisco. But there's no way to avoid having a political voice—it's our common air, destiny.

NG: But some will deny having it—can't see it or will deny having it.
JK: Yes, like a secret.

Drive
—Hettie Jones

Hettie Jones, née Cohen, was born in Laurelton, New York, in 1934 and knew from the age of six that she had to leave home—"Unlike any woman in my family or anyone I'd ever actually known, I was going to *become*—something, anything, whatever that meant" (*How I Became* 10). In 1955, after graduating from Virginia's Mary Washington College with a degree in drama, she headed to Columbia University and then to Greenwich Village, where she found a burgeoning arts avant-garde. Her role in the inception and production of the literary magazine *Yugen* with her then-husband, LeRoi Jones/Amiri Baraka, is now celebrated by historians of the Beat generation. During those years, Jones harbored a secret writing life, but it was not until 1978 that she gave her first public reading. Jones's writing accommodates her self-proclaimed didacticism, which she attributes to her Jewish heritage, combined with her involvement in the civil rights and women's movements. Jones's approach to writing suggests an aesthetic in which the material of the lived life centers the artistic act, which is intended to teach and to validate those denied a voice.

Jones's status as Beat and as a writer is deeply implicated in the particular burdens and liberations of her mixed-race marriage to LeRoi Jones in the late fifties and early sixties. The marriage provided her the

155

opportunity to enter a revolutionary interracial culture, but she was later abandoned by Jones when her whiteness compromised his status as a Black Nationalist and Black Arts writer. Jones's emergence from the marriage and her concomitant development as a writer are the focus of her memoir, *How I Became Hettie Jones* (1990). The very title suggests a personal ethnic and poetic liminality that intervenes in the unstable race categories, which are treated as fixed in establishment discourses of racial difference. Parts of the story Jones tells were told by Jones/Baraka in his 1964 play *The Slave*, which reifies a racial binary as the black father produces and reclaims his "black" children. Hettie Jones's version situates her, a white woman, in an African-American community, disrupting a binary that constructs racial identity along lines of skin color.

The memoir, which includes Jones's own poetry, fiction, and letters to track her emerging identity as a writer, catalogues women unknown to or lost from the male Beat culture hagiographies. The sheer mass of this group of women and their relative anonymity suggest the distortions of official Beat history. Jones is specific in her history, listing, among others, Helene Dorn (128–31), whom she credits with fostering her beginnings as a writer; the poet Sara Blackburn (100, 201); the playwright Aishah Rahman (180); Bonnie Bremser (100); poet Rochelle Owens (111), featured in *Four Young Lady Poets* (Bergé et al., 1962); Rena (Oppenheimer) Rosequist (82); Diane di Prima (98, 190); and Joyce Johnson (80–81, 156). She also enumerates other interracial unions, couples such as Ia and Marzette Watts (169–70), Garth and Archie Shepp (170), Diana Powell and Douglas Turner Ward (202), Carol Plenda and Bob Thompson (135), and Vertamae Smart-Grosvenor and Bob Grosvenor (155, 193). With these names, Jones makes visible the presence of some women and interracial relationships that have gone unrecognized in Beat accounts.

Jones's commitment to exploring the intersection of race and gender finds its voice most powerfully in the short story, a genre that gives her, as she explains in the interview below, "the space that prose offers to tell the stories that race imposes." She employs the form to reveal anger, ambivalence, love, recognition, or redemption hidden in the daily lives of individuals living on the color line, as in "This Time It Was Different at the Airport":

> I was especially conscious of the color business back then, as who wasn't, and for me there had begun to be a new aspect to it, now that my daughters and I were almost the same size. The nature of the hostility I felt when we went out together was changing. (152)

With the short story, Jones documents the evolution of race relations over the last forty years through her own experiences as a single white mother raising two mixed-race children. It is poetry, however, that frees Jones to express what Janine Pommy Vega calls Jones's "mammalian compassion and toughness." An adherent of Charles Olson's theory of Projective Verse—that "form is never more than an extension of content"—Jones uses the page to experiment with long prose and tight haiku-like lines as well as alphabetical and anaphoric catalogues. A theme repeated almost ritualistically throughout her work is the need of a woman to claim her own agency. As the poet reveals in "Seven Songs at Sixty," this project remains necessary for women who came of age in the Beat generation:

> *Once I had*
> *long hair and high hopes*
> *that the pretty boys*
> *would love me forever*
>
> *Now I know better*
> *. . . . .*
> *What do you think*
> *of me, shorn of locks and beliefs*

> *How do you see my*
> *lessening flesh, my grief*
>
> . . . .
>
> *This is what I'll become:*
> *ashheap   bone pebbles   messages*
>
> *If you want to know me*
> *you better hurry*
>
> (*How I Became* 101–3)

Evoking the sermonic, exculpatory, and visionary, Jones's poetry, like that of so much of the Beat and other mid-century poetic movements upon which she was schooled, demands that we see her—and choose to participate with her—in the existential act of becoming human.

In addition to her memoir and short stories, Jones has edited collections of prison writing produced by her students at New York state correctional facilities, including *Aliens at the Border* (1997). She has also written adolescent literature, including *Big Star Fallin' Mama* (1974) and *I Hate to Talk About Your Mother* (1980). *Drive*, published in 1998, won the Norma Farber Award for a first collection of poetry. Her second collection, *All Told*, was published in 2003.

Part One of the following interview was conducted on June 14, 1999, by Nancy Grace at Hettie Jones's home in New York City. Part Two was a telephone interview conducted by Grace on September 26, 2002.

Part I

June 14, 1999

NANCY GRACE: How did you come to write your memoir?
HETTIE JONES: Well, people asked me for years and years when I was going to write the story. I refused for years and years because I

really thought all people wanted to know about was personal information. You know, they really wanted to get between the sheets. And I had no desire to put my personal life on the line like that. But then, after I began teaching, after having run into a lot of young women and realizing that nobody knew this history—nobody knew what the women involved had done—I felt that I had to set the record straight in some way. And then, LeRoi published his book [*The Autobiography of LeRoi Jones/Amiri Baraka*, 1984]. So I decided that I really had to do it. By that time I had been writing autobiographical stories, and my agent sent some of those around to various editors, and they all said they'd be interested. That was about 1985. . . .

NG: In what way were you trying to set the record straight?
HJ: First of all, about the situation of women. A lot of young women at the time had no concept of the fact that prior to the women's movement there were any women who had removed themselves from general cultural expectations, during the fifties especially. I really wanted to show that we had started the whole process, that not enough attention had been paid to the fact that we were here and we had made changes in women's lives. A lot of the people who began the women's movement had some vague idea that we had been out here, although they didn't attribute any real advances to us. They were getting their own apartments and taking off their bras without realizing that there were women who left home as we did and suffered for it.

NG: Both you and Joyce Johnson make very clear in your memoirs that there was great sacrifice, that you gave up a lot.
HJ: I just had lunch last week with Rena Oppenheimer, who is now Rena Rosequist. When she left home to marry Joel, her mother sent for the priest, who tried to bar her way. We were all thought to be lost, but at least we did what we wanted. I don't think I knew any

woman, who, if she was still in touch with her parents, was on good terms with them. Many had just left home and disappeared.

NG: How did your group contribute to the women's movement at that time?

HJ: By physically taking a stand, rather than intellectually or through any particular writing. Simply by saying, "Ok, I'm going to love on my own. I'm going to acknowledge that I am a sexual being, I'm going to have sex, and I'm going to practice birth control. I'm going to be a responsible person comparable to a man—I'm going to live what is generally regarded as a man's life. I'm going to have my own apartment, I'm going to have a job, and I'm going to be self-supporting." Even among the young women that I knew who were slightly younger than I, all this was really considered an accomplishment. It was! You just weren't supposed to leave home until you got married and lived under another man's hand.

Also, I love to mention—clothing! Young women today don't have any idea of the discomfort, and I always talk about this when I make speeches, that to take off your girdle was a radical move—first came the girdle and then came the bra—but to take off your girdle! Ah! To be able to think and walk and move without feeling blistered all the time. To acknowledge that you could have an *ass*. And to wear pants! At my college in the fifties, we weren't allowed to wear pants. In order to work on the stage, to climb all the ladders and everything, they issued us garage mechanic uniforms, monkey suits.

Again—the idea that one could move freely. And taking off high-heeled shoes. I took off my high heels and threw them in the sewer one day when I first came to New York, and then I took to wearing very weird-looking old lady's shoes that I got in the orthopedic shoe store. They were so different. Oh, I remember, my boyfriend loved them—a pair of little, red, old lady's shoes—he thought that they just looked terrific. They were weird! But they were comfortable. And another thing—to stop carrying that little pocket book—the kind that came back into style not too long ago? But instead to wear a shoulder bag and to have your hands free. And what you needed was a big bag anyway if you weren't going to go home at night, you know! . . .

How the women felt about politics back then I can't say. Remember, we hardly spoke amongst ourselves to firm up a woman's opinion on issues. It was all we could do to share information on how to live the lives we'd chosen—practical info about sex, abortion, marriage, divorce. I was grateful back then, as I still am, for the women friends who helped me.

NG: What was the process of writing the memoir like?
HJ: Well, I won't say I didn't cry. I cried a lot, and that, of course, is therapeutic. And of course any exploration into the self is going to be self-discovery. . . . In that respect the process was very healing for me, I think. I'm glad I did it. But while I was doing it, I have to admit, it was difficult. When I began, I really didn't think that I could write more than maybe around fifty to sixty pages. And I really figured out how to do it on my own. Joyce's book [*Minor Characters*] had come out, but her book has a different tone, and it doesn't address the length of time that mine does. She also doesn't get so much into the present as I do. So there was a different process, really because of the different stories involved, and I had wandered my way through.

NG: How does one determine the span of time to deal with? You started your memoir with the memory of being a very young girl at camp weaving an imaginary basket in the clouds.
HJ: Well, it was very, very important to me to show that the decisions I made, when I was a young woman, were a long time coming. They were really an organic part, a progression in the life I had been

going toward from the time I was very small. Because it seems to me that I've always been conscious, or I can remember very early moments of consciousness. . . . So it was a very secret life, and I wanted to reveal in my book that it had always been there. That mine was not a rebellion against any kind of treatment, any kind of repression, but was there simply because I had been destined to do that. If you know when you're six years old that you have to leave home in order to realize your passion, then you just start to look forward to it. And I did.

NG: The book is a lyrical construction of your life, the way it focuses on a place, the way you handle memory and weave in your own poetry and the letters.

HJ: I really didn't know what I was doing. But my memories fell into those patterns associated with place, and then I wanted this to be a woman's book. I thought men would not focus on their homes. But here I mean "home" not just in terms of where we lived, but "home" as the art scene. So it seemed like the likely place to locate not only my life but the literary life and also because of the business of race, where things came together in terms of race. So it seemed very logical. I was a little hesitant of that at first because I thought oh god, people are going to think this is corny. . . .

Then about putting the poems in, well, because of the fact that I had wanted to be a poet. When I wrote the memoir, I had published only one little chapbook of poems and wasn't very assiduous about sending out my poems because I didn't really like the literary scenes that I saw around me. For one thing, I wasn't a Language poet. I was much too logical and much too old-fashioned and much too linear—What are my other faults? But the poems expressed my state of mind, and then I thought the poems that I included by other people expressed the state of mind that was current in the culture at that time, or the culture I was trying to show. So I put them in at some risk, but it worked. . . .

NG: When you began writing as a poet, were you writing within the Beat culture, the alternative artistic culture?

HJ: I can't say that I wasn't influenced by it. Because of the fact that I earned my living as a proof reader, copyeditor, I read a lot of poetry. I worked for Grove Press, mainly, and I read all of the avant-garde stuff, so I was influenced by both prose and poetry of that time. And, sure, I read more of Allen Ginsberg than I did of, say, the more academic poets like Mark Strand or John Hollander—you know, the people that the Beats were sort of in competition with. Yes, I read Robert Lowell as well, but not as carefully maybe. But I read Olson and Creeley and all those people. But what I did not read, other than a few poems by Adrienne Rich and maybe some by Sylvia Plath, was poetry by women.

The models for the form of the poems I eventually wrote were the guys all around me—LeRoi, in particular. But what to say, that was the big question. You know, writing a woman's life. The poem that's in my book that I wrote a thousand years ago—"my dearest darling will you take out the garbage?"[1]—when I wrote that, I never dreamed of publishing it. I just thought no one will want to publish this. That didn't keep me from writing.

NG: Did you go beyond or manipulate the form that the men were working with at that time?

HJ: I don't think so. I think one of the things that influenced me regarding form was a statement that LeRoi made in *The New American Poetry*. He said that there must not be anything that I have to fit the poem into, no form—everything must be made to fit into the poem; that is, the poem itself.[2] I guess if you want to go back to it, it's Olson's

---

1. Untitled poem in *How I Became Hettie Jones*, New York: Dutton, 1990, Penguin reissue, 1991, 209.
2. In "How You Sound??," Baraka wrote, "I must be completely free to do just what I want, in the poem. 'All is permitted.' . . . There cannot be anything I must fit the poem into. Everything must be made to fit the poem" (425).

idea of projective verse—that one thought leads to another, that you don't have to have an initial idea that you follow all the way through. I find that still works for me. . . . That way you learn your own breath.

NG: Do you consider yourself principally a poet, fiction writer, editor, publisher?

HJ: . . . I don't see why, if you write, you can't do everything. I have examples of this all around me, certainly Olson, Creeley, Frank O'Hara, Baraka. Though I was never attracted to writing criticism and still am not. I've done a few book reviews, and I find it very hard. You really have to extract yourself from it, while the fiction that I write is mostly autobiographical. You know Poe said that the short story is much more related to poetry than it is to the novel, and I guess I feel that way about my stories, which are generally fairly short. I think, though, when you write fiction you have to be a little more concerned with gossip, and I've never cared very much for repeating who's sleeping with whom, finding out things like that, so my stories are generally morality tales, and in a way they are borderline essays. Well, I'm a preacher at heart. But I like writing nonfiction too, I think from the same impulse.

NG: What was the position of women in the publishing phase of the Beat movement, particularly your position with *Yugen* and Totem Press?

HJ: We were the facilitators. . . . This is not to say that Roi couldn't have gotten *Yugen* together by himself, maybe. I don't put a lot of things on me that he could have done. But, you know, I did all the real physical work. Plus the question of where I worked was very important. At *Partisan Review*, getting Bernard DeBoer, who was the distributor for all those little literary magazines—that meant that he took us on, a magazine stapled at the spine, only because he liked us. And it wasn't only me he liked; he liked Roi. He was a very open-minded man.

I never did figure out whether he liked the idea that we were married, but he and his wife invited us to their house. We did not get that kind of attention from white people for the most part. But DeBoer brought us to universities, and it made a difference. *Yugen* got out to the West coast.

And then Ted Wilentz, who owned The Eighth Street Bookshop, I remember him loaning us five hundred dollars—ah, such a huge sum of money!—to get things typeset because I couldn't do the IBM typewriter anymore. And he said to Roi, "I'm only loaning you this money because of your wife." And Roi said, "Yeah, yeah, yeah," I mean he didn't want to hear that. But Ted knew that I would get the job done and stuff like that. So, yes, my role was very important. I may not have written the poetry, but I sure did type it! And I sure did lay it out. And people liked me and saw my role in that; I did get a lot of positive reinforcement. That and also, where I worked, I think in a way; although a lot of women worked, not every woman had a good job where she was associated with something that was important and was given a certain responsibility. . . .

NG: Did you or do you consider your writing to be Beat? And what does that term mean to you?

HJ: Well, it certainly reflects a more bohemian approach. Certainly, I don't write about middle-class angst because I don't have any. I don't even know what it is because poverty takes you a long ways from all that. Also, so much fiction goes into the ins and outs of relationships: of marriage, of friendship—I'm really not interested in that kind of stuff. So I'm more interested in telling morality tales and adventure stories that deal a lot more with race. I seem not to deal with race in my poems, and I don't know why that difference occurs. Gender issues find their way into poems but not race. But I do deal with it in my stories. Perhaps because I'm angrier and therefore less immediately articulate about race issues and I need the space that prose offers to tell the stories that race imposes. I don't know whether it's Beat or not, although it certainly grew out of a separation from American fiction in general. Also, I think my writing is political when it deals with subjects that touch on our political lives—race, class, gender issues. It's probably political on most counts because of who I am and the way I think about things. If you want to go down the "beaten down" path, if you want to go to the beatitude aspect of it, writing for me is a spiritual experience. When I said I was a preacher, I was serious. I think that's always what I wanted to be. I wanted to be the cantor, or, in another world, I probably would have seriously thought of becoming a rabbi, if I could have stood the scholarship. I think this preacher/spiritual side is behind my artist impulse, that I'm more in that tradition than, say, your novelist who is in more of a literary tradition. I'm less influenced by literature than what the literature itself was after. The philosophical premise behind it. And we were living then, if you want to start back there, in such a material world, whereas Beat was a spiritual movement. Allen [Ginsberg] used to try to get people to understand this all the time, that we were looking for enlightenment and organized religion wasn't giving it to us. Our parents weren't after that enlightenment either. They were after comfort and security, as far as possible. But there had to be a different way. . . .

NG: Do you see that same search for spirituality amongst young poets today?

HJ: No, I think they're looking for language—language that isn't the language of advertising. And the spoken word is so hot! And though a lot of the work is shallow, it's a facility with language that they're seeking. But the ones that stick with it—they can go below the superficial aspects of language and ask language to carry meaning, not to be just pretty. Then they will redefine something. I don't know—it certainly has upset all the adults, and I find that excellent. . . . If it leads people to the study of language and the possibilities of language, what could be wrong?

NG: But isn't language use an essentially spiritual act in some ways?

HJ: I think all of us—young, old, and anywhere—who write are engaged in an act that could be construed as spiritual, though I'm not sure how to define that word anymore. I know that for the Beats the idea of the spiritual was very much opposed to the material, the original way of defining our own lives, our urges and motions. We were reacting to a material world—and the reaction as well as the position of that post-World War II world was rather clear cut. Nowadays it seems permissible to be an acquisitive venture capitalist at the same time one is a spoken-word poet. But maybe this isn't even a criticism; we don't ever put down Wallace Stevens for having supported himself selling insurance. Anyone in pursuit of art is responding to a desire to make visible that which is not, to offer the unknown self to others. My concern today regarding young writers would have more to do with their failure to communicate through language's first role: that of meaning, of message. . . .

NG: Does your own poetry and fiction manifest, as does some Beat literature, the black street language of the time? There's some of it in your memoir but not as much as what we see in di Prima's early poetry.

HJ: Yeah. I don't mean to accuse Diane wrongly, but I wouldn't have done it that way. She was just being hip. I feel that hers was really an adaptation, in a way. Mine comes out of the language of my young adulthood. . . . I also know, and am more intimately involved with what we—I guess—call black culture than most white adults of my age. I was at a conference last week and began to sing, "Save the bones for Henry Jones, 'cause Henry don't eat no meat." And people looked at me like I was just stone crazy! "What is that?" they said. And I said, "It's a song from the forties." Then I was telling this story to an older black man, and he laughed and laughed—he understood! So, that's what I know, and it comes out in my language. But I don't feel it as an adaptation.

NG: It's organic, the way you talk. Were there any women of color writing in your community, then?

HJ: Yeah. But so few of us actually shared our writing. A friend of mine, Aishah Rahman, became an experimental playwright and now teaches at Brown and has published her memoir. She was writing, and I knew about her.

NG: But you weren't sharing your writing?

HJ: No, I wasn't. People who were publishing more might have, but I wasn't. No. I was writing poetry at that time that I put away in a drawer and wouldn't show to anyone. But a lot of people believe that [that] was somebody's fault.

NG: Did LeRoi encourage you to write?

HJ: He wanted me to write criticism. I didn't tell him I was writing poetry. It was my very private thing. Diane di Prima, who was the person I knew most, was the most accessible of all the women writing then. And there were others like Barbara Moraff and Rochelle Owens. But I couldn't write like them, and didn't want to. Also, when you're having two children, it just takes a lot out of you. But, and I think I said this in my book, nothing but my own voice held me hostage. Also, what I wanted to write about, women didn't write about.

I am, I will admit, somewhat of a perfectionist when it comes to writing—I really work on my things and I didn't understand, because LeRoi was so adept, he would pull a poem out of the typewriter and come running and show it to me, it was perfect. But my poems had to be revised because they're not perfect when they come out. It's getting a little bit better now but not even that much better. There are people who write to say what they think and other people who write to find out what they think, and the latter have to work on it to find out what it's about. But I didn't understand that. Don't forget, this was a time when there weren't writing classes—I didn't know a thing about them—and certainly I did not take any writing workshops in college. There were no such things in my college! I struggled with it, although I wrote prose in college, for my literary magazine, just little articles, little essay things here and there, not fiction. The first fiction I began to write, which was probably in the seventies, was just autobiographical, so it was very little different from writing essays, although I knew much more about form by then and I had read so much more. . . .

NG: You're speaking directly to people, as opposed to presenting the poet in isolation. You establish a community with the reader.

HJ: Well, that's what I feel poetry or anything written ought to be. Why bother to write it down if you don't want to communicate it to others? This is not to say that people are not allowed, as you say, to write for themselves, but what I find when I teach is . . . the very fact that you're in a class and you're reciting this poem to other people, do you want them to get an inkling of what it means? But, again, my impulse is the preachy one—and that requires an audience.

NG: Do you have your students recite their poetry aloud, do a lot of oral readings?

HJ: That's the only way. That's what they do. And prose classes as well. Everyone has to read their stuff aloud. Once people get over their initial fears, and when other people say, "Hey, that was good, that was interesting," it's so gratifying to a person. That's the way you get people to write. You can't get people to write by saying, "No, this is wrong, this is wrong, this is wrong," because you just stop them. But the voice comes from the soul—if I can be very deliberate about this. . . . All you have to do is give it permission.

Part II

September 26, 2002

NG: Did you know or read the work of activists and authors such as Alix Kates Shulman, Shulamith Firestone, Gloria Steinem, or Betty Friedan?

HJ: I never met Alix Kates Shulman until maybe ten years ago. I believe she wrote a review of my memoir in the *Nation*.[3] So subsequently I met her. She was very nice. I think prior to that she'd written about the Beats in an article in the *Village Voice*.[4] We'd never met face to face, though I think I read one of her novels. You know, there were so many different worlds of writers in New York that even though she was probably the same age as I, our paths never crossed. No, I never met Shulamith Firestone as far as I know. I hope I'm not making a mistake. I never met Gloria Steinem.

You know, when the feminists arrived on the scene, I'm talking about the people you mention like Betty Friedan and all those people, I was already "feminist-ized" by my circumstances. There I was, alone with two children, with no help from anybody anywhere. A little bit of emotional support from my in-laws and their love of their grandchildren certainly helped, and occasionally the kids would go visit them and stuff like that. But for the most part I was alone and very poor, supporting us all on nothing. And what these people [such as Friedan,

---

3. Alix Kates Shulman, "Keeping Up with Jones," *The Nation*, March 26, 1990, 425–27.
4. Alix Kates Shulman, "The Beat Queens," *Voice Literary Supplement*, June 1989, 18–23.

Steinem] were demanding seemed to have absolutely no relevance in my life. I took a look at *The Feminine Mystique* years later, and—ahh—I can't even remember what it was that I read, but I thought, "Oh, I don't need to read this." I think that was the way I felt about it, that I didn't need to read it. Of course, you know, I apologize for that attitude, but there were so many other things that I needed to read.

NG: What were you reading? Were there particular texts that fit your life circumstances?

HJ: No! No, no, no, not at all. Nobody was writing about what I was going through. Nobody had ever gone through it as far as I knew. Nobody, nobody wrote about the experience of [being white and] having black children. But racial issues were political, and nobody was writing any kinds of self-help books on what it was like to [be white and] raise black children—or a primer for crossing race lines. When you talk about reading, who had time to read? You know, reading takes time, and you have to have leisure time. When I wasn't working at earning money, I was making clothes, or baking bread—and not just because it was a back-to-the-land time or any of that kind of stuff. I was doing it because I really lived on pennies. So reading was a kind of luxury for people who had time and money.

NG: But how do you evaluate those feminist activists?

HJ: Well, sure, the changes that they made in society, in raising the level of attention, were certainly valuable. I would never, ever, ever disparage them, or say that their contributions weren't valuable. Just because I wasn't reading them didn't mean that they didn't have an effect on me; they made it possible for me to attract more attention.

NG: So your life experiences radicalized you before the women's movement texts were published?

HJ: I just always had my own idea of myself. I don't know whether you'd call that feminist or not. I mean, I wasn't trying to bring other women along with me. I was certainly trying to bring myself along. I think that's probably more to the point. But you know, growing up in the forties really—because by the fifties I'd already gone to college— you didn't have any role models. There was no concept that you [as a woman] were in any way another status; that was just the way the world was. But by the time I started to think about it, I was away from home.

NG: Can you tell me a little more about the significance of your relationship with Joyce Johnson in the fifties and sixties? Did you read her work?
HJ: Well, no, not before publication. We women did not talk about our own work with each other.

NG: Even you and Joyce, being as close as you were, weren't talking about that with each other?
HJ: Right. And you also have to think about closeness: how do you establish closeness with someone. I had a lot of friends, Joyce [was] just one. She was single; I was married. She worked uptown; I worked downtown. I saw as much of her as I saw of my other friends. It's just that we've maintained this close relationship all this time, and a lot of other people have moved away or remained married or something like that. So ours is just longstanding. But you know I worked most of the time, day or night, whatever. And I doubt that we even had time to go out for a cup of coffee. Life was very different then. Especially when I was having two babies. And that's really a lot of work. And a full-time job. And a press to manage.

NG: That's a tremendous amount of responsibility. When did you really begin to share your work with other writers?

HJ: Well, of course I was very pleased and proud of the books that I wrote for children. So all of my friends got copies of those. So that would be like sharing. But prior to publication? I didn't give my first public reading until, oh, I think it was 1978. So it was late.

NG: Where was that reading?
HJ: At PS 122—an important venue now but just then beginning. And I believe it [the reading] was arranged by Thulani Davis. And people, old friends, were astonished that I'd written all this stuff.

NG: Were you reading fiction or poetry at that event?
HJ: Maybe both, because I'd started writing stories, I probably started writing stories in the mid-seventies or early seventies. And I started writing much more poetry. I was a little more settled by then; I had a little more time. I was writing [children's books] for a living and not going out to a job. The kids were older; they were in school all day. And I was just living from advance to advance; in between, I would do copyediting. But life was so cheap then. It was different. I mean, you could live on a pittance. So I had no time to do anything until the mid-seventies.

NG: How then did you finally emerge as a poet?
HJ: Slowly . . . I think because of the subject matter I chose, as I guess I have written [in my memoir]—and this is probably where the feminists did help—*Writing a Woman's Life*, that book by Carolyn Heilbrun, I don't necessarily like that book—but anyway, it's because at first I didn't think the subject was hip. But then I realized it was hip!

NG: To write a woman's life?
HJ: Yeah, yeah.

NG: Who helped in that process?

HJ: I think it was these young guys that I ran into, all of whom were at least fifteen years younger than I. I got to know the next wave bohemia, and that was a group of largely young men who found out who I was. They were students of Joel Oppenheimer, second generation St. Mark's people, living around on the Lower East Side. Their approval of me—and when they finally encouraged me to show them what I'd done, they really liked it. And, of course, the times were changing.

NG: Who were some of the guys in that group?

HJ: Well, Chuck Wachtel, who's now a writer, who's now at NYU. Who else? His partners Harry Lewis and Brian Breger. They had a little press called Number Press, and they published my first chapbook, *Having Been Her*, in 1981. Then there were musicians around too. People who are still around, David Murray and Butch Morris and other jazz musicians that I knew. Stanley Crouch, he probably encouraged me.

NG: So are you a feminist writer?

HJ: Am I a feminist? I'm just a writer. Of course, I deal with women's issues all the time, and I like to write about women. In fact, I write largely about women, although a lot of my poetry is kind of genderless, and I hope men appreciate it as much as women. I don't know how you would define a feminist now in this day and age. But of course I have to be a feminist. I wouldn't say though—I would never say that! But I don't identify myself with any label. You know, that's really probably the answer.

NG: What does feminism mean to you?

HJ: Well, simply in broad terms, it means standing for the rights of women in all cases and in all aspects of life. I'm a feminist because I believe we should help women everywhere who are in need of everything we can give them. I'm not a feminist because I want to crack the glass ceiling. I don't have any interest in that. I seldom run into male chauvinism, and when I do I'm so appalled. But it seems so stupid to me now. It's stupid male chauvinism. Stupid! [laughs] You know?

NG: Yes, I do. [laughs] Can you amplify a bit on what you mean by Beat or bohemian?

HJ: Okay, I guess it's a looser approach to life. I mean what bohemian has always meant to literary and artistic history in general. Bohemians are people who live outside conventions, as most artists do, who are loose. And I don't just mean people who are loose sexually. But e-e-e-easy. Easy with their emotions. More emotionally available. They're more likely to shout and scream and then to hug and kiss and weep. Now that's a very general description, but I don't think I can get any closer. I don't know. I mean, when I read Jack Kerouac, I don't even know that it's Beat. I don't even know how to define that any more, it's been bandied about so much.

NG: Do you see that looseness in your own fiction or in your own approach to writing?

HJ: Well, yes, first of all I don't like forms in poetry. I like word play, that's for sure. But then it's a mixed bag because I don't think I could write anything that I wasn't satisfied had meaning in some way or another. That is, I don't like things that fall apart at the seams, where you finish reading it and you wonder, "What is this that I've read?" So I do have structure, and the structure is involved with the content.

NG: Does that connect with the Jewish cantor tradition that you discussed in our earlier interview?

HJ: Well, I was friends with a cantor in the synagogue where I grew up because I liked to sing. And for a while I played a little foot-pedal organ for the junior choir; but I was playing everything by ear, and that wasn't too great. But, you know, it's not the cantor—it's the scale. The scale in the liturgy was familiar music to me. The scale is more like what you hear in any non-Western music. It's like Indian music, it's like Arabic, it's like African music. If you hear it, you know, like [sings a brief example]. I'm not doing very well!

NG: So when you say the scale is the inspiration, how does it manifest itself in your poetry?

HJ: Well, because that sound feels familiar to my ear and not foreign in any way. So I think that's why I like modern, atonal music. It's mostly why I felt so comfortable listening to jazz. As I explained in my memoir, it wasn't until I heard Thelonius Monk—and the blues were something like that too—that I found those off notes again, those notes you couldn't find anywhere. That was what I liked. It feels as if it expresses my deepest emotions, and it has influenced my writing because I like to hear tones, and I wish that I could write poems on a scale, on a staff the way you write music. But then I thought that was way too precious. Not everybody can read music so they wouldn't know what to do with it.

NG: In some ways when you construct that poetic line, you are charting a musical line in some respects, aren't you?

HJ: Oh, sure! And that's why I like to teach open field composition. I try to explain to my students that you don't have to hug the left margin. And it appeals to people's sense of space. It frees their voices.

NG: How did you become involved with prison writing, and what specifically do you do with the project?

HJ: Janine Vega called me up one day and said, "How would you like to make fifty dollars?" [laughs] She'd been teaching a poetry workshop at

Sing-Sing, and she had just published a book from there, and she felt that the guys in the class needed some other instruction. So she asked if I'd like to teach a prose workshop. This was in 1988. She'd get the prison to put up some money, and *Poets & Writers* would match it. I had a car, so I could drive up there. So I said, "Sure." I'd never been in a prison in my life. But I had been teaching for about ten years by that time. So I found that it [teaching in the prison] was fun, and I did not feel intimidated. You know, I've been in so many situations where I'm the only white person and everybody else is a black person, so I did not feel in any way intimidated by the race thing. [Later] I ran into a woman who said, "Are you interested in teaching women?" And I had grown tired of that all-male atmosphere. You know, because . . . Janine is more imposing than I—she can keep that distance. But one guy started passing me little notes and stuff, and I just didn't want anyone to hit on me. I'm not exactly sure whether I'd taught classes of all women before, but subsequently I have, at the Y especially. And I love teaching classes of women.

NG: What's the difference, or what do you love about it?
HJ: This is not particularly an argument for single-sex education—I went to a women's college, don't forget—there is some value to women in being in a group of only women within the course of their education. I've found that women open up, they're not afraid to cry, for example, or to reveal themselves. Well, usually I'm teaching memoir, and a lot of people cry in my classes. I like teaching women because they would confide, and, of course, there were very interesting women at Bedford Hills. Don't forget, Kathy Boudin and Judy Clark[5] are not uninteresting women. They're women who have been through a whole lot of stuff.

---

5. Kathy Boudin is a former leader of the radical Weather Underground who was incarcerated at the Bedford Hills Correctional Facility for her role in a 1981 armored car robbery. Judy Clark was a member of the SDS and is currently incarcerated in the Bedford Hills Correctional Facility for a 1981 armored car robbery in New York by the Revolutionary Task Force.

When someone has become an extremist in another direction from mine, when you encounter someone who has actually murdered someone, you respect that person for being able to live at all. Because don't think that they don't know what a heinous crime it is. They know better than you and I. So I found it very interesting, and also their writings and the book that I published was very, very important.[6] Also just to bring out to the world the fact that people in prison are interesting, that people in prison have lives. Through the Prison Writing Committee of PEN, I've done that for many years for both women and men—contests that we run. So you can't sit back and say, "Well, somebody else made up the idea 'lock 'em up and throw away the key,' and there's nothing I can do." After Attica in the seventies, there were lots of programs, in prisons all over the United States. And they helped people.

NG: There's a lot of research to show that they did help people. So I'm sure you've observed the effects of writing on the women.

HJ: Oh, it just gives them incredible self-confidence. It's just broadened my outlook on everything, to go into the prisons. I know more [now] than I did—and what can I tell you—maybe a little more about good and evil. And by the way, I've been fired from Bedford. There was no room, they said, for my program. And I didn't fit into any category. You know, prisons like things neat, so you either have to teach in the college or represent a religion. But there are teens, children, in a women's prison now. Girls of sixteen in a maximum security prison. It's totally wrong. So the effect on me was to raise my level of outrage. People have asked on various occasions if I would write about my experience in prison, but I never felt that that was my role. I felt that my role was to go there to help the women and to bring out their voices, not to be a voice for them.

---

6. *Aliens at the Border: The Writing Workshop, Bedford Hills Correctional Facility.* Edited with an introduction by Hettie Jones. Segue Books, 1997.

In the Night Café

—Joyce Johnson

With the 1983 publication of Joyce Johnson's *Minor Characters*, a memoir of her experiences as a young writer coming up in the nascent Beat scene in New York City, women associated with the movement became visible. Johnson was born Joyce Glassman in 1934 in New York City, and after an adolescence devoted to theater and the piano, she quit her composition studies and declared her intention to write. She left Barnard College in 1954 one course short of the degree requirements, found a job in publishing, and began to focus on becoming a novelist. She earned a book contract in her early twenties—before becoming involved with Jack Kerouac in January 1957—and, as Joyce Glassman, published her first novel, *Come and Join the Dance*, in 1962.

The first Beat novel written by and about a woman, *Come and Join the Dance* claims the seminal status of comparable texts such as *On the Road*, *Howl*, or *Junky*, all of which represent the Beat generation through and as a male preoccupation. Johnson gives the lie to this exclusive assumption by telling Beat culture as the life experience of her female protagonist. Out of print for many years, the novel crucially fills in narratives of the Beat emergence by instantiating women in the scene and by representing women's integration of Beat ethics and aesthetics into their existential and personal beliefs and conduct. While Johnson does not practice the free-form composition processes advocated by Kerouac, weiss, or di Prima, her attention to the psychological dimension of experience, a mark of her early apprenticeship to the fiction of Henry James, has enabled her to produce both fiction and memoir that with a haunting, lyrical tone document aspects of human consciousness overlooked in the writings of male Beats.

Minor Characters focuses on a small number of people, defining Beat as the people Johnson knew, and integrating into Beat history those women who were her friends and colleagues on the scene. Her narrative of Beat New York introduces Elise Cowen and presents Cowen's poetry. Johnson represents the central role played by Edie Parker, Jack Kerouac's first wife, in forming seminal early connections among those who would comprise the Beat generation. Placing Parker and Joan Vollmer Adams Burroughs in the first chapter of her account, Johnson assigns them priority in the Beat genesis, foregrounding Joan's often overlooked killing by William S. Burroughs in 1951. Johnson claims for Beat the sculptor Mary Frank, married in the 1950s to photographer Robert Frank, and Hettie Jones, whose writing was not well known at the time of Johnson's publication. Johnson tells these women's Beat stories, their struggles to write and be recognized, to raise children, to produce art, and to survive on the subsistence economies and downward mobility of Beat culture. Her narrative of female commonweal establishes a canon of women writers as well as corrects the incomplete record by insisting on the presence and significance of Beat and outrider women of the 1950s.

Johnson's memoir inscribes against their elision a historiography of women as Beats and Beat writers—not as auxiliaries to Beat men—which includes herself. Indeed, had she not written *Minor Characters*, Johnson's novels—*Come and Join the Dance, Bad Connections* (1978), and *In the Night Café* (1989), which emphasize the ambivalent reality of redefining female subjectivity—might still be eclipsed. Her novels and especially her hipster protagonists reconfigure the dominant Beat discourse and intervene in reactionary Beat-culture as well as establishment-culture constructions of female inferiority and marginality, thereby enlarging Beat movement radicalism. *Come and Join the Dance* insists that young women of the fifties had deeper ambitions than the M-R-S degree. *Bad Connections* depicts the confusion and controversy accosting the white, middle-class protagonist in the sixties as she struggles to maintain a home for her child and participate in the liberation movements of her day with a free sex life and enlightened political and spiritual consciousness. *In the Night Café* returns to more explicitly Beat themes and venues via the life of a young woman married to a destructive and talented abstract expressionist painter in the fifties. These three novels form a trilogy spanning Johnson's life in hipster and hippie New York and critique Beat as well as sixties countercultures and discourses.

Johnson has also written a nonfiction book, *What Lisa Knew: The Truth and Lies of the Steinberg Case*, her controversial 1990 report on the murder of six-year-old Lisa Steinberg, the trial of her adopted father, and the ordeal and complicity of his lover, Hedda Nussbaum, a story that drew heated national attention. In 2000, Johnson brought out *Door Wide Open*, the correspondence between herself and Jack Kerouac during the fifties and sixties. This book provided a return to the documents from which Johnson wrote the memoir that first brought her to Beat attention twenty years ago. All her books— memoir, novels, nonfiction documentary, letters collection—bear her signature tone and style: restrained, ironic, witty inflections in a cool discourse of withheld promise and insight; an understated scrutiny and consideration that refuses easy compromise or needless effusion; a beat weariness of inflated emphatic claims but still an openness to possibilities of redemption and relief.

Johnson has written regularly for magazines and newspapers and has also contributed significantly to the promotion of other writers through her work as an editor at William Morrow, Dial Press, Atlantic Monthly Press, and McGraw-Hill. At the latter house, she edited for posthumous publication Kerouac's masterwork, *Visions of Cody* (1972). She has ushered into literary history several seminal New Left books, including those by Abbie Hoffman, Ron Kovic, and Anne Moody.

Part One of the following interview was conducted by telephone on May 15, 1999, by Nancy Grace. Part Two was conducted by telephone on October 3, 2002, by Grace. For both interviews, Johnson was at her home in New York City.

Part I

May 15, 1999

NANCY GRACE: What prompted you to write *Minor Characters*?

JOYCE JOHNSON: Ah, well, a kind of mysterious urge. I was still working in publishing at the time and it was in, I guess, 1980 or '81. Anyway, they sent me off on a business trip to England, and I arrived very jet-lagged and some friends who met me immediately said, "Even though you're jet-lagged, we have to go in and hear this great musician, a Kansas City piano player, in this café in London. Pizza Express, it was called. So I went out with them, and in came these old guys, very nattily dressed, who played this wonderful music, and I began reflecting on the fact that here were these . . . septuagenarians, still on the road, [while] others in their generation are dead—people like Charlie Parker are dead and so on. Then I began thinking about people who I had known who had sort of perished young, and suddenly I thought I wanted to write a memoir. That was how it happened. That's the way one gets an idea for a book, sort of all at once. That's been my experience. You know, had I written that book, say, in my late twenties or early thirties, I probably would have written a novel about a sad love affair.

NG: In your late twenties and early thirties, were you thinking about a memoir at all?
JJ: Oh, absolutely not. I was thinking solely about fiction. You know, I think it's probably a good idea to write a memoir at a sort of a twenty-five-year remove. You can see with Virginia Woolfe, for example, in her book *Moments of Being*, she writes about the same events at twenty-five, and then she writes about them again, remembering so much more, it seems, and being able to recreate them so much better at the age of fifty and being able to see around the events, things that happened to her. To have the recognition that she and her siblings were Edwardians, whereas her father was Victorian. That was the kind of thing she could not have realized at the age of twenty-five.

NG: What's the place of fabrication in memoir writing? How far can one go in terms of remembering?
JJ: There are things you do for the sake of form. For example, I could have put in everything that happened to me during the years that I was writing about, but there was a lot of stuff I simply left out because I wanted to have a focus. For example, the fact that when I was a child I was in the theater. Well, somehow that was very interesting, but it would have taken me away from what I was really writing about, so I didn't put that material in. As much as I could, I really tried to remember what happened as close as I could get, apart from when one has lapses in memory. I didn't consciously invent in that book. I sort of recreated, which is different.

NG: Do you have particular processes for remembering as accurately as you can? I'm thinking of that one scene in which you write about remembering your parents' room with the red couch with a green slipcover, the baby grand piano.

JJ: You know, I can close my eyes and see that room.

NG: You don't have any particular process that you go through in order to visualize places?

JJ: No. There are some things that are stamped on my memory. There are also a lot that are simply lost. Can't remember it at all. I forget whole people whom I used to know rather well. I'm a very selective rememberer—as opposed to Jack who was very inclusive.

NG: His mind was unusual in that regard.

JJ: Well, it was unusual, and I think his very extraordinary full memory definitely influenced the way he was able to write fiction. If you want to call it fiction. I think it's closer to call them true-life novels.

NG: Did you ever experiment with some of his techniques, such as spontaneous prose or the sketching?

JJ: No.

NG: Do you think those are worthwhile methods to practice?

JJ: I think they're interesting theories. I think there's not one kind of writer. The reason Jack was able to [write that way] was his fantastic memory which was so available to him. . . . And also his amazing verbal fluency. He was somebody who really could write at speed. I guess, obviously, the letters that I wrote him were more spontaneous—written faster.

NG: Does the process of writing a novel prepare one to write the memoir?

JJ: Oh, I think it does. There are a lot of the same techniques that go into writing a memoir. I brought what I learned writing novels into the memoir. Know how to tell a story, know how to recreate a scene, all of that.

NG: Why do you think there is so much interest now in memoir writing?

JJ: Well, I think for one thing, it's the age of confession, where confession has become the norm. When Allen [Ginsberg] and Jack were first writing their rather confessional literature, it was a strange thing to be doing—shocking. But we have become very accustomed to it. Another thing is that, in a way, very often the stories that memoirs tell are often more surprising and more interesting than a lot of the fiction that's around. If you read a lot of contemporary fiction you seem to feel after a while that the same kinds of things are being endlessly written about. Where real life is full of quirky surprises, messier. I think, especially, people are really casting about for content right now. In the days of, say, Edith Wharton, there were so many restrictions on life and class differences and so on that inherently dramatic situations were created. If you wrote a novel about a woman who had an affair, it was really a life or death situation. Nothing is as loaded now. We don't have as many taboos, and a lot of novels are about people who are kind of unhappy and wish they were happier. There are good new fiction writers, but I think they have that content problem. That's one reason why you'll find a lot of good fiction writers turning to historical novels. They go back into the past to get those situations in which there is more inherent drama.

NG: Do you think it's the end of the novel then?

JJ: I don't know that it's the end, I would never want to say that. The novel always surprises us, but the content problem is a big one.

NG: What were your major influences?

JJ: Henry James was terribly important to me. And when I began to read Henry James's novels, well, before that, I had thought I would write plays, also a carry-over from my years in the theater. Then I began to realize more and more that the stuff that really interested me was not the kind of stuff you could write very well about in a play. It was what was underneath the action that I wanted to write about, which is what Henry James did superbly.

NG: Were there any particular memoirists? You mentioned Virginia Woolfe.

JJ: Virginia Woolfe, Nathalie Sarraute, Vladimir Nabokov. Actually, when I wrote my memoir I wasn't reading memoirs. I began to read a lot of memoirs after I wrote my memoir, when I was asked to teach a course in memoir. . . .

NG: Do you think you would have written a different memoir if you had studied the literature prior to writing it?

JJ: No, I don't think so. I've always felt that somehow your content and the story that you want to tell and its inherent problems sort of, for me, always determine the form. For example, I remember one of the problems I was concerned about when I started writing the memoir was that I knew I had to tell the reader about Jack's life, so that it wouldn't interrupt the memoir. Then I hit upon the device of following myself and following him as two separate streams, that then converge . . . then diverge at the end. That was the form of that memoir. I think one thing that was an important influence on that book was thinking of the women's movement. Suddenly the recognition that my story was important, and the story of the other women was important.

NG: Have there been any particular women or events in the women's movement that have been important to you?

JJ: Oh, the whole abortion rights movement is particularly meaningful to me. People don't realize how it used to be. We can go back to that. You can easily go back to that. It's interesting. I definitely have a debt to the women's movement in terms of my seeing my story as an important story, but I was also always a little bit out of step with them. I guess because a lot of the things they were talking about I had already done.

NG: Let's talk about your three novels: *Come and Join the Dance, Bad Connections,* and *In the Night Café.* Are they a trilogy of sorts?
JJ: In a sense, they are sort of about me in different stages of my life.

NG: Do you consider your first novel, *Come and Join the Dance,* to be a Beat novel?
JJ: I don't know. At the time, I thought of the male writers as the Beat writers, but I felt part of the Beat scene, as in sympathy, and I felt that it was a novel those people would understand. I see now, in hindsight, that it was much more of a Beat novel at the time, but I had conceptualized the whole thing even before I got involved with Jack, working on it for a year, and I had the whole idea for the novel in mind. A lot of it grew out of my Columbia experiences and knowing this group of people through whom I eventually met Allen and Jack. These were people who were perpetual graduate students, somewhat ten years older than I was, who were experimenting with a lot of stuff, moving around campus, in pad-like situations.

NG: Does the term "Beat novel" have any critical meaning for you?
JJ: I think it defines a certain unconventional bohemian attitude of the 1950s, you know?

NG: Yes, the focus on individual freedom, sexual liberation, rejection of some white, middle-class values, and a critique of cultural mores. *Come and Join the Dance* certainly has that.

JJ: It wasn't the kind of novel that young women were writing at that time. Not many of them were writing novels; it wasn't the kind of story they were telling. Another big influence on that novel was *The Counterfeiters* by Andre Gide. I was very interested in the whole idea of the gratuitous act, you know. So in *Come and Join the Dance*, the young woman, Susan, decides to go to bed with someone as a gratuitous act. See what it was about. That fascinated me.

NG: Certainly at the time it was a radical gesture. Were you satisfied with what you were able to do with that act in the novel?

JJ: Oh, I wrote that novel with so much uncertainty. I could hardly believe I was actually writing a novel, I was so scared. And also, I was quite nervous. I was quite aware that I was writing about things that a nice young lady should not write about. If you wrote about those things people would think you had experienced them yourself—that my parents would read it and be shocked—and various people did read it and were shocked. Reviewers were shocked.

NG: What about *Bad Connections*? You experimented with narrative perspective in that novel, moving back and forth from the first person to the third person. Did you accomplish what you had hoped for with that experimentation?

JJ: Yes, I wanted to be close and then distant. . . . Sort of like a camera moving, you know, moving in and moving out.

NG: *In the Night Café* appeared to have a more explicit attention to history than did *Come and Join the Dance* and *Bad Connections*.

JJ: Actually, both *Bad Connections* and *Dance* were written very soon after the experiences that were the basis of the book, whereas *In the Night Café* was written around twenty-five years later. So it was more reflective, and it was a novel that I had tried to write, made a couple of attempts to write, before that. Because I was actually widowed, and I wanted to write about that experience and that man, Jim Johnson, and in a way, too, remember him. So I first attempted that book early in the sixties shortly after he died. Then I had a long hiatus where I really didn't do much writing. I married again and I had a child, I had a divorce, I had a very demanding job, and it wasn't until my son was five and I left my husband and I really sort of tried to write again and I wrote the good part of a version of what eventually became *In the Night Café*, but it was actually written in the third person and it was too distant and too elegiac and I still don't think I had totally comprehended what had happened, and I knew something was very wrong with it. I showed it to Tillie Olson actually, and she said that it was just too distanced, it wasn't working. I knew in my heart that she was right. So I put it aside and I started *Bad Connections*. Then I went back to *Café* in the late eighties. I still wanted to write that novel, you know, and I went back to it with a very different perspective on it. Distance of time, and various other things that had happened to me. I suddenly thought in a very different way. The emphasis on people's childhoods, that was something I wasn't really capable of doing when I first attempted it. I didn't understand fully the whole impact of those things. And, also, I saw the relationship much less sentimentally.

NG: The book does have an elegiac quality. In fact, all three of the novels have this sense of longing, something which seems to have matured in *In the Night Café*.

JJ: I guess I consider *Night Café* my best book.

NG: What are the major differences in writing fiction and nonfiction? What about the composition of *What Lisa Knew*?

JJ: It really depends on the book and its particular problems. *What Lisa Knew* was all based upon a huge amount of fact that I had to absorb, and I had to let it all sort of pass through me. . . . I just wanted to figure out what on earth had happened in the Steinberg household. . . . In a way, I almost had to re-experience it in order to write it. That was pretty harrowing, actually. But with nonfiction, you're working with a whole lot of received information, and within it you sort of have to find the story. . . . That's a faster process for me. And the other, fiction, is something that takes me a long time, and I have to dredge it up out of myself, out of my own sort of imperfect memories, out of what I make of them; it's a much slower and deeper process.

NG: Are there other stories you could have told about that event?
JJ: Well . . . other people wrote about Hedda [Nussbaum] very sympathetically, and so on. I don't think I would have wanted to write a book about it at all if I hadn't seen that some terrible distortion of the point of the whole case was going on. It had a lot to do with the politics of the women's movement. . . . On the one hand, women are being proclaimed the equal of men. On the other hand, "No, no, we're victims, we're too weak, even if we let a child die, you mustn't judge us." There's also something terribly wrong with that thinking. So that's what led me to write the book.

NG: How do you respond to reviewers, such as those reviewing *Bad Connections* and *What Lisa Knew*, who felt you were not feminist enough.
JJ: It's painful. It's upsetting. I think it's the orthodoxy of the women's movement that really began to get me down. That you couldn't have a counter [position] that was at all passive, or you couldn't do this or you couldn't say that, or you couldn't have the views that I had and Susan Brownmiller had about Hedda Nussbaum. It was like the Thought Police. And I had a big encounter about it with Gloria Steinem

on *The Larry King Show*. It was when *What Lisa Knew* came out. She was a real Hedda supporter. . . . I don't think she had even read my book. . . . She totally trashed the book, told people not to read it and so on. It was unbelievable. . . . I had always respected her, and . . . I was very lady-like. But I wish I would have taken her apart.

NG: You've long worked as an editor. What was the most satisfying editing experience for you?

JJ: That's a hard one to answer. They were very uphill experiences in terms of the authors and so on. But I did some really important books. I was especially interested in doing a lot of New Left books. That was my contribution. I did Abbie Hoffman's book *Revolution for the Hell of It*, and I did a very important book by a man named Harold Cruse, *The Crisis of the Negro Intellectual*. I did *Born on the Fourth of July* by Ron Kovic, which was a book I rewrote from stem to stern. Another book that was important in the civil rights movement was *Coming of Age in Mississippi* by Ann Moody. They were important books at the time. I'm proud of them. I really felt I was making a contribution, helping to get these books out into the world.

NG: What was it like to edit Kerouac's *Visions of Cody*, since it came out from McGraw-Hill three years after his death?

JJ: Well, that was a book where I couldn't do much, I couldn't do any editing. What I mainly did was conform all the names because the book had been written at different periods of time until the names and characters were inconsistent. But I had a pretty good sense of who they were, so I was able to do that. Then I commissioned Allen Ginsberg to write an introduction. I put the whole package together. Had I been Jack's editor, I would have recommended some cuttings.

NG: And what would he have said to that?

JJ: Oh, he would have absolutely refused! I think I could have made a somewhat more readable book. But I'm very proud of doing it. It has some of Jack's most remarkable writings.

NG: Why do you think there's so much interest now in the Beats?
JJ: It's always been there; it's never faded. But somehow Jack continues to be a kind of reference point for people. I think this is a period, in some psychic way, like the fifties, where people's lives feel very circumscribed. You almost have to, in order to survive, buy into the system and make money and have your whole life consumed by your job—or else! So this whole idea of sort of dropping out and being free and having all these experiences and not buying into the establishment—the opposite of the prevailing ethic—I think it's very potent. And probably, also, it's such a very materialistic period, you know, the spirituality of the books is also very potent to people. And there is such a lot of sort of, oh, imitations of life style. You're always looking backward and imitating something of the past—something retro. When I was going to college, we were all hung up on the twenties, we all wondered if we were like F. Scott Fitzgerald and Zelda—we weren't, but. . . .

NG: Is there anything else you would like to add?
JJ: It's always interesting that people ask me questions about my writing as though it's a very conscious process. You know, like, well, I've got to sit down today and write—what's my process? Okay. It's just sort of not like that. Not like that at all!

NG: You just do it?
JJ: Just do it! On really fortunate days, it's as though there are voices inside your head. And other days, you don't have them, but you sit down at the computer, you try to start them going. You know, that's

about all I can say. Half of it is getting across the room to the computer—that can be a very long walk!

Part II

October 3, 2002

NG: You recently published your correspondence with Jack Kerouac, *Door Wide Open*. What was it like for you as a twenty-two-year-old to write those letters to Kerouac?

JJ: Those letters that Jack and I wrote to each other were a good sort of, uh, occupied a good percentage of our relationship. He kept going away for long periods, and that's how we corresponded. He was not a man to pay for a long distance call! [laughs] And he didn't use the phone very much. He really preferred to write. So that was how we communicated with each other. I was actually quite bowled over when I got the very first of his letters from Tangier because when he went off I didn't know if I'd hear from him or not. And suddenly we began this correspondence. I was working on my novel *Come and Join the Dance* then, but I think the experience of writing the letters to Jack . . . I was trying to write up to him. I began to feel its effects upon my voice in writing. I think it had an effect upon my writing that has sort of stayed with me. Writing up, writing in a looser way, writing with a longer breath. Yes, I think that's stayed with me. And I actually did a great deal of writing in my letters to Jack, almost more in periods than I was doing on my novel. My novel was going very slowly, and I seemed to be rewriting every sentence thirteen times. I think in the last parts of the novel some of that [loose] voice came into it.

NG: What was the process of editing the letters for publication?

JJ: Well, I didn't really edit the letters very much as such. The letters are in there as they were. There was very little left out. What interested me when I was able to get my letters back—because I hadn't seen them in forty years, whatever it was—to put them together with Jack's letters, which I had always kept, I was excited to see a real dialogue going on between the two letter writers, a kind of narrative. [John] Sampas¹ had said, "Oh, you can make a book of this," and I wasn't so sure. But then when I interwove the letters, I saw that I could. There was movement in it. I thought it was an interesting form. And I didn't really think of myself as editing. You know, it wasn't a book that I edited. It was a book that in a way I wrote, my found materials. And I have a long introduction, but then I wanted to make the voice of the commentary another dramatic factor in the book and also to play with the whole question of what I knew then and what I know now.

And I still hadn't quite finished the book when the second volume of Jack's collected letters was published. And then I saw letters to other people that Jack had written during that period. Some of my letters were in there, but also letters that he wrote to Allen and Gary Snyder, some of which had to do with our relationship and were rather shocking to me. And, you know, Jack was sort of a different person when he wrote to me than he was when he wrote to Allen, say, about me and so on. It was a jolt to read some of these things, but I also felt that I had to include this, and so I put in those discoveries, and I put a certain amount of that in—I was sort of playing with the footnotes. They were part of this whole process of learning more years later and dealing with it.

NG: How did *Door Wide Open*, then, fit with *Minor Characters*?

---

1. John Sampas is the literary executor of Kerouac's estate.

JJ: It was a going back to the documents, and it was also much more narrowly focused. Because *Minor Characters* was a memoir, I was looking at a good piece of my life development and looking at other women's lives and the whole Beat scene. *Door Wide Open* was focused very minutely upon my relationship with Jack almost blow by blow, bringing it forward. And actually I felt very fortunate that the book of Jack's letters came out so I was able to consider that material and weave it in.

NG: Did Kerouac encourage your writing when you were working on your first novel?

JJ: He took it very seriously that I was writing. And I think to him the fact that I was also a writer was an important, special part of our relationship. And somehow, even when our interpersonal stuff wasn't going so well, we could always have a dialogue about writing, and I think that's reflected in the letters. He kept trying, exhorting me to take more chances, to go out—he felt I should follow his path—go out in the world, not be tied down to a little secretarial job, and, you know, have the kind of life he had. Of course, that was impossible . . . for me. I think I was both brave and innately cautious. And I always had to make sure that I had enough money to take care of myself—I was good at taking care of myself and I wasn't going to jump off the deep end.

NG: How did he exhort you to do that?

JJ: Well, for example, there was this idea that he and I would go to Mexico, that when he was in Mexico City I would come down there. And I would be there with him, and it would be an important part of my "education," as he put it. And I thought so too, but I never got there! [laughs] And I always sort of regretted that.

NG: Did you and Elise Cowen talk about writing? Were conversations about aesthetics part of your relationship?

JJ: Yeah, we did talk about writing, and I showed Elise a lot of my writing. She'd seen a few early pieces of the novel. But she did not show me hers. She was secretive about her writing. She, well, it's a conversation that I actually wrote about in *Come and Join the Dance* that she considered herself, what she called, a *mediocre*. You know, that was horrible. But she was always writing secretively in notebooks.

NG: Did you find those conversations with her important, and what was your reaction when you finally read her poetry?

JJ: The conversations were important. They were affirming and encouraging. And I *was* surprised, and I was very moved by [her poetry]. It is fragmentary. And, ah, Elise, if Elise had been born ten years later it would have made a tremendous difference. The world treated her very cruelly because she was such an odd girl. She didn't care about being pretty. She was, you know, very bright and she was eccentric. She kept going to shrinks, and they kept sort of "firing" her, saying we can't help you. And having bad experiences with men. She was really out of—not in the right time. And it was very poignant to me that when she was released from the mental hospital into her parents' care—and taken out of there [the hospital] much too soon— well, of course, being back in the house of her parents was an absolutely poisonous environment for her. And they had this idea that they were going to take her down to Miami with them. The idea of Elise in that condition in Miami—sort of unbearable.

NG: Were there any other women at the time that you were talking to about your writing?

JJ: I don't know that I talked with Hettie about my writing. She knew that I wrote, of course. She didn't talk with me about hers. I didn't talk with Diane di Prima about my writing. I knew Diane.

I had known Diane in high school; she and Audre Lorde were on the literary magazine there, at Hunter High School.

NG: Had you contributed to that magazine?

JJ: I had, I had. I was rather in awe of Audre Lorde. Everybody thought she was brilliant. I remember she wrote a poem that was sort of a refutation of *The Wasteland*. You know, this is how the world ends: not with a whimper, but *bang*. And she was right!

NG: So you really weren't talking with anybody at that point about your novel?

JJ: Well, no, I wasn't. My novel didn't seem to fit in with what people were doing on the scene. It seemed something separate from all this experimental Beat writing around me. It didn't seem to be anything that the people that I knew and hung out with would really be interested in.

NG: Did Kerouac read parts of it?

JJ: He did, and he liked them.

NG: That's interesting considering his own experimental style. Who were some of the published women writers that were important to you at that time?

JJ: There weren't many books by young women being published at all. It was a very lousy time for women writers. It was before the women's movement. You know, of course, there was *The Bell Jar*. I didn't read that until much later. And the then-contemporary women writers who were most important to me were people like Carson McCullers. Then another writer who was important to me was Jane Bowles. Not her fiction but a play that she'd written, *In the Summer House* [1953], that I'd seen about the time I'd started at Barnard. And that play, which was very much about mothers and daughters, showed me that that was worthwhile material.

NG: How did you feel when *Come and Join the Dance* came out?

JJ: Well, it was one of the biggest disappointments of my life, because I had worked on it for years, and, you know, living this sort of chaotic life, and I was thinking that at least my novel would come out. And finally it came out, and so what? It came out in such a way that people months later would ask me, "Did you ever finish that novel you were writing?" And then I got these very peculiar reviews in different places. You know, reviews to the effect that to think that a girl from a good home and with a good education would come out with something like this. Well, the idea that a young woman would deliberately decide to lose her virginity to see what that was like, that was not a popular notion at that time. You know, these moralistic reviews. But then, the only good thing that really happened was that—the book had been out for two or three months—I got unexpectedly a very good review in the *New York Times*.[2]

NG: What was the impact of all of that on your writing?

JJ: It was discouraging. It was discouraging because it was, you know, I had written this book and I'd put so much effort into it, and then it had all sort of evaporated. And I wasn't connected to any literary scene that supported me. I felt very alone with what I was doing. Then right after the book was published, I met James Johnson, whom I married. And he had a lot of problems, and I was very caught up in all of that. And my life with him was so intense. I think it was probably impossible for me to work when I was with anyone. I needed to be alone to write. But I couldn't write. And he was

---

2. Gerald Walker, *New York Times Book Review*, January 28, 1962, 38.

obsessed by that. He was troubled by the fact that I wasn't writing. And then after he was killed—we'd been married for a year, and he was killed in a motorcycle accident—I wanted to write about him, and I went off to Europe as soon as I could, about three months later. I began writing about him there. I then came back to the States, but I didn't go on with it. I met another man, Peter Pinchbeck. I got involved with him, we had a child, I was working. I was so tired. I had this small child; there was a babysitter who came during the day, but then I'd sort of stagger home from work, take care of the child, make the dinner, and do the dishes, and my husband would go off to the artists' bars, and I would just practically black out. There was just no possibility, no space in my life for any work of my own.

NG: When did that begin to change?
JJ: When I left the marriage.

NG: Was working to make a living something you always expected to do?
JJ: Yes, oddly enough I never imaged that anyone would ever support me. I always thought that I'd always have to make my own way. But that had a long history with me because my mother and her sisters had worked. Although my mother didn't work after she was married, her sisters continued to be working women.

NG: What did they do?
JJ: Well, bookkeeping and secretarial work. And I had taken the secretarial course one summer right after I'd entered Barnard. And this skill, this trade of being a secretary, gave me the means to leave home and find my independence. And I had worked my way up to being an editor, and I was quite involved in other people's books. But it was painful to me, the fact that I wasn't writing. Particularly once the

women's movement really got rolling, and I saw other women publishing their work. The whole atmosphere had changed so much since I'd published *Come and Join the Dance* that I felt very bad about it [not writing]. And so when my child was five, I broke with my second husband, and suddenly I was able to create some space in my life for my own work. So I went back to the novel that I'd started about my first marriage, and worked on that for two or three years. Then by around 1976, I began writing *Bad Connections*. So *Bad Connections* was really the beginning of my second career as a writer.

NG: Had you been reading anything like *The Feminine Mystique?*
JJ: Oh, yeah, I was reading all those books. I was editing some stuff that had to do with the women's movement. So I was very much under the influence of those ideas at the time. And those ideas were partially what led me to get up the courage to leave my husband.

NG: Were you active at all in any consciousness raising groups?
JJ: No, I've never been one for groups very much. My contribution to the politics of the time was to do a lot of New Left publishing.

NG: You talk a little bit in your memoir about your own experiences with anti-semitism. You don't present yourself as someone who was terribly discriminated against, although you do recall one incident.
JJ: Oh, no, I never felt terribly discriminated against. It was still the time, in 1950, if you were a Jewish girl, it was a big deal to be accepted by a place like Barnard. They had a quota. Friends of Mother would say, "Oh, she'll never get it." That's what that was about. And then when I was in publishing, I had some sense that it was a genteel, WASP-y world. That if you were going to get ahead, you would have to be a certain class. And I remember applying for a job at Doubleday, and it was very clear that they weren't interested in me because

of my Jewish name. But it wasn't a big part of my life, the feeling that I was going to suffer because of racism. That wasn't an idea that consumed me. But once I started hanging out downtown, I had black friends, and I was very hopeful that the kind of social interaction we were having in the downtown scene—because there was a lot of ease and friendship between people—that would spread out through America, that we were beginning something that would take hold in the culture.

NG: Well, you did. But how do you as a writer get at what's going on in a person's mind?
JJ: There's no conscious process. Things occur to you. I find writing a very mysterious process. You sit down and maybe you don't even have an idea in your head, and things you don't even know you're thinking about pop out. Or memories come back. But it's very much something that happens in the process of writing things down—the process of thinking about what you're going to write is something else. I can't say I sit down and think things out. Ideas for books I want to write or stories I want to tell or pieces of what I'm working. It's like a door suddenly opening. You could be doing something else, like watching TV or washing your underwear or walking down the street. Of course, I've written very much from life. I always have. The process of writing is like a form of very deep meditation. And when I'm doing a lot of that, when I'm doing a lot of writing, I feel balanced in a certain way that I don't feel when I'm not writing. It's the same with what I call fiction and with what I call memoir writing.

NG: Does your writing then fit with any spiritual practice?
JJ: My writing does not deal with spirituality. I don't think I'm exactly a spiritual person, as it's usually defined. I was distressed at some aspects of Jack's spirituality. For example, I felt that he was misusing

his interpretation of Buddhism to kind of—it was preventing him from actually trying to deal with some of the tremendous problems and confusions in his life. You know, we're all going to die, or we're all headed for the void, or birth is death. I felt all that was nonsense. I think Burroughs felt so too. There's a letter of his in the collected volume.[3] And I absolutely agree; I agree. I guess I'm not very interested in things like Buddhism, Judaism. I'm just not. I never have been.

NG: What's the focus of your new book?

JJ: The new memoir is about three different periods in my life that are thematically related. The title of the book is *Missing Men*. The first part of the book is about my grandfather. The second is about my father. The last part of the book is about my second husband [Peter Pinchbeck], who recently died. And it's all thematically connected.

NG: So it's really different from *Minor Characters*?

JJ: It is. I really am proud of *Minor Characters*, but I also feel cursed with it. I feel that people can't see me past that. And although I think it's nice there's all this interest in Beat women, I also feel impatient, very impatient with that whole designation. I really want to be seen as a whole writer, and to see the Beat part of me is only to see a small part of who I am and what I've done as a writer. My other work seems to get forgotten in the shuffle, and I find that very disturbing. So I'm hoping that this new book will somehow broaden the whole picture.

---

3. The letter is dated July 24, 1958, Paris (Harris 392–94).

The Story and
Its Writer

—Ann Charters

Ann Charters is responsible for initiat-
ing a canon of Beat writers and writing through her prolific scholar-
ship, criticism, and literary history focused on the Beat generation.
Charters is Jack Kerouac's first biographer and bibliographer, and the
only one to have worked with him to establish a record of his work.
She is the editor of major anthologies of Beat literature including *The
Beats: Literary Bohemians in Postwar America* (*Dictionary of Literary
Biography*, 1983), *The Portable Beat Reader* (1992), and *Beat Down to
Your Soul: What Was the Beat Generation?* (2001), texts which have
mapped compelling arguments for the continued attraction that
Beat writing, and the writers themselves, hold for academic and lay
audiences. Charters's personal story of being a young woman who
avidly read Beat literature is also powerful testimony to the way in
which Beat writing, and eventually some women Beat writers, contributed to the development of women's consciousness in the postwar years before the second-wave women's movement emerged.

Charters was born in Connecticut in 1936, and her family moved to
California when she was twelve years old. On a blind date in 1957 with

Peter Orlovsky, Charters, a self-described nice, square Jewish girl, was in the audience of the gathering commemorating the first anniversary of the monumental 1956 Six Gallery reading, in which Allen Ginsberg had first declaimed "Howl." It was not, however, fraternizing with these male poets that turned her into a Beat aficionada and later scholar. Rather, the catalysts were her reading of Jack Kerouac's *The Dharma Bums* (1958), whose San Francisco setting reminded her of the California she had known as a girl, and Diane di Prima's *Dinners and Nightmares* (1961), whose courageous and humorous portrayal of poverty and art in the Beat bohemian scene intrigued Charters. After completing her doctorate in literature at Columbia University in 1965, a rare feat for a woman in the closed environment of academia in the early and mid sixties, Charters bucked academic conventions that favored canonical writers and followed her own path to study the writers she admired, first compiling *Bibliography of Works by Jack Kerouac* (1967) and then *Kerouac: A Biography* (1973). Her editing of the two volumes of Kerouac's selected letters (1995 and 1999, respectively) has helped to recuperate the writer's battered reputation by lending the weight of her critical acumen to studies of his work.

Charters's discernment about Beat writing provides a crucial link between the experimental Beat art and the academic critical establishment dedicated to the evaluation and preservation of a culture's literary works. Her selections and advocacy of writers and their works have satisfied critical standards while permitting the latitude necessary to the recognition of a true avant-garde. Charters's inclusion in *The Beats* of Bonnie Frazer, for instance, not only expanded the purview of the Beat canon beyond the limits described by its men—by including a woman practitioner of the movement—but also judged the value of Frazer's writing in the absence of an antecedent critical consensus. Similarly, in her latest collection of Beat writing, *Beat Down to Your Soul*, Charters orders her choices in alphabetical, not chronological, order, achieving a provocative unsettling of old hierarchies. For example, she exploits the quirky connections of Anatole Broyard and Robert Brustein, Ken Kesey and Joanne Kyger, John Updike and Anne Waldman—all because their names rest in proximity alphabetically. Further, she does not reprint Kerouac in this volume, though many of the works she chooses are about him, which permits him a ghostly pervasiveness in place of a needless redundancy since his work is so widely collected. Charters's astute choices of the obscure yet significant essay by Broyard, "A Portrait of a Hipster," or of the understudied poems of Joanna McClure, or of the review by Joyce Carol Oates of Kerouac's selected letters give dimension and nuance to Beat studies. Just so, Charters's work as Beat critic and scholar has established a foundation for increasingly serious and diverse critical study of the Beats in our time.

While not a poet or novelist, and in fact claiming to be a "reader, not a writer," Charters as an editor, a scholar, and a professor of English at the University of Connecticut-Storrs, has produced an ample body of work that establishes not only interpretive paradigms but also visible cultural-artistic milieus. Through her attention to the preservation of what she determined to be seminal works of art from the Beat era, Charters created a Beat canon that eventually came to include both male and female writers. Her candid discussion of that process not only adds to the history of Beat scholarship but also contributes to larger discussions of canon formation. Her example demonstrates that a literary canon is a fluid form guided by aesthetic taste, personal preference, and community connections. Charters's career evinces the work of the scholar and literary critic undertaken with integrity, imagination, sympathy, and vision.

The interview below was conducted on March 13, 2000, by Ronna C. Johnson and Nancy Grace at Ann Charters's home in Storrs, Connecticut.

NANCY GRACE: Because you've had many different roles—you're a writer, musician, historian, friend—how do you see yourself in the Beat generation?

ANN CHARTERS: The thing that makes me situate myself in the fifties most clearly is the simple fact that, of all Kerouac's biographers, I was the only one who actually spent time with him working with his books. I was his biographer; I saw him in the context of the books. Not as a friend. I didn't go on the road with Jack.

RONNA JOHNSON: That's the interesting thing. You weren't on the road. You were there working.

AC: Right. Another difference in my relationship to the Beats is that I actually was interested in them early on. When I was first with Peter Orlovsky as a blind date going to that poetry reading in Berkeley in the spring of 1956, the repeat of the Six Gallery reading, I was very impressed by what I saw on stage of all the poets. And Allen's reading "Howl." I wasn't interested in continuing to see Peter or getting to party with them. I absolutely was, well, nineteen years old. I was going to be twenty in November of 1956, and they were all a good decade or so older. I had a roommate whom I really loved—Carolyn, whom I've written about in the afterward of Brenda Knight's book. I saw what her life was like as a hip—she wasn't Beat, but she was definitely a bohemian—art student. I admired lots of it, but not the sexual part. I thought she put herself in danger with abortions. It was abortions, that was the issue here. I was also really involved emotionally with Sam [Charters], even though he was married. So I wasn't looking the same way that I might have been if I was twenty-six or twenty-nine.

It's very strange because there's that wonderful Harry Redl photograph of Allen in the tree naked, you know in back of his Milvia cottage. I was thinking that that was the same day that I later went to his cottage with Peter. Allen gave a spaghetti supper before the Berkeley reading in 1956. I didn't get there earlier in the day for all the shenanigans, the naked shenanigans. Didn't do that. But that evening at the Berkeley theatre, the sight of them in the Robert LaVigne drawings making love, the men, I just really didn't know men. I was so sheltered from being brought up in a Jewish community in Los Angeles closely guarded by my parents. It wasn't shocking in the sense of "oh how could they?" It was more like "this I don't even believe it." [laughs] I was so innocent.

So I never wanted to go back there. I was never attracted to the idea of hanging out. Peter understood this immediately. I was a nice girl, a nice, square girl. I really came to the Beats two years later when I was a student at Columbia University in William York Tindall's class on William Butler Yeats, in the fall of 1958, after Kerouac had published *The Dharma Bums* and I had read it. I didn't really respond to *On the Road*, frankly, because I had been on the road a lot myself. My parents had moved from Connecticut to Los Angeles when I was twelve, and we used to make those cross-country car trips back and forth all the time to see [my mother's] folks in Boston. It was the picture of Berkeley and those cottages in *The Dharma Bums* that really was the first book that opened me up to what Kerouac was doing. I loved that book because it was my experience with my little cottage and my poetry reading with Peter and my friend, Carolyn, who at that point had also left California and had married a graduate student in sociology at Columbia—her life became a nightmare. All this stuff back in California was like a dream. I had left it, I was in New York, my friend was in New York, and the past was like some sort of picture postcard memory.

The point is that I came to Kerouac without anybody telling me this was a great book. I found it myself. And it had been about what I remembered sentimentally my life had been like in this little idyll of the two years I spent in the cottage, really only one year, the last year. And I got the Woodrow Wilson graduate fellowship in 1958 and everything went well. In 1957, I got my job teaching at the high school in San Lorenzo, California. I hated teaching there, but Sam came from New Orleans, and we got together, and then I got a crazy little part-time job or two. So it was like a Beat life I was living in '57, '58. And that's what Kerouac was describing. I had nothing but total sympathy for what he was doing. [But] I never thought that I would specialize in the Beats. I hadn't had that idea when I was going to school. I read very earnestly and got good grades and zipped right through graduate school. But I never did any thinking about what I was going to do until I finished. Because I was always so apprehensive about what questions they were going to ask me, what papers were going to be due, what their responses were going to be. So why would I ever have the mental time to think about anything until 1965 when I graduated, finished the requirements for the Ph.D. By then, I was living on the Lower East Side, very interested in music by Country Joe and the Fish, taking drugs, we were in the folk music movement, and we knew a lot of people in New York, the folkies. So it was absolutely, like, 'course I'm going to turn my back on the academy and I'm going to start doing research on the Beats.

RJ: You came to this unlike anybody else.
AC: I know, it was weird. I think because I was married. That's all I ever really wanted. I didn't start when I was fourteen years old thinking—like Susan Sontag perhaps—that I'm going to be the leading intellectual woman of my generation—no, no, no—I was just going to be free of my parents' influence and make a life, startlingly like theirs! [laughs] But on my own terms. "Like theirs" meaning married, and having kids, and having a nice house, and a nice secure life.

So square, square, square. On the other hand, I was the rebel girl, breaking away.

RJ: You would have had to be. How many women got Ph.D.'s with you?[1]

AC: There weren't many women. Couldn't even really count them in hundreds. At Columbia University, perhaps five or ten that year in all the departments. Yes, it was unusual. I must also say that part of my rebellion—it was always a personal rebellion—in other words, until the Vietnam War I really wasn't that critical of the country because I had it so good. A Woodrow Wilson for a master's, then I went off and taught at Colby-Sawyer for a couple years, realized that if I really had to make my living, I would not want to teach freshman composition for another forty years. So I needed a Ph.D. to have upper division courses. And so when I wrote Columbia saying I wanted to come back for a Ph.D., they said fine, we'll pay it, all the tuition, we'd love to have you back. It was very generous. But it wasn't personal; it was just a form letter. Then I wrote a dissertation and completed the requirements for the degree. I thought this system was working for me. After I finished school in '65, and I lived on St. Mark's Place while Sam went around the world, my first thought was "I'll have a baby now." I mean, I didn't want to do any books, I wanted a baby because I'd finished my doctorate. Sam said, "Give me some time." You know, like I put you through grad school, paid the rent, got the food. Why don't I go around the world as a reward? I said fine. You do that. I was teaching at Columbia, a freshman course. We had an apartment, and he left me there with an Irish setter puppy so I could see whether I liked taking

---

1. Approximately 260 doctorates in American Literature were granted by graduate schools throughout the world in 1965. James Woodress, *Dissertations in American Literature 1891–66*. Durham, NC: Duke UP, 1968, vii.

care of something. He went around the world for five months. While he was away, there was a poetry reading at St. Mark's Church—Poems for Peace. This was '66. I realized that Sam wasn't around, but the tape recorder was—[I thought] I know how he does it. Why don't I just record this reading and I'll put it out for Folkways.

RJ: So here you're doing fieldwork.
AC: Yes. The Beat poets interested me; they were my culture. I thought instead of going down to Tennessee to record Sleepy John Estes, I'll just do St. Mark's Church. That's when I met Ginsberg. He kindly let me take photographs and talked to me. I thought to myself, he'll never want to talk to me, why would he talk to me? I live in his neighborhood. I have a Ph.D. from Columbia, but I'm nobody. I thought I'll tell him that I really love reading the Beats, and I think there are really only two important Beat writers from my perspective. I've been trained, right, to be a reader? So from my professional perspective, after William York Tindall's class, I would like to tell Ginsberg that in my opinion, of the two who are most important—him and Kerouac—I frankly respond more to Kerouac, because he seems to reflect my own experience, since I'm not gay. I've been profoundly moved by *Kaddish* and I love "Howl," but on the other hand, Kerouac speaks to me. Because I come from Bridgeport, Connecticut. Kerouac comes from Lowell, we are both working-class first generation Americans. That does it. So I say this to Allen. The first thing I say to him, coming in through the door is, "Mr. Ginsberg, I would like to get your permission to use your poetry on my record, and I want to tell you thank you so much. I'd also like to tell you that I think Kerouac's the most important Beat writer. Now, how do I get Jack's address?" I thought Ginsberg might just pay attention if I say something totally off the wall like that. What do I have to lose? If I bore him, I'll never get my foot in the door. In retrospect, thinking back, it was such

a dumb thing to do. Allen didn't remember. I asked him once kind of nervously to forgive me. And he said, "For what? I don't remember you said that." But I remember. Some things are just so unusual that they stay in your mind. So anyway, that's how it started.

RJ: Did he know you had credentials? Did he know you were a literary critic?

AC: Well, I wasn't really, I mean I'd written my dissertation on American writers in the Berkshires, and while I was living in Pittsfield I was trying to write articles about Kerouac's *Dr. Sax*. But they just didn't work. You know, I could write about Melville, but for some reason, there was a real block. I was going to write about Kerouac and *The Shadow* and how he read *The Shadow* magazines. Again because I was interested in American culture. So I had even found out where Walter Gibson, Lamont Cranston's creator lived, and I had driven to New York state to do an interview with this man, which I wrote up in a paper subsequently.

So anyway, I approached Allen Ginsberg a year or so later, and he gave me the idea that I could go and talk to Jack. Then, my friend Robert Wilson at the Phoenix Bookshop was publishing bibliographies and I had decided to collect Kerouac because while I was working at Colby-Sawyer I used to go to the Dartmouth library all the time. They had a wonderful lobby full of Erskine Caldwell books in little glass cases. This must have been in 1961–62—I had never thought of anyone collecting books that were in cheap paperbacks—just for the covers. All of my friends, when I was a grad student, liked Henry James first editions or Joseph Conrad. Those were the things you collected—with all the leather bindings and the glass-fronted bookcases. Yet here were these cheap paperbacks of Erskine Caldwell, and I thought, "Yes! for Kerouac. I can do that for him." So I started collecting him. Most of his books were remaindered. They didn't sell at all. I didn't even have to pay full list price for the first hardcover editions. Sam went around the world with a mission to collect Kerouac, any foreign editions. He brought me back books from England and France and Germany and Italy and so forth. And so that's sort of how it all got started.

RJ: So it was always evaluating the work, preserving the work, collecting the books, not as, even though you became, friends.
AC: No, never friends. With Ginsberg, but not with Kerouac.

RJ: Well, where is that collection now?
AC: It's at the Berg Collection at the New York Public Library. This was, oh, my proudest moment. I approached the Berg Collection at the New York Public Library where I had worked on Kerouac manuscript notebooks a long time ago. I did an article about that in the seventies, early eighties. I had been in London and done a lot of work with Carolyn Cassady, who's a friend. She had a copy of *The Town and the City* that Jack signed to Neal and her. Such a marvelous inscription. I said, "Really, you shouldn't just let this lie around your apartment. It should be in a good library. How about the New York Public Library? Would you like me to ask them because I'm in New York a lot." So I went and asked if they wanted to buy it. They said yes, but it has to be appraised and they told me all about that. I said, well, I'll pass on the word to Carolyn. Something just made me ask, "You wouldn't be interested in my library, would you? I've got all the Kerouac books that he signed when I did my work with [his] biblio." And Francis Mattson, who was then the curator at the Berg, said, "Yes, I'd buy that." I said, "Well, I won't sell just the signed Kerouacs." He said, "I don't want just the signed Kerouacs." I said, "Well, what do you want?" He said, "Everything."

RJ: How many pieces?

AC: Almost four thousand. They wanted a scholar's library. That's what they said. I was really honored: The Ann and Samuel Charters Collection of Beat Literature and Memorabilia.

NG: Which women writers are included in that collection?

AC: Well, there's of course di Prima, who's the main one. And Carolyn Cassady, whom I also enjoyed. I like Anne Waldman. I was interested in her work early when she lived on St. Mark's Place. She lived across the street from our apartment when she was with Lewis Warsh. I took some pictures of her then. And she was doing a lot of work.

RJ: Is that the one of Waldman in *Beats and Company*?

AC: Yes. That's where many of those pictures were published. I took them while Sam was travelling and before our first daughter, Mallay, was born in '67. When Sam came back and I got pregnant, we moved out of the Village because we needed another room for the baby. We moved to Brooklyn Heights because I'd gotten a little tired of the Lower East Side. I didn't want to raise Mallay there. It was in Brooklyn that I finished the Kerouac bibliography and I started working with Charles Olson because our friend Robert Hawley in Berkeley wanted a book about Olson. I said, "I'll write you one about Melville and Olson," because I knew about Melville and I thought it'd be fun to learn about Olson. I had a lengthy correspondence with Charles.

RJ: That's one of the reasons we wanted to interview you. You're the person with the Ph.D. who was able to be in that intermediate place of Beat's development. You were able to legitimate them as writers in a way that the fans and other people writing about them, you know, "I drank with Jack, I hung out with Burroughs," couldn't do. I'm so impressed that that doesn't kick into your work anywhere.

AC: It's wonderful to hear you say that because I've always felt something was wrong because I couldn't hang out. So I really have, all the time since then, wished that I could have just been looser. I don't think that anyone ever took me personally as somebody whom they had to bother with. The only one who did was Charles Olson. Olson once said to me, "You really run a tight ship." That was his comment. Charles was so charming.

RJ: Well, Melville and Olson—they're canonical. And the notion of linking them together—that's a scholar's project, that's not a fan's project.

AC: No, no, no. I never thought of myself as a fan. Everything I wrote always had a focus. With Kerouac and the interviews I was doing. But first there was the bibliography, which I was asked to do. I mean, I worked on projects. I'd get an occasional idea, like *Scenes Along the Road* or my concept for my textbook *The Story and Its Writer*. But I always am very receptive to other people's projects if I think I can do them. Or like [John] Sampas saying, "Would you like to do [the Kerouac] letters?" I say, "Yes, if I can do a portable Penguin reader of Kerouac." You know, it's always project-driven.

RJ: Well, you single-handedly brought professional academic respect to bear on this group of writers.

AC: Even though they were very literary themselves. I mean Ginsberg, Kerouac, Burroughs—I never felt that I was in a world where I didn't belong. That's probably one reason why I didn't respond to some of the writers, like Jack Micheline, for example. I just couldn't—or even Gregory Corso—I just simply—well, with Corso, it's personality. But with somebody who is coming off the streets, it doesn't, I'm not there. I'll collect his books, but I don't read them really. Whereas with the major [Beat] writers, they do know about literature and you can have a talk. So that's good to hear. Thank you for that perspective.

RJ: Well, which women writers have you paid attention to? How did you decide which ones to include in *The Portable Beat Reader*? Or in *The Dictionary of Literary Biography* [*DLB*]?

AC: Okay, here's what happened. With the *DLB*, this is another one of the projects that I didn't initiate. It was George Butterick. He was approached to do the whole thing. After my Kerouac bibliography did so well, I got the job here [at the Universtiy of Connecticut–Storrs]. But also Oxford University Press approached me to write a biography of Olson. I knew George was giving his life to Olson, so I went by his office at the library and said, "What should I say to these Oxford University Press people?" I work for hire. I could do a biography of Olson. I said, "This would really disappoint you—you want this?" He said, "Yes, please." So I said, "Okay, it's yours." I just wouldn't dream of muscling in because no one could do a better job than George either. When he was approached by Gale [Research Company], he called me and said, "You know, I don't have time for this. I'll work for you, but you're the best one to do this." So he told Gale that I was going to do it. So thanks to George, I got to do this project [the *DLB*], which I loved doing.

NG: Of the women Beat writers, which ones resonated for you?

AC: The women writers that I chose for this book were Bonnie Bremser, and, of course, Carolyn Cassady because I loved her autobiography [*Heartbeat*]—I hadn't met her at that point—now I have, we're very good friends. I didn't get a good response from Carolyn Cassady when I tried to fact check the material on Kerouac when I first met her in 1972. But I just thought that she was a very important person and she belonged there too. And so the next woman is, of course, Diane di Prima, and Butterick wrote on her. That's a nice essay. He liked her work too. Lenore Kandel—because I loved *The Love Book* [1966]. That was very important. It was really on the cusp.

That's really why she's in the book. And Jan Kerouac because [Gerald] Nicosia was writing for me, and he loved Jan Kerouac. And I thought, of course, she's written a nice book in her father's image. And then Joanne Kyger because I liked her cool California poetry. And I thought that *The Japan and India Journals* were fascinating. There is Joanna McClure because Michael [McClure] said, "Joanna's a poet too." And he wanted to write about her. I thought that was good. Then there's Janine Pommy Vega. Rlene Dahlberg, who I met with the Olson material, wanted to write about her. I guess she was fascinated with her rebel sensibility and her generally sad life. Dahlberg had a close feeling for that. Then I wrote about Anne Waldman. And that's it. The editors at Gale Research really didn't have any input at all. As my editor at Viking Penguin didn't with the [*Portable Beat*] *Reader* because no one knew about this stuff.

NG: In what ways do the women exemplify your understanding of Beat writing?

AC: I still don't think of Beat writing as primarily centered in the women at all. I think that the Beat community was largely not supportive of women's efforts. Diane di Prima is the stunning anomaly. She really is very special. She's always been independent. I learned a lot from her. The others it really seemed to me were following the men. And the irony here is that in the fifties, women, American women, did great writing. That's when Flannery O'Connor is writing. That's Sylvia Plath's time. We have [women] writers—extraordinary breakthroughs—none of them would have been caught dead within a mile of Kerouac and Cassady. These women are not attracted to the little thing that's going on in the boy gang. And it really was a boy gang. If you were a really talented woman, and you need a strong mind for that, I just don't think that you drift into their orbit. Because they're going to clobber you. They're going to eat you alive. I think part of that, of course, is the fact that they're gay and they don't really need women. I also feel that part of it—certainly Allen and Jack—is that their immigrant background has always placed women in a non-intellectual and subservient position. So you're not going to find the men encouraging and supportive, polite. They just want the standard, traditional women's role. Whereas I married someone from a very different social background who had a totally different sense of supportive, independent women. It was one of the things I was looking for. Quite clearly. Obviously. That I didn't have to conform to a traditional role when I married him [Sam Charters].

RJ: So there's a strong woman like di Prima who manages to hold her own.

AC: She does it because she's coming out of a situation at home that was even worse than mine, in terms of lack of support for her, lack of the sense that she could make a contribution, an intellectual, or any kind of contribution. She's from an Italian home and apparently a very overbearing father and a weak mother. They wanted very conventional things for her, but didn't give her any sense of self-esteem. She was fighting much harder than I was to break free of what they expected. To the point where she was—I don't know if I want to say this, but I think she would say it about herself after growing up in that household—she was emotionally a very battered person.

She's much more open about that now. For a long time, I was often comparing myself to her sense of freedom because [I was] not hanging out, [but] running the "tight ship." The life I was living was not as wild as my friend Carolyn's or di Prima's. She slept with many, many guys. When I interviewed di Prima about fifteen years ago, I finally got up the courage to say, "I really respect you and admire you for having been sexually so confident and being so free." She said,

"Well, thank you very much." Then I said, "But, can you explain how you came to that, you know, state of mind. Was it yoga?" She just looked at me, "What are you talking about?" I said, "Well, I admire that independence." She said, "You do understand, don't you, that I never felt anything for any of these people?"

RJ: But that's the revolutionary aspect of Beat for women. It's anticipation of women's liberation and the sexual revolution.
AC: Exactly. So I said, "You really mean it." And she said, "Yes." And I said, "You mean, and I'll try to get it straight, you mean if you had fallen in love with someone at seventeen, and he loved you too, you wouldn't have been wild and crazy?" "Of course not," she said.

I thought *Dinners and Nightmares* was one of the greatest books I'd ever read. That was the one. No Beat book has ever moved me more. If I could write one book, I'd want to write *Dinners and Nightmares*. I'm not sure I would today, but that was true for a long, long period. It could even be said that if that book hadn't existed, I might not have gotten so excited about the Beats. [It shows] that there was a life for someone who was a woman in this, otherwise, why I just couldn't feel it at all. And then when I found Sylvia Plath's *Ariel*, then it unfortunately made it impossible for me to give my heart to, say, Anne Waldman, because I was aware that you could be rebellious, you could go into a confrontational stance with conventional women's lives, but you didn't have to do it as a Beat. You could do it in other ways. *Ariel* was the most important book of poetry for my generation. For women.

RJ: What about Levertov?
AC: I thought she was very interesting, but I never felt that she was as passionately engaged, emotionally engaged. No, I was interested, but she ultimately bored me. [But] if you're gonna pick a figure like

that ... of course, Adrienne Rich. She's the great writer. She's the great poet of Levertov's generation.

RJ: Levertov had a small moment of intersection with the Beats. But she disengaged from them.
AC: Exactly. And I thought that was wise of her because she's much more English and in a different tradition. Whereas Adrienne Rich— that was *the* poet—got engaged in the feminist struggle, which was the most momentous thing that's happened in literature. Not the Beats, I'm afraid. They're up there, but there is something much more influential to our century or half-century, and that was the women's movement [in literature] led by Adrienne Rich. So after Plath's suicide in 1960, then came Adrienne Rich in the late sixties and seventies, eighties and even today. She's much more radical than any of the [Beat] men. The heterosexual society that they're rebelling against is an issue, but it's much bigger. The audience is much bigger; the stakes are much bigger with what Rich is doing.

NG: What is it about *Dinners and Nightmares*, though, that you admired?
AC: The style. The looseness of the style. The fact that she could find a language and a form that was so hip, so street-oriented, and that she could present it in a way. The only people that I've read or the only books I'd read about poverty, that way, was Orwell's *Down and Out in Paris and London*. Di Prima's book was such a different approach to the experience of having no money and doing what you want to do. It wasn't political; it was for art's sake. I just thought it was absolutely charming. I loved the humor in it, and I felt that she really had a lot of courage to do what she did. This is again when I, in a way, had a fatal attraction for the bohemian lifestyle, which I couldn't live, couldn't hang out, couldn't take endless lovers, couldn't ball homosexual guys.

I could never give myself over to them the way that I would never dream of writing a sentence while I was stoned. I couldn't play the piano when I was stoned, why would I try to write when I was stoned?

RJ: What's your take then on *Memoirs of a Beatnik*?
AC: I thought it was just a book for money. I never took that one seriously, except there's some good writing in it. But as far as taking it as a portrait of the time, I thought, well, she's just over the top because that's what they asked her to do.

RJ: But what about the parts of the book that are not the love-making sections? The people living in apartments together, crashing, reading each other's books.
AC: Exactly. The city was so different. You can get a sense of the times, her own times, in the fifties. But Joyce [Johnson] is probably the closest to how I lived, in terms of her middle-class Jewish background, the fact that she also, like me, rebelled. She really fell heavily for Kerouac, in his time. She really primarily thinks of herself as a novelist.

NG: But you did include her in *The Portable Beat Reader*.
AC: In *The Beat Reader*, I wanted to do a book that would cover the whole field as I saw it—the canon. Starting with the East Coast Beats, who formulated it, and then the importance of Neal Cassady, especially how influential he was on Kerouac's compositional practice. Then the importance of the California Renaissance poets, not only Ferlinghetti, McClure, the people at the Six [Gallery], but also the Rexroth connection. I really was trying to have it clarified that "Howl" was coming out of San Francisco. He couldn't have written "Howl" in New York, because he'd read "Thou Shalt Not Kill," that poem that Rexroth wrote in memoriam to Dylan Thomas; that has

exactly the same theme, even uses the word "Moloch" in it. When *The Annotated Howl* came out—that's another reason why Ginsberg was down on me—when *The Annotated Howl* ends with all the poets who had inspired him to write "Howl," and he didn't put in "Thou Shalt Not Kill" and Rexroth, I got on Allen's case. I said, "Allen, how come you left this poem out?" "Well, I don't think it had anything to do with 'Howl.'" I said, "But you know, really, have you read it recently? You forget that it talks about Moloch as the great god." "No." "Well, you oughta look at this." But I wanted all of Rexroth's poem in *The Beat Reader*, and I say something about the "Howl" connection. I had to take a little bit out because I ran out of space. I wanted to put some haiku of Rexroth's because Snyder—that was the only change I made—Snyder said, "Hey, not just 'Thou Shalt Not Kill,' because I know what you're trying to do, and it's fine, but there's something else that Rexroth represented to me and that was the haiku as a poem for the seventies." So that's the connection.

There's a section in the book [*The Portable Beat Reader*] titled "Fellow Travelers" because I wanted it to be the political theme as well as the fact that there were a lot of people who came afterwards. And the only women there are di Prima, Brenda Frazer, and Anne Waldman. Part 5, that's the part where the women come in because what I really felt was that, as a lifestyle, it [Beat] was so unfair about what the women's lives were like, just before the feminist movement starts getting rolling.

RJ: Do you think of those women as precursors to feminism?
AC: No, no. I really don't. It's because the ones who were precursors to feminism just wouldn't have been attracted to these guys.

RJ: What about Johnson's contention that the male Beat model was the only available model for her?

AC: Well, that's arguable.

NG: I think Hettie says that too.

AC: Yes, I think Hettie would say that. That's how they experienced it. Whereas I felt that [those] guys were too risky. I really had places to go also. I mean, I was going to graduate school. And it was because I really enjoyed the classroom. I never saw it as a social issue. I don't think they [the women Beat writers] did either, except they lacked that other necessary component of professional graduate school education. My friend [Carolyn] was the only woman I knew who wasn't going to be a doctor or a chemist or so messed up alas that they didn't really do much of anything except get married disastrously and have kids, and then have breakdowns. So those were the models. How weird I was. I just thought that I could write. [But] I never thought of myself as a writer; I was a reader, not a writer.

NG: What's your sense of the importance of race in the Beat movement? Hettie talks about the race issue in many of her stories and poems. Were you seeing race in any way?

AC: Well, growing up in a Jewish family in Los Angeles, I knew no black people; they didn't go to my high school. I went to John Marshall High School in L.A., which was middle class. The prototype for it would have been *Rebel Without a Cause* because that took place when I was in high school, and in the film they went up to Griffin Park Observatory, which was the neighborhood of my school. You look at the yearbook and there are no black faces or Hispanics either. Bizarre. 1953 is when I graduated. I went to Berkeley not knowing much about blacks at all, except that I knew that I responded to jazz and ragtime as much, or not quite as much, as classical music. I was trained as a classical pianist. Sam played me black jazz—he had lots of records and he knew a lot about it. He was interested in recording black musicians. So this was the first time, in the late fifties, that I went into this.

But again, it was an exotic world, and I had no black friends. In New York, one of our friends, who was a white designer, was going with a black woman, and this was an amazing thing. This was in '58 when I was first at Columbia. At the same time, I was acutely aware when you traveled in the South that they would have "White Only" on drinking fountains, and I couldn't stand that. This led me years later, when I was teaching at Colby, to my first book which was about Bert Williams, a black entertainer who died in 1922.[2] Anyway, I published this book with Macmillan, and I showed it to my friend who was running Folkways Records—Moses Asch. He looked at it and he said, "Why would you do such a thing?" I mean, he was happy for me. "This is a great job," he says, "I'm sure it's a wonderful book. But why would you—a nice Jewish girl—do such a thing?" Moses Asch, okay. Jewish beyond the Pale. I really, for the first time, thought about it. Why had I spent two years at the Schomberg Collection, researching all those black newspapers to get Bert Williams's career, going through vaudeville, going back to the minstrels? Why was I so fascinated with the minstrel show? I wrote my first article on the minstrel shows.[3] Why? Because I was so offended by race prejudice.

RJ: But was there an interracial scene?
AC: I surely didn't see it. No. Although people would go to black jazz clubs in the Village, and there'd be people sitting at tables and mixing, and no one thought anything of it.

RJ: Did you ever consider writing a memoir on some of the anecdotes you've just told us?

---

2. *Nobody: The Story of Bert Williams.* New York: Macmillan, 1970.
3. "Negro Folk Elements in Classic Ragtime," *Journal of Ethnomusicology*, 1961.

Tracking the Serpent

—Janine Pommy Vega

Janine Pommy Vega was born in 1942 in Jersey City, New Jersey, into a Polish-Prussian family. Reading Jack Kerouac's *On the Road* in 1958 inspired her to search for an elusive intensity of experience in the Beat world. Leaving home at the age of sixteen after graduating from high school, she headed for Greenwich Village, where she met Herbert Huncke; Allen Ginsberg; Peter Orlovsky, who later became her lover; and Elise Cowen, her roommate. Within the next five years, she met and married the Peruvian painter Fernando Vega; traveled with him to Paris, Israel, and Spain; endured his sudden death in 1965; and returned to the United States. Since then, she has taken pilgrimages throughout the world, writing, teaching, and studying sacred practices.

A protégé of Ginsberg, Pommy Vega has developed a poetic practice grounded in the commitment to political activism that came to characterize Beat writers, such as Ginsberg, Waldman, di Prima, and LeRoi Jones, as they matured into the sixties and seventies. Pommy Vega's stance, which she calls "bare-knuckled warrior poetics," a term that she derived from observing Ginsberg, allows her to use language to challenge the status quo, particularly through her work over the last twenty-five years teaching writing to inmates in the New York, California, and Peruvian prison systems. For Pommy Vega, language is the medium for change, an essential element undergirding her life as teacher, writer, and soul-seeker.

Her first book, *Poems to Fernando,* was published in the City Lights Pocket Poets Series (no. 22) in 1968. These delicate elegies to her husband are also a portrait of the woman artist coming into poetry. The book illustrates a crucial moment of enfranchisement in which the woman Beat writer exercises the capacity to transform herself from object to subject. An untitled poem dated "summer/paris '65," soon after Fernando Vega's death, turns from love to the art of writing:

> *this pile of Pot, like grandmother's leavings*
> *the lamplin girl leaves love at the doorsill*
> *every pen*
>   *starting; leaking out–*
> *a freak of nature this poem* (43)

The matrilineal line moves through the pen, positing the poem "a freak of nature," what's there when love and its obsessions are superceded. The collection moves on, settling in California in three poems from 1967, the apex of the Haight-Ashbury counterculture. In one of these, dated "5/67 s.f. [San Francisco]," the eve of the Summer of Love, the poet addresses the existence and character of the poem as entity:

> *That it live by itself, a locked key*
>   *opening, the*
> *poem in its footsteps on the page*
>   *has a power*
> *to make known its own secret, chattering in the*

> *Ancient tongues, hierarchical code messages,*
> */magic cantering in its own block print*
> *,intuitive signatures.* (47)

Reveling in the mystical "I AM" that writes itself, the poem enacts the poet. As the poet comes out of her mourning, her kaddish for Fernando has led to, among other destinations, a self-possessed clarity through language.

This clarity is the kind achieved through meditative practice, establishing Pommy Vega as an heir to the romantic tradition of Ginsberg, Whitman, Wordsworth, and Coleridge. Within this tradition, the poet's role is to use the natural world as emblem upon which to focus the mind in order to transcend the physical and temporal universe and achieve an awareness of the holy. The sublime quality of such a vocation is seen in "Poem/Exhortation, marin county, cal 5/67." The poem, partially written while Pommy Vega was riding on a motorcycle, exhibits romantic exuberance in its celebration of the world and the formation of its line:

> *flickering forest leaf shadows passed*
> *down into depths of sleep*
> *imprinted.*
> *(everything the eyes have seen*
> *imprinted.*
> *EVERYTHING.*
> *everything, everything, Everything, everything, everything*
> *everything, everything.* (55)

True to its lyric ancestors, the poem relies upon visions to prompt an understanding of the sanctity of god's creation: "What more? / What less / What else is there, ever?" (59) the poet wonders, returned to herself, a temporal and corporeal being, enhanced.

Over the years, Pommy Vega's poetic language has become less elevated, and her lines somewhat shorter and less dependent on idiosyncratic punctuation. Her love of truth and beauty has remained steadfast. In its service, her poetry becomes a method of problem solving that stimulates reflection and action, the woman poet assuming responsibility for her own salvation and that of the greater polis. Poems in Pommy Vega's *Mad Dogs of Trieste* (2000) cry out for political action. For instance, the speaker of "Out of the Reach of Children" angrily confronts the Nuclear Regulatory Commission (49–50), and in "The Draft," she intones an elegant sermon on the humanity of those incarcerated in the penal system (267–68). Elegies to longtime Beat companions, such as Elise Cowen, Ray Bremser, and Bonnie Frazer, must honor the living and the dead, particularly those who were ignored or mistreated.

Pommy Vega's work articulates the refraction of feminist politics through New Age spirituality, romanticism, liberation theology, and open sexuality. These dynamics meet in *Tracking the Serpent: Journeys to Four Continents* (1997), her prose memoir/travelogue that refits the road tale to white feminist goddess-based spirituality and post-sexual-revolution free sexuality. The text, drawing upon the peripatetic, questing, and confessional heart of Beat culture, chronicles Pommy Vega's treks throughout Ireland, Peru, and Nepal which began in the early eighties in search of the divine as the great Mother. Her road stories are distinguished by her fierce independence; her keen awareness of race, gender, and class prejudices; and her triumphant conclusion that "[t]he source of power resides in the interstices between one world and another, between the known and the unknown, between who we are and who we are becoming" (10). The memoir draws on this power to further define the woman artist through the ancient source of female divinity.

Pommy Vega has authored fifteen volumes of poetry and prose, the most recent being *Mad Dogs of Trieste*, and edited eleven anthologies, including *Voices Under the Harvest Moon: An Anthology of Writing from Eastern Correctional Facility* (1999). She is also at work on a novel and a collected edition of her poems.

This interview was conducted by Nancy Grace on January 29, 2000, in New York City.

NANCY GRACE: Can we talk a bit about the genesis of *Poems to Fernando?*

JANINE POMMY VEGA: When Fernando died, I did a lot of traveling all through Europe. How long was I in Paris? A year and a half. And I was a year and a half in Jerusalem. I must have been gone three years and maybe three months or so. And that's when the book starts. This is it, the mourning, running from place to place looking for him. Through the French Alps, through Geneva, through . . . of course he wasn't anywhere. You know what I mean, you're just wildly in love. And then I came to New York. I must have come here maybe in March. When I returned it was '66, yes. And I stayed in New York a year or so.

NG: When was the last time you looked at the book? [hands JPV a photo copy of *Poems to Fernando*]

JPV: Geez, I looked at it last year, you know Ray Bremser died, and I remembered that I wrote a poem for him, and I went back to see [what I'd written].[1] Yeah, so here they are. Wow . . . [looks at the poems]. Have you read Peter Coyote's book [*Sleeping Where I Fall*]? It's very instructive because he remembers back to one of those times and identifies with the person he was at many of those times. It's not that I don't identify with myself there, but what I'm looking for is ecstasy. I really want to get it on my own. I want to get it through my

---

1. Ray Bremser, 1934–1998. *Poems to Fernando* contains two poems written to Bremser: "to Ray: Poem to the Old Man" (49) and "to Ray: Junk [& the old man] changes" (50–52).

practices. [In these poems] there really was a sincere desire to get to the heart and depth and extent, furthest extent, of everything. To encompass it, to understand it fully and totally. I must say, that's one big reason for all those drugs we all took then.

NG: Did you revise the poems a lot?

JPV: Yes, I reworked them a lot. I think that part of that process is the pursuit of your own voice, the actual specific voice. I also think that part of it is anal retention. When time gets shorter, like now, fifty-eight times short!—it's not that I don't go over the poems now. It's that they come out more closely aligned to the way they finally will be. I also cut. That always happens when you put together another book. You know it was always good, but now suddenly in the great harsh light of day it still has that problem, whatever it is. So then you go back, and it's another whole set of revisions.

NG: Did you show any of them to Allen [Ginsberg]?

JPV: Yes. I wasn't using plain speech, and I know he must have been strong enough in his comments for me to feel hurt by it, but when I came home—I was living with Fernando—and I was crying, and he said, "You know who he is, and you know who you are, and I don't understand what the tears are about. That's his opinion, that's all it is." Because he [Fernando] was clear about who he was. He wasn't starting out as a painter; he was a painter. And then the ones after that, I don't know if I showed them to Allen or not. They were written while I was in Paris, while Fernando was alive. Yeah. Wow, what a time!

NG: What's the process to try to understand something as you did with these early poems?

JPV: Yes, reaching the place in the consciousness where you really are part of the totality; the totality is part of you. That's like when a particular chemical touches or releases that capacity in the self. The disciplines, such as chanting and meditation and japa[2] and contemplation, also release; you get to the same place. When you're drenched with love and certitude, you know that you've gotten to that place. Sometimes shorter times, sometimes after a lengthier period of getting there, but it seems to me that that's the way. I think that the desire of the soul, or the being, to fulfill the life's purpose of becoming part of that totality is inherent in all of us. And in some more than others. The people that I saw during that whole time—everyone was pushing the envelope really. We pushed the envelope to the absolute maximum. So many people, more than 75 percent of the people, did not return. They died. They went mad. And the people that did return, or the people that are still here, [of them] I don't know anyone who isn't involved in some kind of practice. I think that's such a normal progression because that yearning, that desire, doesn't go away. You may disagree with the method that you used through all that intense yearning in your youth, but, and even for love to answer, love from another person, finally it has to come home to this is where it began, this is where it's answered, and this is the only vehicle you have to reach it.

NG: Is writing part of the practice?
JPV: Absolutely, absolutely. There are very few ways that you can disappear—where your ego is—and I think writing is definitely one of them. Writing, loving, walking, meditating. What else? The chanting, the japa. I've started a practice—I have a problem with my heart—I don't have as much power [mountain] climbing [as I used to have]. So what I do is I climb with the japa. It's as though there's a cable car line and the japa is the teeth that pull you up. So by the time you're at

---

2. Japa is the practice of repeating a mantra or the name of god.

the top, there's no one there. You're just part of everything you perceive.

NG: Is that a daily practice for you?

JPV: No, it's not daily, it's whenever I get a chance to. I have certain positions that I go to and refer to, get my reference point, yes.

NG: What's your practice in writing like now?

JPV: I write any chance I get. My writing life is right now divided into being an editor and writing about, like if someone asks me for an article on a particular kind of teaching or school, I'll write about that. And then there's the poetry. There's also the story I'm writing now about the hooker in New York in 1966. And also I bring a notebook with me wherever I go. I write in it.

NG: Have you always used a notebook like that?

JPV: Oh absolutely. Yes. That's why I have the dates on all those poems [in *Poems to Fernando*]. It lets me know where I was. I may have memories, but I can't necessarily chronologically pinpoint where they were.

NG: So you're always jotting down in the notebooks?

JPV: It depends. Now I'm working on the story, so depending on how closely aligned I am with the story, I'm working on it all the time. For instance, if I'm working in schools—I do poetry in the schools, that kind of job—then starting out in the morning I still have some mind. And if I have any thoughts, they can go on my clipboard. But after that, all my attention and energy is entirely given over to the teaching. So when I come home at night, there's nothing left unless I take a nap and don't need to get up the following morning very early. Then I can actually maybe squeeze something out. But whatever you have to do, whatever you have to do to get it out there and get it in motion.

NG: How does your process of writing poetry differ from writing narrative fiction?

JPV: Well, the techniques are very different. In this particular story, for instance, I'll have a knowledge of the next thing that's coming up. I won't know anything about how we'll reach that point, and then it's a matter of subsuming the character, where I'm always—not astonished—but I'm certainly not aware of what's going to happen before it does. It's the process of swimming out in that. You're swimming in the process until it finally gets your two or three or four or five pages. Rarely five.

Whereas with most of the poems I've written recently, a lot of them are written in prison or about prison or dealing with prison. Just because I always go there once a week for three hours. For three hours we have a time where we're all concentrating on writing. So I know if I have no other time, I'll have that time to write that week. Or if somebody asks me to do a particular thing, like recently I wanted to underscore the importance of a persona poem when you absolutely take on the character of someone else that's not yourself—and I don't mean a part of nature or an animal; I mean another human being. So to that end, I remembered my own nephew whom I'm very close to. He's had many jobs in his life and one of them was as a CO—correctional officer—and he wrote to me about what that was like. So that's what this CO says in the course of [my] poem. Now I didn't write it on command, but I was moved to it by the necessity of addressing a particular problem.

Allen did that. That's something that I really learned from him. This capacity that he had to, on his feet, use whatever platform was available to put forth his own belief systems in a cogent and convincing manner, he did that. I have a line for him— "bare-knuckled warrior poetics." That's it—where you just hop on a plane and you jump off and you're there and you do whatever—that kind of readiness to not lose sight of the truth as you see it and bring in facts that will help you put that across to whomever it is you may be facing is something that he did again and again. It means doing. You have to be there and there's work that needs to be done and you do it. That's it. And when I say "bare-knuckled," you cut through the bullshit; you cut through everything you need to get to what the heart of the matter is. You know, all the traveling can be called bare-knuckled warrior poetics. And going to a gig when you're below par and you suddenly jump out of your skin, jump outside of yourself. Bare-knuckled warrior poetics is going beyond the limitations of the ego. And hence you become the warrior that you actually are. Bare-knuckled warrior poetics is something Allen really taught me—not from living with him, not even from talking about it, but from the way I saw him do it. And really, since taking my own direction, causing my own direction, it works for me as it mirrors what he does, not as it follows what he does. In other words, I can do it in my way—the way I saw him do it is his way. I can't do it his way.

NG: You're making it yours.

JPV: Right. For instance, the business with the prisons that I fell into totally accidentally when a friend asked me to help. I've been doing it for twenty-five years, starting at Sing-Sing teaching poetry writing workshops, and it's a long process of dealing with people who are incarcerated. It's also a long process of making people outside the walls aware of it, and making people inside the walls aware of their absolute requirement to get their words out there. It seems to me that not everyone is gifted as a poet, but everyone who's thinking can make some kind of statement that might make sense to someone who hasn't got a clue.

NG: How does your version of "bare-knuckled warrior poetics" compare to Allen's?

JPV: Well, Allen had notoriety and exposure to the world from a very young age. So that's what I mean. He used his notoriety, his high profile. He always used it on TV, wherever he was, always to put forth his own view as he saw world politics. But I don't have that kind of notoriety or exposure, and the difference is wherever I find an audience for anyone who's interested in knowing what my point of view is, I'll definitely put it across. I'll even try to galvanize people. If I lecture or read or do a full day at a university, that's one of the things I bring up: "Hey, what are you gonna do about it? What are *you* gonna do about it? The way it is ain't workin'. We can see that. It is not working!" And the cynicism of the youth faced with the culture that has only taken advantage of them monetarily, let's say, and swayed their thinking and so forth through life—it's not surprising that some of them are saying, "Listen, what can we do? We want to *do* something." Then I give them a couple of possibilities: "You don't have to go to your local lock-up. What you can do is make a friend who's not like you, who's not your color, who's not your culture. Start there." Because as long as there's "the other," we're a civilization divided. One has two million people behind bars; the rest are out here. And we need to bridge these two civilizations. So when I give workshops, like for women, there's always a component of "what are you doing about it now?"

NG: For you, then, is every poem a political act?

JPV: Oh, you could say that. Even though they're love songs? Even if they're . . . is that true if they're religious? If they're spiritual? Well . . . is every poem a political act?

NG: That depends on how you define "political." Even a love poem can attempt to shift the power structure. *Poems to Fernando* are poems of grieving, mourning, moving out of those stages, controlling the situation.

JPV: And then taking on the power or being empowered to make changes within yourself or outside yourself. I guess they are all political acts then.

NG: Perhaps not in the sense of actively critiquing American culture the way many of Ginsberg's poems do.

JPV: Right. But "Wales Visitation" doesn't. Or "Father Death" [sings title]. Is that a political act? Sure it is.

NG: What writers have most strongly influenced you throughout your life?

JPV: Blake, certainly. Gertrude Stein, who now I can't tell you why because I'm not fond of her. I'm just not. She's so ego-bound. I remember reading Melville, *Moby-Dick*, in Allen and Peter's room, so I guess I hadn't read that before. And John Wieners, I read that. And, of course, Herbert Huncke.

NG: Any other Romantic poets? *Poems to Fernando* really reminds me of Shelley.

JPV: I read some Shelley, not a lot. Fernando loved Shelley. He really did. Ah, gee. You know who loves Shelley is Gregory [Corso]. Gregory love[d] Shelley. Now the poets that I heard at that time— Lew Welch, Albert Saijo. I remember listening to Barbara Moraff, whose work I didn't understand very much, but I was really taken with her. She knew what she was saying, that was clear. She was very adamant and very intellectual, I thought. And also Bob Kaufman and Jack Micheline. Let's see, I did read Bonnie [Frazer] when she wrote

Troia. The writer who has shown me so much, though, is Rabindranath Tagore.[3] He's so great. He's a poet from India—Bengal—I encountered him through his work in Paris at Shakespeare & Company in 1964.

NG: What do you admire about his work?

JPV: His ability to capture the devotion of a heart in love with god. The way he uses the lower-case "y" for "you" when he addressed god. Without any soppiness, just like Kabir, whose work I also like, as well as Rumi and Cesar Vallejo.[4] Lorca, certainly. Lorca I've been in love with since I was sixteen or seventeen. I can also say Hettie Jones.

NG: What is it about Hettie's poetry that appeals to you?

JPV: Hettie's poetry is direct, as is her prose. It has that mammalian compassionate and tough stance. She's been through a lot of changes, and she's become very strong because of it. And she has the ability to laugh at herself, which so few people do—like in her "Seven Songs at Sixty!" [1998, 101–3]. Also Isabelle Eberhardt.[5] You really have to read her. The intensity of her passion, her quest for the infinite, simultaneous with her tremendous passion for her lover Salmene. She was called "The Little Nomad of the Desert." She dressed like a man—she drank with the Legionnaires. She's a great role model, along with Alexandra David-Neel and Madame Blavatsky.[6] All those women— you could even call it an extension of a woman's desire to travel and to take in all these experiences. From a woman's point of view, you had to do it in two ways: you had to go after your thing, but you also

3. Rabindranath Tagore (1861–1941), Indian poet and scholar.

4. Kabir (1398–1518?), Indian poet, mystic, and philosopher. Mowlana Jalaluddin Rumi (1207–1273), poet and founder of the Mawlawi Sufi. Cesar Vallejo (1892–1938), Peruvian poet.

5. Isabelle Eberhardt (1877–1904), Swiss-born adventurer; joined secret Sufi brotherhood.

6. Alexandra David-Neel (1869–1969), French-born adventurer. Madame Helena Petrovna Blavatsky (1831–1861), Russian-born esotericist and a founder of the Theosophical Society.

had to do it in a man's world at that time. I really identified with that. You know I spent a long time, must have been from '69 to '71, reading all the writers of the Golden Dawn Society.[7] Arthur Macon and Algernon Blackwood. Then Sax Romer and Violet Firth.[8] I guess what really fascinates me about the Golden Dawn people is that they were reviving the Western mystery tradition, and they were also expressing the unknown. And the people they wrote about were real people. I followed the Golden Dawn people quite literally for years.

NG: That's a rich background. Did Kerouac's writing influence yours in anyway?
JPV: I can't say that his style of writing influenced me. It was his idea of the desire to go. You know, for years, geez, that's mainly what I did.

NG: Yes, your poetry is definitely from the world and of the world—written all over the world.
JPV: And now I haven't of late, just short journeys, partly because of less time away from my desk and partly because of my physical capacity—I just need to do it differently now, you know? I'm a reader. You know who influences me, I think, in terms of prose, who has taught me a lot? Hemingway! Just to leave out as much as you can. And also Henry Miller—all that exuberance, you know.

NG: So do you consider yourself a Beat poet?
JPV: No . . . I mean to say . . . I was there then. I was writing, and I was listening. I was certainly imbibing. I was reading. But I didn't show anybody anything I was working on. I didn't even show Elise

---

7. The Golden Dawn, founded in 1888 by Dr. William Wynn Westcott and Samuel Liddell MacGregor Mathers, was a magical society dedicated to the philosophical, spiritual, and psychic evolution of humanity. Others associated with its development include Alastair Crowley and Madame Helena Petrovna Blavatsky.
8. Violet Firth (1890–1946), Welsh writer, member of Golden Dawn Society, aka Dion Fortune.

[Cowen]. I lived with Elise—a year and a half or something. She was writing, and I was writing. I think I showed her one poem.

NG: Did she show you any of hers?

JPV: No, not a thing. In fact, when Brenda Knight's *Women of the Beat Generation* came out, that's the first time I saw her writing. And one of her poems was to me. It's the one about the orange, the one about "Dr. Death." Did you see the one I wrote to her, the one in my book *Mad Dogs of Trieste*? You'll see how it matches up.[9]

NG: In the Knight book, though, you mention that you showed Elise some of your poems.

JPV: In the memoir I say I showed Elise some poems. Make that one poem that I remember with any clarity. It was a poem written while listening to Beethoven, and she commented. She did not show me hers, kept a notebook, was private about it. The fact that we did not, as roommates, share what today's young women might take for granted I think speaks for an era when what women were going through in terms of their own chosen art seemed unimportant next to the art of the men. I don't mean in my own mind for my own work, which was to me the most important, but out in the air with others. The young lover Ray Bremser had in the slam, who came to the Lower East Side when he got out, called Rimbawd [sic], as far as I can recall, was asked to read his poems aloud in the company of all of us, and they were amateurish and wanting depth. Nevertheless he was encouraged, and I remember thinking, "Hmmmm, there it is. We're both the same age, I'm a better writer, the only difference is he's a cute guy."

---

9. Vega refers to the poem "Death" by Elise Cowen (Knight 162–63) and to "Elise," which she wrote in 1996 (2002, 256).

NG: If not Elise, who did you share your work with?

JVP: I showed it to Huncke. He was always helpful in saying that he thought I was very talented, strong-minded, independent, truthful. Now Allen did a criticism of my work once in Paris. You know who really helped me as an elder? Thomas McGrath.[10] I was living near him in Spain, and he was very gentle, very patient, and very straightforward.

NG: Did you spend any time then with women writers?

JPV: I talked to the women. Diane [di Prima] was out there. Now I don't remember if I heard Diane di Prima [read] or not. I remember knowing her, meeting her. And Joyce Johnson was a published writer. But I'm talking about the coffee shop scenes that I would see. When I talked with this group of women that I was with, none of us were, at that time, Beat writers. That we came out of that time is true, however.

NG: That's one way of defining Beat—that particular group of people you were hanging out with.

JPV: Right. And breaking through at that time. For me to take that bus in from New Jersey, on 48th Street in Union City, and go twenty minutes to the Port Authority was a complete and total change of consciousness in itself. The old way of holding on to family values and all that stuff which I just was breaking away from—I wanted to get on with it: "Let's get to where the poets are! Where they're really living!"

NG: When did you realize that you wanted to write?

JPV: Since I was ten or eleven. It's seemed to me that I've always been a writer. And reading *On the Road*, where those people were so alive as compared to my own life with the high school kids, my boyfriend— who in fact gave me *On the Road*, he was a much older person than

---

10. Thomas McGrath (1916–1990), North Dakota poet, founder of the literary journal *Crazy Horse*.

me—my house, the railroad rooms. There was one room that was mine, next to the living room, and I thought that if I could really make this room bohemian, I would have a better life. So I changed everything in the room. I painted things, and had a little table and this, that, and the other, and I made what my vision of a New York pad would be. When it was finished, I sat in it, and I realized that not only what I wanted was *not* there, but that I could never be in that room—because I had painted myself out of it. The stuff I had was no longer there, and I wasn't there either. I was looking for something else; it wasn't there, I knew that.

NG: You had to leave that place and find a new physical environment?
JPV: Absolutely. And when I moved in with Huncke, I embraced the new way wholeheartedly, jumped into it.

NG: How did you meet him?
JPV: I met Allen and Peter in 1958, and then they went to California. My friend Barbara was hanging out with Gregory. I was working in a coffee shop in the Village one night when Huncke came in. I thought he was so wonderful. I loved his face. I loved the way he approached life.

NG: Were there particular ways in which Huncke influenced your writing?
JPV: His way of seeing. His observations of details were something I always noted. But it was his point of view, the point of view of some-one who can relate to every point of view. You know, he really had that, well, you could say, a sense of compassion. And it was egalitar-ian. He was the only man in that scene, that I met, who was not a sex-ist, by today's standards, I would say. They were living according to the lives that they were brought up with, you know. I'm not blaming anybody. I'm simply saying that he perceived people as individuals.

I remember in 1966, when I came back from Europe, and we were coming down the stairs in some tenement in the Lower East Side, and I was explaining to him why I was in love with this Italian crazy person, very smart guy. I was saying, you know, sort of basically I can't help myself, I'm just a woman. Using those words. And he said, "Just a person. Just a person. I mean, you're just a human being. And it's natural for a human being to want to desire love. And you're just a human being. A woman, uh-huh; that's not it." I learned a great thing like that from him. He had that capacity: he was really able to take on the possibility of everybody else's trip. That's what made him such a great con man! He could always insinuate his way into your point of view, so you would understand it. You would understand why this five dollars was meaningless to you and meant a lot to him. [laughs] This typewriter was only worth the pawn ticket; it didn't have any other value.

NG: His egalitarian nature is unexpected.

JPV: Oh absolutely, absolutely. He really could see that. He really was my teacher in that way. Through the last years, I may have disagreed entirely with his lifestyle, because it was no longer mine, but he never ceased to be that way. And let's call that "god," if you want.

NG: How's that egalitarianism manifest itself in your writing?

JPV: Well, I try—as a person as judgmental as myself—I try to do that same thing. For instance, I don't think that you can create a work of fiction if you don't take on all those roles. There's got to be something you can identify with or love about every character, no matter how repulsive. I only know when it's true. That's all I know. I know when it's true. Or I know when it's tending toward truth. You know what I mean? I know when I'm there. I can feel it. And then my job is to hack, hack, hack—to take everything out that's not there.

NG: Does that happen with your poetry too?

JPV: Ah, I think, I think it does. Yes. Poetry, it's not the same. You're not ensouling a character through time. Or you're not looking with the character through time. It's another thing. The process of trying to arrive at a truth, whether you know what it is or you don't, that's really not the issue. You may never know it. You may know it twenty years later. You may never know just what it means. You just know that it's right—that's all you know. The poem itself will define itself. All you can know is that it's clear. You may not understand it. It's true. But you've been swimming in it. You know what's clear or not.

NG: Is that different from fiction, where you're creating a character who takes on a palpably real form?

JPV: Well, I think you have to cut out the shadow, no matter what, the writer's shadow in the midst of it. Things become revealed in prose at their own pace. You know, the way the verbs work, they pull the train. Whereas, with a poem, you stand revealed in a certain space, which is that poem; it's not necessarily through time. It is: this is it; this is it. It has its own reality. It shines in its own truth, and all you really need to do is swim out there selflessly enough so that you can hack away everything that isn't it, that isn't that truth.

NG: Has your poetic voice changed over the years?

JPV: Oh sure, sure. Like the influences here [in *Poems to Fernando*], some of the long lines are like Allen's lines. And there's a lot of the influence of the Bible in there. A lot of influence: "thee" and "thou." And there's a male. God in here is considered male. It's very Jehovah, Christ, Judaic, from reading the Bible. So that's changed. See, like this "Poem/Exhortation." I was riding a motorcycle, and I was writing it as I was riding.

NG: You were writing as you were riding!?
JPV: Yeah, I was on the back, and I was writing as I was going along. All these three-liners. Now the three-line thing happens a lot in my work. That's still true. Of course, the punctuation has changed considerably. [laughs]

NG: I rather like those commas and backslashes at the head of the lines in the Fernando poems. They're consistent in the collection.
JPV: What does the punctuation mean?

NG: What does it mean?! [laughs]
JPV: You can only guess! But it seems to be integral, so she must mean something. I think the idea of the images overcoming, coming from within, or cropping up from the inside out, rather than like an opinion—outside in, that's continual in my poetry. I rely on the same source for my work: dreams and all that stuff having to do with the total unconscious. I think trying to capture an emotional moment with the small lines—I still do that.

NG: Do you find gender changes at all in your poetic voice, writing from the perspective of a he or a she?
JPV: Oh yes, the poetic voice was "he" in my earlier work. You'll see it in *Journal of a Hermit*. *Journal of a Hermit* is "he," and also the one that comes after, the *Journal of a Hermit &*, where there are a few tales in which the character is a "he." And I'll tell you why—because all my teachers were male, up to that point. That's why. That's what happened. So in terms of my own voice, if the female was the passive or the receptive or any of those other things, this voice was not. This voice was assertive. It was a complete eye-opener one day when I took the idea of "he" and changed it to "she."

NG: When and how did that happen?

JPV: The idea of creating the voice as female, I think, has its inception when I read about the Holy Mother [in 1970]. Ramakrishna's wife [Sarada Devi] is called the Holy Mother. There's a picture of the Holy Mother in the story about her life. That was the first time that anybody had mentioned to me that god is *her*. *She* is god. She is here. Ramakrishna was devoted to Kali, and the whole thing just blew open my mind. It made me so happy. I was just so grateful that it filled a whole corner of my life. A whole sterile land became rained on. It's a matter of you the writer, you the controller, taking that thought and bringing it to the concept of you the writer [as] female.

NG: How did that change your writing?

JPV: Well, first of all, you own your sexuality. You own your own motivation. Like my book *Tracking the Serpent*, that narrator is a female. She's going out, and she's having these experiences because she's looking for something, and everything else is peripheral. Any guy that comes up is somebody that she fucks because at that time, that's what's happening. And then she goes on. There are places where she stops and gets involved. But the involvement is a reckoning back to how one uses oneself and the involvement, and how she's dealt with that through the years. It's very female. But before that time, because the only ones who were speaking with any authority were men, when I was speaking with authority the voice had to be male. I guess that's how I perceived it. Until I myself was going out. That's it. And I was a female—period—end of story. And yes, the male characters that come into the story are rather peripheral, just as in a male's adventure story the females would be peripheral. It's just like, hey, you lead, that's it. But then it's really bigger than that. You're looking for something yourself, and by "yourself," I mean the total self. You'll always be looking for that. You're a human being. I just don't see the difference.

NG: You just mentioned *Tracking the Serpent*, your memoir of spiritual journeys. What materials did you use to write it?

JPV: Oh, journals, absolutely! And poems. I always have a notebook with me when I travel. Well, in that particular case, that book took over twelve years to write; the book itself two years; the journeys took twelve years. And each one of them has a specific quality about it. I saw that that was so when I began to put it together. I hadn't seen it until then. So one is the sexual imperative in the jungle: How far can she go? How many layers can she peel off, really? And then there's the healing of the mother, and the shamanic way of the Indian mountains. And then there's the sudden recognition of the mother or the presence of god as the mother in this ancient place called Nepal in Asia.

NG: Were you trying to make an accurate record of what you did or were you more interested in going back and playing with narrative forms?

JPV: It isn't exactly memoir, nor is it autobiography, because the person involved in that story is being used as a character by you the writer. You know, that's really so. It's true! For instance, if you want to point up a certain experience, and your character happens to be you, there's a certain point where you can't go at it subjectively. You're not going to get anywhere. You have to go at it objectively. And I always consider the character to be "her" once it's out there.

NG: The narrative of *Tracking* relies heavily on description and not extensive reflection. Are there reasons why you did this?

JPV: I don't agree. I think the reflection in it is exactly proportionate to what is going on.

NG: So you became the person you were in that past as you recreated her?

JPV: Absolutely, absolutely. And also, like in the novel, whomever that person is who is supposed to be generated, the life they assume, and you're living it through them.

NG: When did you start to hike?

JPV: Well, I've always hiked; I've always been a walker.

NG: It's unusual for women to take off on the solitary treks as you did. When Ginsberg and Orlovsky made their trip to India in the sixties, did you consider going with them?

JPV: Of course I did. Was I invited? No. They told me that they were going, and I was going to stay and take care of Lafcadio [Orlovsky]. And I was working, and I thought, "Geez, they should have at least said, 'Why don't you save up your money [to go].'" Later when I asked Allen about it he said, "You know, I was just being a real shithead. I was being really self-involved." So that's that.

Fast Speaking Woman

—Anne Waldman

Entering poetry late in the Beat move-
ment, Anne Waldman encompasses diverse literary schools and eras
in her work, embracing Beat and New York school poetics; drawing
from Sappho, Stein, and the Mazatec shaman Maria Sabina; and performing slam poetry. Her works are produced from a profusion of
media and art forms, many inspired by collaboration with writers,
musicians, and dancers, and created to be performed. Waldman
balances an aesthetic that advocates both personal expression and
political activism; her longstanding practice of Buddhism merged
with her affinity for postmodern literary theory and praxis to
produce a poetry of complex visual and linguistic structures that
seek visionary existential points on the edge of the noumenal. She is
the author or editor of more than a dozen works, including *Giant
Night* (1968); *Baby Breakdown* (1970); *Journals & Dreams* (1976);
Talking Naropa Poetics, volumes I and II (1978); *Helping the Dreamer:
New and Selected Poems, 1966–1988* (1989); *Kill or Cure* (1994);
The Beat Book: Poems & Fiction from the Beat Generation (1996);
Iovis, volumes I and II (1993, 1997); *Vow to Poetry: Essays, Interviews &*

Manifestos (2001); and *The Angel Hair Anthology* (with Lewis Warsh, 2002).

Waldman was born in 1945 in Millville, New Jersey, grew up in Greenwich Village, and graduated from Bennington College in 1966, where she edited the literary magazine *Silo*. Waldman's coming of age in the 1960s allowed her to benefit from the pressure to integrate women writers into the academic curriculum and from the influence of a generation of male writers who began to see women poets as peers. She met the poet Lewis Warsh, with whom she founded the literary journal and press *Angel Hair*, at Robert Duncan's reading at the 1965 Berkeley Poetry Conference (Charters, "Anne Waldman" 528–29). The conference was a powerful germinating experience for Waldman, who credits Charles Olson's wrenching extemporaneous perform-ance with galvanizing her to dynamic public readings of her work ("My Life" 297). She also mentions the importance of hearing Lenore Kandel read at the conference, where Joanne Kyger appeared as well. Waldman became involved in grassroots poetry efforts throughout the late sixties and early seventies. She has also been acclaimed for her offices as director of the Poetry Project at St. Mark's Church in the Bowery from 1968 to 1977, and, since 1974, as founder and director (until his death, with Allen Ginsberg) of the Jack Kerouac School of Disembodied Poetics at Naropa Institute (now Naropa University) in Boulder, Colorado. Waldman participated in the antiwar movement of the sixties, and, through her poetry and activism, has been an out-spoken opponent of nuclear energy, helping to close Colorado's Rocky Flats power plant.

Waldman is not cut in the image of the coolly silent "girls" in black who signified the feminine in early Beat generation discourses. Rather, she exemplifies the nonconformist promise of Beat's "wild self-believing individuality" by bringing to the Beat generation's antiestablishment impulses the resistances of second-wave feminism.

Waldman embodies Buddhist spirituality and Beat's spontaneous, confessional poetics, cut-up methods of composition, and penchant for oration and public performance. But she brings a woman-centered sensibility to her Beat poetic praxis, consciously taking the works of women poets as models—among Beat writers she acknowledges di Prima, Kyger, and Kandel (Charters, "Anne Waldman" 530–31)—and embodying a belief that, in spite of signs to the contrary, "feminine energy is . . . in the ascendant in this culture" (*Fast Speaking Woman* 157).

Waldman's woman-centered ethic is linked to her refusal of female stereotypes of Beat "cool." Her most obviously Beat-indebted work is the long poem "Fast Speaking Woman," published in 1975 by City Lights Books in *Fast Speaking Woman: Chants and Essays* (number 33 of the Pocket Poets Series), which came out in a revised edition in 1996. This poem of over thirty pages is based on vibrating incantatory repetitions of the declarative enunciation "I am," an anaphoric proliferation of limitless claims for women listed in the following manner:

> *I'm a shouting woman*
> *I'm a speech woman*
> *I'm an atmosphere woman*
> *I'm an airtight woman*
> *I'm a flesh woman*
> *I'm a flexible woman*
> *I'm a high-heeled woman*
> *I'm a high-style woman* (3)

Fast Speaking Woman reveals a hybridity of historical moment and poetic influences that typifies Waldman's work: the urgent exclamatory poem places her as a second-wave feminist of the "hot" school of Beat generation writing. Fittingly, the poem was, Waldman reveals, for some time in a state of being unfinished, "interminable" ("My Life" 315); it was a work to which she added intermittently and altered in performance to suit the venue (*Fast Speaking Woman* 38–39). The poem is indebted, as is evident from its look on the page and from Waldman's performance of it, to Ginsberg and "Howl"; it, as do many Waldman "list" poems, visibly descends from Beat styles of Whitmanic declamation and prophecy as interpreted and epitomized by Ginsberg. Its signifiers ever exchanging among themselves, it is a poem as seemingly "interminable" in the motion of its lines as in its composition.

The ultimate feminist or woman-centered innovation on Beat poetics in *Fast Speaking Woman* is the work's relationship to its sources. The poem is interwoven with a text of the chants of Maria Sabina. Waldman, "appropriating shamelessly, as poets do," constructed her work intertextually, using Sabina's "refrain"—"'water that cleans as I go,'"—"as a place to pause and shift rhythm and acknowledge the cleansing impulse of the writing" (*Fast Speaking Woman* 37–38). In this, Waldman constructs a poem that speaks with multiple voices, enacting by the pastiche of others its claimed relation to women as a caste. Now, the poet recognizes what she calls the "cultural colonialism" of this practice. Yet, Waldman's collage of Sabina into her Beat poem accomplishes the transfiguration of Beat aesthetics by the infusion of a woman's material discourse that integrates women into the male-exclusive Beat mythoi.

Waldman's masterwork, *Iovis*, published in two volumes with a third in progress, turns from Beat poetics to the multivocal pastichings and typographic calligraphies more typically associated with late high modernist and full-blown postmodern texts. Although the look and substance of the epic seem to deviate from Beat movement writing, the poet fills the numerous texts of *Iovis* with concerns continuous with her earlier works' political and poetics discourses. *Iovis* in some instances seems destined to be sung/performed, as in Waldman's homage to John Cage; it demands action, as in the numerous unan-swered letters that were sent to the poet and which she collaged into her visions; it self-reflexively and self-consciously erects and per-forms the consciousness that it calls "poet." *Iovis* is a long epic poem that instantiates the contemporary poet in an ancient tradition of metanarrative declamation.

The following interview took place on July 3, 2001, in Boulder, Colorado, at Naropa University and was conducted by Ronna C. Johnson and Nancy Grace.

RONNA JOHNSON: Let's start with what you think of the recent recovery work related to women Beat writers.

ANNE WALDMAN: The value is inestimable. It is necessary to bring the female persona, the feminine principle, feminist concerns, the sense of women's struggle as wives, lovers, mothers, artists, breadwinners— as well as taking into account the literal existence of living breathing thinking creative women—into the whole macrocosm that is the Beat literary movement. It thickens the plot. It complicates and gives depth and power to the record, the annals. We need the full story. Certain sites, configurations, occasions excluding women. The female body—while perhaps "liberated sexually" in its ability to experience pleasure—still held one back. The reclamation has to re-figure the sites, the publish-ing and public reading scenes historically. Why did the men willfully exclude them? The writing and the life narratives exist; let's examine them. The relationships between the women—those particular soul-sister camaraderies—exist as much as the relationships to the guys; let's look at that. What was it about the fifties that went so retro, especially after the examples of Gertrude Stein, Hilda Doolittle, and others? The framing of how writers positioned themselves is also important and it's important to keep in mind the differences, the particularities. Some of the women were more adventuresome than others perhaps.

Some were outlaws, or literary outriders. How far did they go in their *dereglement des sens*? Not make assumptions that once again narrow the field, as has been done to some extent with the male writers. The Beat zone is still problematic in easy summation. It's richer than ever now.

NANCY GRACE: How did what you are saying now about the women influence the way you constructed *The Beat Book*?

AW: I was working with pre-existent texts—texts somewhat "out there" in the world—and I was troubled with space constraints. I held primarily with a sense of the official literary parameters, as well as personal favorites: Joanne Kyger, Diane di Prima, and Lenore Kandel. Di Prima and Kyger each command a strong body of work. Lenore less so, but her work had been radical at one time and in a way was quintessentially what we think of as "Beat," with its confessional sexual appetite. Joanne is amazingly herself, resilient and consistent. A maverick person shines through, as in Frank O'Hara's sense of Personism, or the poet as seer. Her magnificent journals resemble the observations and vicissitudes that manifest in *The Pillow Book* of Sei Shonagon. Likewise Diane, the incantatory mode soars. Kyger's and di Prima's writing—because they have worked steadily at it for so many years in so many myriad forms—in a way defies categories. I could also make the case about William Burroughs being a category of his own. These writers all are symbols of themselves, in the Buddhist sense. We reify these categories because of the necessity of being able to articulate the particular time frame, the personal associations and so on. It's easier to say what they are not: not safe, not "academic," not formal. Their lives inform the writing—their sexuality, drug experimentation, travel, Buddhism, relationships all have impact. Some have self-destructed—men and women both.

John Wieners's inclusion in *The Beat Book* was very deliberate. He resides in an interstice of the whole scene. And has a very particular "mad" ear. I made a case for Bob Kaufman with whom the editor was less familiar. I love the surrealist play of the *Abomunist Manifesto*—its very particular peculiar wit. He's an important figure for a number of reasons: his lifestyle, his vow of silence, his ethnicity, his relationship to jazz, his spiritual integrity. There was no room for Herbert Huncke or for Janine Pommy Vega. I especially admire her *Fernando* poems, which would have worked beautifully in this book. Or for Philip Lamantia, which are serious omissions considering this particular grouping.

RJ: Getting Kandel in there was a real coup. She's almost invisible.
AW: It's heartening that she resurfaced in San Francisco a few years back in time for the Book Fair when *Women of the Beat Generation* came out. A recluse now, I gather. What does she remind me of? She's ur-feminist, radical. Her work seems trapped in amber at times. I've also had recent contact with ruth weiss. Her hagiography is fascinating: Jewish, escapee, family in camps, self-proclaimed outrider, lived in Vienna until she was five years old. She's poignant in performance, reminds me of Edith Piaf—her physical stature. I like that she claims another thread, another defining line, on the map. Her work is stronger voiced than on the page. We're talking about a time when a woman might be whisked away to mental institutions, lobotomized through electric shock treatment because of an affair with a person of color, or a lesbian relationship, or for supporting Adlai Stevenson and hating Joe McCarthy.

NG: You mentioned your role as an editor of *Angel Hair*. What was that experience like?
AW: It was edited in collaboration with Lewis Warsh. We started it in 1966. We were mutually respectful of each other's styles, tastes, and I think were learning from each other. Lewis had spent more time on the West coast and knew Spicer's and Duncan's work. I had been at

Bennington and brought the printer I used there for *Silo* into the mix, and my friend from high school, Jonathan Cott, whose line "Angel hair sleeps with a boy in my head" inspired the whole Angel Hair project. I was familiar with the Beat writers, of course, and was becoming more familiar with the work of [John] Ashbery, [James] Schuyler, Barbara Guest. We started this project when we were twenty years old, which shows some kind of perspicacity of mind and energy.

NG: How do you see your place in this tradition of women writers who have edited literary journals? I'm thinking about women like Margaret Anderson and Jean Heap who edited *Little Review* and Harriet Monroe who edited *Poetry*.

AW: *Little Review* and *Poetry* shaped the whole modernist moment, which continues as influence to this day. They were extraordinarily intelligent, prickly editors, really honing in on the work. Not without advisors of course, but they knew they were serving a poetics with great sophistication. Non-provincial. These were not just volunteer church ladies, or do-gooders or idle housewives looking for some hobbies. They were literary visionaries, unique in their time. And being middle class with some wealth and entrepreneurism, they could make these things work. So a strong can-do woman thrust. I wish women like this would get more credit for standing outside their time and place. For me, it's often the "Little Red Hen" syndrome—somebody has got to roll up sleeves, be a witness, and get this stuff done. There was also the idea that you couldn't wait around to be published. And you had an immediate audience of the alternative community of friends and other writers who were all over the country and even abroad. Even if it was only two hundred folks, like *The Floating Bear*, a newsletter sent to friends and avid readers.

I was already editing magazines as a child—we had a home publication that my mother and I produced from Macdougal Street. And then there was *The Stove* I edited from Grace Church School and *The Oblivion* newspaper at Friends Seminary during high school years. Distinctively handprinted *Silo* at Bennington was produced by the printer we also used for *Angel Hair*. Robbe-Grillet was in an earlier issue of *Silo*. I published Robert Kelly, Gerard Malanga, and others. I suppose I was a natural editor—certainly drawn to the job—or enjoyed the power of putting these things together and, of course, deciding who's in, who's out, erring on the side of inclusivity, however. I simply loved projects and, of course, later felt an urgency about getting young writers and the overall outrider community into print.

NG: In that light, then, how do you conceptualize your work as an editor?

AW: Well, all of the above comes into play, but maybe most essential and gratifying is the tactile element. Rolling up your sleeves, hands on the work, getting it organized. Who sits next to whom at the party? [William Carlos] Williams describes the participants in magazines as "bedfellows." Like that. And then getting it around and continuing the dialogue with the writers, more response, more manuscripts. Getting the right cover artist for the project. So poesis—the making.

RJ: What kind of contribution to literature do you think editing makes?

AW: Invaluable. It's like a flank in an army. It's a measure of the "siddhi"—or "accomplishment" in Sanskrit—of a body of writing, how it is selected. What context it's given. How it holds itself up next to others. Standing by the word and the community enough to make copies and flash them out. That's for the magazines. The books: how a writer will move into the world. The maiden or solo voyage. It's wonderful how many prominent writers list their small press pamphlets and self-published volumes as milestones in their careers. I certainly do. The early offerings are introductions, calling cards, show you are committed, serious, have confidence in the work you both write and publish. As a small press editor, it is often an exciting collaboration with the writer. You help writers shape and edit themselves. Arrangement and design are crucial. The launch is exciting, and then you are generating support and feedback for the person. It will help them continue.

NG: Since an editor of a journal helps make a group of writers cohere and become visible, an editor virtually functions as a creator of literary canons, right?

AW: I would agree. The ventures I've been involved with are becoming canons or reflect preexistent canons—like *The Beat Book* or the anthology I co-edited from Naropa: *Disembodied Poetics: Annals of the Jack Kerouac School. Nice to See You,* the tome for Ted Berrigan, was a labor of love and personal archivism—a socio-historical-literary homage that centers around a pivotal figure on the New York scene. It manifests a lot of what needed to be said about the life and times of all of us. My friendship with Ted shaped that book in a very deep way. It was a book he would love.

RJ: Was there a canon of *Angel Hair* writers?

AW: It was a far-reaching amalgam of talents—this canon—you could say it was the canon of our two minds. Most of the writers we published exist in larger canons, or sub-canons. You could say it was a consortional moment.

RJ: When you were coming up as a writer, were you aware of the work of the women writers now associated with Beat?

AW: The writing was available, primarily in small press format. My family frequented the Eighth Street Bookshop and we knew Ted and

Eli Wilentz, and I must have seen some early smatterings. Ted Wilentz published Barbara Moraff, Barbara Guest, Diane di Prima and later my *Giant Night*. Donald Allen's *The New American Poetry* had scant women. I had met Diane earlier at the Albert Hotel in New York, when I was seventeen. She was *in situ* with child, shrines, library, magical accoutrements, an entourage that made me even more curious about her work. *Dinners and Nightmares* from the early sixties is a classic. Hip, sophisticated, projective, great details from inside her life. I heard Lenore Kandel at the Berkeley Poetry Conference in 1965 and liked her gutsy delivery, and met Joanne Kyger first in 1967 when I visited her in California and was reading her mytho-poems in *The Tapestry and the Web*. I was already corresponding by then with Philip Whalen who was close to Joanne. By 1966 I'd been hired by the newly envisioned Poetry Project at St. Mark's and became director in 1968. As a curator you naturally stayed in touch with the work of the people you were inviting to read and perform.

Bonnie Frazer was living at Cherry Valley, married to Ray Bremser. She'd written *Troia*, which is an extraordinarily brave book. Passionate, heartbreaking. She's a natural writer I think. We became close in Cherry Valley—our families knew each other. She and I went to the Zen Center in Sharon Springs; she was practicing shamata meditation. Here we were "back to the land" for a brief spell. We're in Cherry Valley—a kind of red-neck bohemian scene, an odd syncretism—in upstate New York—but then her life took a different turn. She was more of the eccentric farm housewife. Her life had been hard with Ray. Later, I saw her as something out of Grant Wood—pioneer earth mother, somber, deep, repressed even, a slower clock, farm lady with her pitchfork out there in the dirt. She always has had a philosophical/melancholic cast of mind. She wasn't ready to step out as a writer and have a career and perform, but she wanted to have her work there.

NG: So how do you define the term "beat"?

AW: Well, it's beatitude, beatific, being blessed because you actually get outside your neurotic head and have a kind of satori or epiphany about your own existence in the larger maelstrom. You might therefore be grateful because you see how precious your imagination and a life in writing is.

I never wanted to be a man although I would have liked the presumed safety or armour that identity engenders—but that's only metaphorically skin deep. I never envied a man for his so-called privilege, although I admit to a lot of masculine energy or "skillful means," which is the Buddhist notion of what the masculine principle is capable of, that is, making things happen. Navigating the larger constructs. But as so-called Beat you find yourself inside the sacred life, the sacred conversation, the action, the most interesting game in town. It's beat in the Buddhist sense of being exhausted with samsara, the endless meat wheel of suffering—you're exhausted with phenomenal reality and your own habitually-conditioned patterned life. You have a certain insight. You just let go in a way. You see through the hype, the guys and their trips, the come-ons, the put-downs, the endless condescension, and you are up for the challenge. I came up a bit later and maybe I could meet the challenge head on. In the early days, I was constantly fending off men, my own college teachers. Luckily I had a few male—and female—soulmates and lovers. There was parity. In my early salon at 33 St. Mark's Place, I was surrounded by the guys.

And you're just beat anyway, whatever your literary school. You are this human bag of bones, "gone beyond gone" as they say in the Paramita Sutra, and it's the moment when there's a gap and the mind can open up and spontaneous thought and language can occur and you're re-charged. You're so world-weary that actually there's an opening or shift in your experience—fresh air gets in—so instead of going toward nihilism or eternalism, it's somewhere between the two. But it's complex, the parrying around the term "beat." How important is it to come up with a reifying definition? I like that you can't nail the word down or compartmentalize it. I'm also always drawn to the sense of "beatitude" because of the image from old Italian paintings of *sacre conversatione.* A poetics of inquiry. I speak with Diane and Joanne about our work, our friends' personalities, cultural history, politics global and local, loss, heartbreak, our health, financial picture, work, and so on. It's been going on for centuries, the conversation between women.

So I define Beat in my own way because I need a working definition that applies to my own work. And being a kind of cultural historian in that I'm asked to reference these things, I would say also that there's a frame within the frame: I grew up with jazz. I was growing up on Macdougal Street; it was all around me. Then there are the tropes— the image of bongo drums, chianti bottles, black turtlenecks—those tired but "minute particulars" of the Beat tropes, and because we live in this representational culture of artifacts, you have to work with those as well. These are the associations, and as we see things commercialized, you have to deconstruct those tropes or allow them to enter, whether it's the turtleneck or the beret. At least it's an alternative to the man in the gray flannel suit and to the fifties housewife with her deodorant spray. So you constantly have to use those, but again it's a lot of work to contextualize them.

RJ: You were a young woman in the sixties, and the feminist movement was there and the anti-war movement.
AW: Right. That's absolutely true, and I was involved with both of those—more so the anti-war movement. But it was the beginning of all that, and being a person who had grown up in Greenwich Village there was a certain artistic privilege and expectation. I sat on Leadbelly's knee. And the lineage through my own mother was a weighty legacy

to carry around. That must have given me strength. [I] felt bohemian, and "bohemian" is the word I would use because of my parents. My father had met Allen in the fifties. Allen and I had spoken on the phone when I was at Bennington in the early sixties, I met him in Berkeley in 1966. Sure I wore a lot of black. I met Thelonius Monk in high school. It was an ethic, surely, that appealed to me. My friends were somewhat Beat. John Hersey's son carried around a copy of *Naked Lunch* in a guitar case. I was close to David Amram early on and going around to parties and concerts and events with him. Allen—because of our mutual connection to dharma and politics—and later than this, was the bigger link. And by 1974 when we founded the Jack Kerouac School, with Diane's help, we were already in a kind of death-do-us-part mode around this huge all-consuming visionary undertaking which was the poetics program at Naropa. So my association with him and getting published by Lawrence Ferlinghetti's City Lights made me a qualified Beat. Of course, by then I knew Joanne, I knew Philip, Gary Snyder, Gregory Corso, everyone—although I never met Kerouac, missing my chance to go along with Ted Berrigan for his *Paris Review* interview— and was also very much affiliated with the second and a half generation of the New York school as well, which is a whole other history. Why is the concept "beat" so important? There seems to be so much invested in this term.

RJ: Does "beat," then, have any importance for the women writers?
AW: Within the women's psyches you probably had the situation of not resisting those modes and models yet still trying to discover a way beyond the onus of the patriarchy and male dominance. So there may have been acting out, role playing, trying to be more "hip" and liberated than they felt. I'm always delighted when I think about the camaraderie between men as being one positive aspect of that scene because that was a trope out of the army or workplace—real guys

sharing the struggle—that they didn't have together in those particular zones. They had missed out on that so had to invent it for themselves. Allen Ginsberg had enormous capacity for generosity and empathy—a blind spot perhaps early on for recognizing talents in various women.

NG: What's the place of memoir in the work of the women Beat writers, including your own work?

AW: I would say the memoir, which has become an accepted, high genre, is one of immense possibilities, the way you work with cross genres and documentation. My own work is more around poetics, but there's a lot of autobiographical material in there, and memoir too. There could be more, if I had more time, more stories to tell. And then memoir can be so imaginative. There are so many of these smarmy memoirs, but [writing a memoir] isn't therapy. Yes, it does help you to tell these stories, but it's not a self-help reality. So that should be distinguished. You have to broaden the definition of the writing because even within the guys there was a kind of cross—the prose, the dream work of Kerouac, Burroughs's dream journal, you have Burroughs's letters, cut-up, and the culture, because this definition between fiction and poetry is not addressing [their work]. I wanted to say also that *Dinners and Nightmares*, the way di Prima is working with genre, is radical. Just the way the thing looks on the page and the stream of consciousness and the tracking of the grammar and the punctuation have to be looked at.

RJ: Would you call *Fast Speaking Woman* a Beat work?

AW: Yes, the litany. I consider it a performance piece. I feel it's a female proclamation, reclaiming the body, and also being Everywoman. It's in a lineage with Christopher Smart, Walt Whitman, and Allen. Do you know the story of Lawrence Ferlinghetti coming up at the end of a reading of that poem in '73 or '74 in San Francisco? I think Allen and I were doing a Buddhist benefit, and Lawrence rushed up and said, "I gotta see that poem. I want to publish it." That's how it happened. Had he not been there at that performance, I don't know. But *Fast Speaking Woman* was written in '73 or '74, and I wasn't that interested in it on the page, even though it was fine on the page, and there was the Maria Sabina recording. And then Lawrence wanted to take this photograph of me for the cover, you know, this whole thing, the manifestation of *woman*.

RJ: I see that as feminist, though, collaging and working with the Maria Sabina text; you're creating a female lineage in that poem.
AW: I agree.

RJ: You also wrote it on the run, is that right?
AW: Right. I was traveling in South America, I was writing it on planes. It was a road piece. I also thought of it as something that I can add to.

NG: Is that a sort of "kinetic aesthetic" then?
AW: Well, it has lots to do with performance and getting up and not starting at the beginning. The sense of the narrative as A to Z just wasn't interesting in performance. I wanted something that was fluid, and the very simple anaphoria/litany you can do that with. You can jump around. There are certain pieces that I can move within and repeat and get on a riff here and a roll there. So it was the performing and extending the sense of narrative and delineation of time. I'm not very good with memorization either, but with *Fast Speaking Woman* I can trust myself sometimes, and it's easy. And I loved the time when Allen and I were backstage with the Dylan show, the Rolling Thunder tour [1975–76], with Mohammed Ali, and he had these nine body guards in their pastel suits, and Dylan introduced me as a woman poet, and Ali says immediately, "Well, let's hear some poetry!" I'm on the spot and we were leaving the room, the performance is ready to start, and I'm going

"I'm the woman walking down the backstage with Ali." I mean it was
terrifying!

RJ: And he was a master of rap!
AW: I know! That to me was one of the highlights of my life as "fast
speaking woman!" You couldn't get better than that. And these beautiful guys with their pastel suits, this whole entourage, and I was the
only woman in the room.

RJ: But you're often the only woman in the room.
AW: Less and less so, because there are many more women poets now.

NG: What was that like, though—for you to develop and mature as
a woman poet?
AW: Well, at least Bennington was a woman's college, and although
the teachers were male, they were models of active writers, which is
one of the credos here at Naropa; everyone is an active writer. If I'd
gone on to graduate school, that was a possibility. But it seemed like
the last thing to do. There were certain lifestyle decisions that have to
do with the work, since you were asking about the work. You know,
we had a real salon on St. Mark's Place. That became more fluid and
more women started to enter. I also had some connection with Diane
Wakoski, Carol Bergé, and these women were also ancillary to,
although not categorized with, the Beats. I also had a voice in designing
the curriculum for the Church. There's also my mother's generation,
[people like] Jean Boudin. There was also a little nexus around the
New School that took classes with Frank O'Hara and Kenneth Koch,
so there were women. In fact, Hannah Weiner was in those classes;
Bernadette Mayer and my mother were in them. Patti Smith was in a
class at the New School!

RJ: The art scene of the sixties was more communal, the hierarchies were collapsing, it was tribal. So what you're saying fits with the era. What about people of color in these movements? Who was around?
AW: Lorenzo [Thomas] was around. David Henderson. The Umbra Group, because they were doing work at St. Mark's. I'd say Lorenzo was my closest friend. I'd also met Al Young and Larry Neal. I was aware of them, but if you were just creaking out your magazine, there were these little nexuses—multiple spaces. There were also readings at the Church in the late sixties, early seventies; I intersected with Sonia Sanchez and Nikki Giovanni. We were in a kind of avant-garde poetry world with readings starting to happen.

NG: Could we backtrack a little bit and discuss the modernists?
AW: Okay! The problematics of the modernists!

NG: You've often mentioned Stein in your earlier interviews, so I'm curious about how Stein has influenced you.
AW: I think of her as being a catalyst, and, in fact, her relationship with art and her art inform my work to a certain extent. She bought art and supported others. So there was a kind of romanticism. Well, you know, you speak of the icons of the Beats, there's a kind of icon style of Stein.
    Then the liberating quality of Stein's work that you couldn't define in terms of these categories of genre. Her egoless quality has to do with the way she seems to track her thinking—but it's not self-centered as such. In fact, it's like the place where in Buddhist practice "thinking" is just "thinking," whether you have the urge to go kill someone or travel to China or eat a gustatory meal—you can be all over the place, but it's not one thing over the other. Her sentences aren't showcases for character or emotion particularly. It's unemotional as such, and the thrust is towards the words as notes, as things, as paint swatches, as landscapes, as blocks of time that are convoluted in a way. Surprise all the

time. And there are her personal codes, jokes, and references that you start to pick up but they aren't identity politics.

RJ: Nancy keeps telling me that *Marriage: A Sentence* is a very Steinian work.

AW: Absolutely. The obsession with the sentence, what is prose, what is poetry, what is the dynamic between the two. There's also something about the Buddhism in Stein. It's like looking down at a landscape from a plane and from a distance everything is equaled. So even the value of the words, even the words that semantically, grammatically, aren't doing their usual job—nouns become verbs, you foreground prepositions, so, for example, "a little of Pauline." They set up funny contradictions. I read her Buddhistically because although she was egoistic and egotistical, you never feel with her writing that there's ego in the play of the language. So that drew me to her.

RJ: What about *Iovis*? That strikes me too as a return to modernism, or perhaps postmodern modernism, a real collage and melange of styles and discourses and textures and voices.

AW: I really wanted to take on the epic. By definition, the epic is a male form, but who knows, so many of these epics were first in oral form. Which is why Sabina's text is so important to me because you got a hint of the woman shaman, the woman storyteller, the woman scribe, and when you look into indigenous cultures, women are holding those roles. But I felt I had to reconfigure and deal with my ancestors, and I had to also take on these wars, and thinking of a form for this. It had to be rhizomic, montage. And the epic was a way to tell a story, although it was also metanarrative. The *Iovis* project demands research, the attention of my troubled psyche, imagined personae, dreams, the war machine, history, the tracking of certain planets [Mars] and other celestial bodies—space stations, birds. And some playful tasks in the composition with numerology, recurring themes. Hints and murmurs of resident leit motifs, *roman a clef* doings. References to Roman military wiles as resonant with U.S. government machinations. Quite layered. The recent sections—one from a trip to Vietnam in 2000 and another reflecting the events of the last year entitled "War Crime" [2002] have a kind of intensity that is very demanding emotionally. There's also a section in *Iovis* where I rewrite Heraklitos. This is once again an ironic bow to Charles Olson or the whole Greek inclination of epic. There's a feminist rant in the works, all posited as questions. Does doubt exist? There are Buddhist ceremonies where you cut off the head of Doubt. I want my epic *Iovis* to soar and be told. And I want it to be ritualistic—to save myself. Does that make sense? Should writing be any less?

RJ: You're talking about techniques that have been shaped by your spiritual practices?

AW: I guess it's a more Tantric view—that I work with color, sense perception, objects/images in the mind that become pregnant with power that release that power, that you want some kind of efficacy there that helps, magnetizes, destroys mind-sets. Through the language as well. That you can penetrate fixation, your own and others. So this is a Tibetan Buddhist practice, visualizing yourself as the deity.

RJ: You really have ranged widely in form as an artist moving through a lot of different influences. You sometimes call yourself a second-generation New York school poet. How do your poems fit in that movement?

AW: Well, some do, like "How the Sestina (Yawn) Works," or even "Revolution" or even others. A lot of people of my generation are really interesting hybrids.

RJ: In addition to the New York school, then, what features of your writing, and that of the writing by women Beats, set the work apart as Beat?

AW: Beat in the writing? Honesty, "istorin"—to find out for one's self, in Charles Olson's sense—long breath lines, composition by field, lyrical wit, gush, influence of jazz strains, questioning authority, paranoia, attention to detail, dream, memory, travel, eschewing traditional form and grammar, passion of language, response to relationship, frankness on sexual matters, general candor of mind, tracking wild mind. Anaphora. The list could go on and on.

As for the writing being specifically female, the body as a site for language, more emotive stream of consciousness, vulnerability. Well, I've spoken a bit about the memoir as a genre of women associated with the Beat movement, that the women were the scribes, the keepers of the records, more straightforward in that regard than the men. And initially the diary is hidden, secret, like the pillow books of the Japanese courtesans. Perhaps you have to initially keep the journal from the male gaze until you have mounted the offense and recaptured the history for yourself. And I think of Kyger's *The Japan and India Journals*, which really examines a relationship occurring in a very constricted— though exotic—part of the world. That book holds the measure of the woman against the collective "guys." She has her journal as her ear— the things she is either too startled or too stunned or too humble to blurt out, say, as Allen might. The list of Gary's admonitions at the end is classic. I had a list like that from a former partner. Was it common for men to write down their pros and cons about the women and leave these tallies around for the women conveniently to discover? How cowardly! In any case, the memoir may be a brave form if it transcends self-pity and egotism. Bonnie Frazer's *Troia* is heart-wrenching, tough. The book is a kind of salvation for the indignity and loss she suffers. It's a torqued testament, surely, to the man [Ray Bremser].

Both of Diane's memoirs examine her and the scene with great humanity. In the latter book she is generous to the men. But she tells it her way. I am sure the account of the relationship with LeRoi [Jones] is very different from a version he would proffer. Hettie's *How I Became Hettie Jones*, Joyce's *Minor Characters*—these are invaluable sociological texts; they locate the person in their time, they take on detail that's telling, intimate, and coded.

RJ: Do those qualities manifest themselves in your work?
AW: As you know I resist categories. I never want to find "my own voice" as such. The possibilities are wildly various and my mind is of many minds, diverse imaginations, and sounds. And the *Iovis* project is a vast "conglomeration of tendencies" of rhizomic possibility. Within it are "hints and murmurs"—a phrase of William Burroughs's—from all quarters. A rhizome is an underground system. Instead of growing down, as roots do, rhizomes grow horizontally. Roots may grow from the rhizome as may leaves, flowers and other stems. So this eight-hundred-page epic is endlessly exploratory, inculcating a range of language and talk and vision and song. I am telling my story, I am telling all our stories which revolve around war and patriarchy. You might view *The New American Poetry*, which includes the Beat generation, with this kind of paradigm in mind as well. Many flowerings/hybrids off the stem of the writing being the experience. It's all working right then, although you might take it further.

On the other hand, around the disclaimer of voice, my work is recognizable and strongly individualized in performance. And it's my body out there and the particular patterns of my mind-grammar and psycho-physical system. I'm the timeless hag or girl or daughter or wife or mother or great-grandmother or whore or whatever. And the sounds that come out of me are sprung from words and actualized at the energy-height of the room, or space or zone. The role of priestess comes to mind—mad Cassandra that no one will listen to? That kind of thing. Seer. It sounds corny, but it's actually very real and not without humor and dramatization. I like to shift the modal structures around. "I am throwing the words around," I sing somewhere. More and more, I am writing pieces that include parts for others—dancers, musicians, other voices. Some of this inspiration comes out of the performance work I've been doing with the John Cage performances and the Gertrude Stein Players in Boulder, a loose confederation of writers, performers, Naropa students that materialized out of classes I was teaching during the Summer Writing Program.

Themes are important to the Beat trope, surely. And the female Beat trope has to do with themes of liberation, sexualization, or a fierce claim on the body away from the patriarchy and commodification. Personal visions play in here, dreams, accounts of moments of heightened awareness, though not the singular epiphany—sometimes it's all epiphany—themes of female outrage, injustice, which climax in rants against Jesse Helms, John Ashcroft, and others. But more important is the form of the content: cross-genre, spontaneity, confession, hypnogogic states, free-associating, influence of jazz, anaphoric structure, cut-up. There's also research, study involved with what I do. Documentary/investigative poetics.

So I would say I carry certain distinctions and affinities within the Beat matrix, of course. And guilt by association, and being part of a consociational milieu. And all the work with Allen, and the political and Buddhist thrusts, and the friendships with Philip Whalen, Gregory Corso, William Burroughs. The intersections with Diane, Joanne, Helen Adam, Janine and even more recently ruth weiss are all important. The shared reality and the sense of having lived through some of the same strange times and thus informing and responding with passion.

Notes

"Mapping Women Writers of the Beat Generation"

1. Quoted in Peabody 1.
2. Feminist criticism that recovers unrecognized women writers has consolidated a body of work whose importance to literary history is now seen as axiomatic, while at the time of its recovery the work seemed obscure. A limited survey of recent research shows that women Beat writers share the status of other twentieth-century women writers who have been marginalized in their heyday (Shari Benstock on women artists in modernist Paris); recognized in their time but written out of narratives of literary history (Linda Kinnahan on modernist female heirs of Williams); under-recognized throughout the prevalence of their artistic cohort (Ann Vickery on Language school poets); elided because they are female (Rachel Blau DuPlessis, Ellen G. Friedman and Miriam Fuchs); misread and undervalued because their narratives departed from aesthetics and mythoi of those of men of their immediate context and cohort or school (Sandra M. Gilbert and Susan Gubar); problematically conflated with and so subsumed by understandings of postmodernism (DuPlessis, Marianne DeKoven, Teresa de Lauretis, Diana Fuss). Feminist criticism has integrated into literary canons "lost" women writers and their texts as essential components, an eventuality this study intends for women Beat writers.
3. Usage of "Beat" and "beat" in this essay is as follows: "Beat" modifies movement, generation, aesthetics, poetics, literature, and so on, indicating the historical era of the counterculture and its expressions; "beat," the signifier from which the

279

movement was given its name by Jack Kerouac in 1948 ("Origins" 362), is postwar bohemian slang for a state of mind or being that is related to hip and hipsters and that has numerous manifestations and interpretations.

4. This sound bite was reverentially coined by Paul Krassner, and seized on by Beat writers and mainstream media alike, at the 1982 conference at the Naropa Institute to celebrate the twenty-fifth anniversary of the publication of *On the Road*. See Ronna C. Johnson, "Celebrating."

5. See Johnson and Grace for an initial discussion of the three generations of women Beat writers.

6. A survey of Johnson and Grace, the Peabody and Knight anthologies, and Charters ("Anne Waldman") illustrates that there is some disagreement about which women writers should be included in the lists of the Beat movement.

7. For example: Lenore Kandel studied at Los Angeles City College and the New School for Social Research in New York (Charters, *The Beats* 271); Joanne Kyger attended the University of California at Santa Barbara and was one unit short of an undergraduate degree (ibid. 325); Elise Cowen attended Barnard College, where she and Joyce Johnson met (Johnson, *Minor Characters*); Diane di Prima studied for a year and a half at Swarthmore College (*Pieces* 198); Hettie Jones graduated from Mary Washington, the woman's college at the University of Virginia (*How I Became Hettie Jones* 10); Joyce Johnson was one gym class shy of graduating from Barnard College (*Minor Characters*); Brenda Frazer attended Sweet Briar College (Peabody 226). Ann Charters earned a Ph.D. in English literature from Columbia University.

8. See the following commentators, who blame Joan for her own murder: in Howard Brookner's interview with Allen Ginsberg, Ginsberg claims that Joan "challenged him [Burroughs] into it [the shooting], led him into it . . . us[ed] him to get her off the earth because she was in a great deal of pain"; Burroughs himself wrote to Ginsberg in 1995 that his killing of Joan, or "Joan's death" as he calls it, occurred "as if the brain *drew* the bullet toward it . . ." (Harris 263).

9. Beat memoris also include Herbert Huncke, *The Evening Sky Turned Crimson* (Cherry Valley, NY: Cherry Valley Editions, 1980); Harold Norse, *Beat Hotel* (San Diego: Atticus, 1983); and Broyard.

"Interviewing Women Beat Writers"

1. Interviews with women Beat writers include the following:

Diane di Prima: "Interview with Diane di Prima," Anne Waldman, *Rocky Ledge* 7 (Feb.– Mar. 1981): 35–49; "Diane di Prima Interview," Joseph Matheny, 28 Oct. 1999 http://www.imedea.com/works/diprima.html; "Diane di Prima," David Meltzer, in *San Francisco Beat: Talking to the Poets*, ed. David Meltzer (San Francisco: City Lights Books, 2001) 1–21.

Anne Waldman: "Vow to Poetry: Anne Waldman Interview," Randy Roark, in Waldman and Schelling, 33–67; Waldman's *Vow to Poetry* (2001) contains four previously published interviews.

Joanne Kyger: "Particularizing People's Lives: An Interview with Joanne Kyger," Linda Russo, *Jacket* 11, 2000 http://www.jacket.zip. com.au/jacket11/kyger-iv-by-russo.html; Interview, David Chadwick, 29 Sept. 1995, in *Crooked Cucumber* http://www.cuke.com/interviews/kyger.html; "Joanne Kyger," David Meltzer, in Meltzer 122–32.

2. Interviews with male Beat writers include, but are not limited to, the following:

Multiple authors: *Beat Writers at Work*, a collection of *Paris Review* interviews, ed. George Plimpton (New York: Random, 1999; includes only male authors); *San Francisco Beat: Talking to the Poets* (includes only two women).

Allen Ginsberg: *Spontaneous Mind: Selected Interviews 1958–1996*, ed. David Carter (New York: HarperCollins, 2001).

William Burroughs: *Conversations with William S. Burroughs*, ed. Allen Hibbard (Jackson: UP of Mississippi, 1999); *Burroughs Live: The Collected Interviews of William S. Burroughs, 1960–1997*, ed. Sylvère Lotringer (Los Angeles, CA: Semiotexte/Smart Art, 2000).

Gary Snyder: *The Real Work: Interviews & Talks, 1964–1979*, ed. Wm. Scott McLean (New York : New Directions, 1980).

3. E-mail correspondence from Tony Moffeit to Nancy Grace, 4 Nov. 2002.

Works Cited

Adam, Helen. *San Francisco's Burning: A Ballad Opera*. San Francisco: Oannes Press, 1964. New York: Hanging Loose, 1985.

Allen, Donald, ed. *The New American Poetry*. New York: Grove, 1960.

Benstock, Shari. *Women of the Left Bank: Paris 1900–1940*. Austin: U of Texas P, 1986.

Bergé, Carol, Barbara Moraff, Rochelle Owens, and Diane Wakoski. *Four Young Lady Poets*. New York: Totem/Corinth, 1962.

Berkson, Bill. "Joanne Kyger." Charters, *The Beats*. 324–28.

Breines, Wini. *Young, White, and Miserable: Growing Up Female in the Fifties*. Boston: Beacon, 1992.

Bremser, Bonnie. *Troia: Mexican Memoirs*. New York: Croton Press, 1969.

Brookner, Howard, dir. *Burroughs: The Movie*. Citifilmworks, 1983.

Broyard, Anatole. *When Kafka Was the Rage: A Greenwich Village Memoir*. New York: Random, 1993.

Cassady, Carolyn. *Off the Road: My Years with Cassady, Kerouac, and Ginsberg*. New York: Penguin, 1990.

Charters, Ann. "Anne Waldman." Charters, *The Beats*. 528–33.

———. *Beat Down to Your Soul: What Was the Beat Generation?* New York: Viking Penguin, 2001.

———. *Beats and Company: A Portrait of a Literary Generation*. Garden City, NY: Doubleday, 1986.

———, ed. *The Beats: Literary Bohemians in Postwar America*. Detroit: Gale, 1983. Vol. 16 of *The Dictionary of Literary Biography*.

283

———. *Bibliography of Works by Jack Kerouac.* 1967. Rev. ed. New York: Phoenix, 1975.

———, ed. *Jack Kerouac: Selected Letters 1940–1956.* New York: Viking, 1995.

———, ed. *Jack Kerouac: Selected Letters 1957–1969.* New York: Viking, 1999.

———. *Kerouac: A Biography.* San Francisco: Straight Arrow Books, 1973.

———, ed. *The Portable Beat Reader.* New York: Penguin, 1992.

———, ed. *The Sixties.* New York: Viking, 2003.

———, ed. *The Story and Its Writer.* 2nd ed. New York: St. Martin's, 1987.

Coyote, Peter. *Sleeping Where I Fall.* Washington, DC: Counterpoint, 1998.

Cruse, Harold. *The Crisis of the Negro Intellectual.* New York: Morrow, 1967.

Damon, Maria. "Victors of Catastrophe: Beat Occlusions." *Beat Culture and the New America, 1950–1965.* Ed. Lisa Phillips. New York: Whitney Museum of American Art, 1996. 141–49.

de Certeau, Michel. *The Practice of Everyday Life.* Trans. Steven Rendell. Berkeley: U of California P, 1984.

de Lauretis, Teresa. *Alice Doesn't: Feminism, Semiotics, Literature.* Bloomington: Indiana UP, 1984.

———. *The Technologies of Gender: Essays on Theory, Film, and Fiction.* Bloomington: Indiana UP, 1987.

DeKoven, Marianne. "Male Signature, Female Aesthetic: The Gender Politics of Experimental Writing." Friedman and Fuchs 72–81.

Deleuze, Gilles, and Felix Guattari. "What Is a Minor Literature?" Trans. Dana Polan. *Out There: Marginalization and Contemporary Culture.* Ed. Russell Ferguson et al. Cambridge: MIT P, 1990. 49–59.

di Prima, Diane. *The Calculus of Variation.* San Francisco: City Lights, 1972.

———. *Dinners and Nightmares.* 1961. New York: Corinth Books, 1974. Expanded ed. San Francisco: Last Gasp Press, 1998.

———. *Loba.* Parts 1–16, Books 1 and 2. New York: Penguin, 1998.

———. *Memoirs of a Beatnik.* New York: Olympia, 1969. San Francisco: Last Gasp Press, 1988.

———. *Pieces of a Song: Selected Poems.* San Francisco: City Lights, 1990.

———. *Recollections of My Life as a Woman: The New York Years.* New York: Viking, 2001.

———. *Revolutionary Letters.* 1971. 3rd ed. San Francisco: City Lights, 1974.

———. *This Kind of Bird Flies Backwards.* New York: Aardvark Press, 1957. New York: Paper Book Gallery, 1963.

di Prima, Diane, and LeRoi Jones, eds. *The Floating Bear: A Newsletter, Numbers 1–37, 1961–1969.* La Jolla, CA: Laurence McGilvery, 1973.

Douglas, Ann. "Strange Lives, Chosen Lives: The Beat Art of Joyce Johnson." Johnson, *Minor Characters* xiii–xxix.

DuPlessis, Rachel Blau. *The Pink Guitar: Writing as Feminist Practice.* New York: Routledge, 1990.

Dworkin, Andrea. *Intercourse.* New York: Free, 1987.

Ehrenreich, Barbara. *The Hearts of Men.* New York: Anchor, 1983.

Ellingham, Lewis, and Kevin Killian. *Poet Be Like God: Jack Spicer and the San Francisco Renaissance.* Hanover, NH, and London: Wesleyan UP, 1998.

Felski, Rita. *Beyond Feminist Aesthetics: Feminist Literature and Social Change.* Cambridge: Harvard UP, 1989.

French, Warren. *The San Francisco Renaissance.* New York: Twayne, 1991.

Friedan, Betty. *The Feminine Mystique.* New York: Norton, 1963.

Friedman, Ellen G., and Miriam Fuchs, eds. *Breaking the Sequence: Women's Experimental Fiction.* Princeton, NJ: Princeton UP, 1989.

Fuss, Diana. *Essentially Speaking: Feminism, Nature, and Difference.* New York: Routledge, 1989.

Gaddis, William. *The Recognitions.* New York: Viking, 1955.

Geneson, Paul. "The Real Work: Interview with Gary Snyder." *Ohio Review* 18:3 (1977). 76–105. Rpt. in *The Real Work: Interviews and Talks 1964–1979.* Ed. Wm. Scott McLean. New York: New Directions, 1980. 58–92.

Gilbert, Sandra M., and Susan Gubar. *The Madwoman in the Attic: The Woman Writer and the Nineteenth-Century Literary Imagination.* New Haven: Yale UP, 1979.

Gilman, Charlotte Perkins. *Women and Economics: A Study of the Economic Relation Between Men and Women as a Factor in Social Evolution.* Boston: Small, Maynard, 1898. New York: Harper, 1966.

Ginsberg, Allen. *Collected Poems 1947–1980.* New York: Harper, 1984.

———. *Howl.* Ed. Barry Miles. New York: HarperCollins, 1995.

———. *Howl and Other Poems.* San Francisco: City Lights, 1956.

Gitlin, Todd. *The Sixties: Years of Hope, Days of Rage.* New York: Bantam, 1987.

Grace, Nancy M. "ruth weiss's *DESERT JOURNAL:* A Modern-Beat-Pomo Performance." *Reconstructing the Beats.* Ed. Jennie Skerl. New York: Palgrave, 2004.

———. "Snapshots, Sand Paintings, and Celluloid: Formal Considerations in the Life Writing of Women Writers from the Beat Generation." Johnson and Grace 141–77.

———. "Women of the Beat Generation: Conversations with Joyce Johnson and Hettie Jones." *Artful Dodge* 36/37 (1999): 106–33.

Grele, Ronald J. *Envelopes of Sound.* New York: Praeger, 1991.

Gruen, John. *The New Bohemia.* Chicago, IL: a cappella, 1966.

Harris, Oliver, ed. *The Letters of William S. Burroughs 1945–1959.* New York: Penguin, 1993.

Haverty Kerouac, Joan. *Nobody's Wife: The Smart Aleck and the King of the Beats.* Berkeley, CA: Creative Arts Books, 2000.

Heilbrun, Carolyn. *Writing a Woman's Life.* New York: Ballantine, 1988.

Hicks, Emily D. *Border Writing: The Multidimensional Text.* Theory and Hist. of Lit. 80. Minneapolis: U of Minnesota P, 1991.

Hoffman, Abbie. *Revolution for the Hell of It*. New York: Dial, 1968.

Holmes, John Clellon. *Go*. New York: Scribner's, 1952. Rev. ed. New York: New American Lib., 1980.

———. "The Philosophy of the Beat Generation." *Esquire* Feb. 1958: 35-38. Rpt. in *Nothing More to Declare*. New York: Dutton, 1967. 116–26.

———. "This Is the Beat Generation." *New York Times Magazine*. 16 Nov. 1952: 10, 19–20, 22.

Hutcheon, Linda. *A Poetics of Postmodernism: History, Theory, Fiction*. New York: Routledge, 1988.

Johnson, Joyce. *Bad Connections*. New York: Putnam, 1978.

———. *Come and Join the Dance*. New York: Atheneum, 1962.

———. *In the Night Café*. New York: Dutton, 1989.

———. *Minor Characters: A Young Woman's Coming-of-Age in the Beat Orbit of Jack Kerouac*. New York: Penguin, 1999.

———. *What Lisa Knew: The Truths and Lies of the Steinberg Case*. New York: Kensington, 1990.

Johnson, Joyce, and Jack Kerouac. *Door Wide Open: A Beat Love Affair in Letters, 1957–1958*. New York: Viking, 2000.

Johnson, Ronna C. " 'And then she went': Beat Departures and Feminine Transgressions in Joyce Johnson's *Come and Join the Dance*." Johnson and Grace 69–95.

———. "Celebrating Jack Kerouac and the Beats." *Boston Globe* 12 Aug. 1982: 57–58.

———. "Lenore Kandel's *The Love Book*: Psychedelic Poetics, Cosmic Erotica, and Sexual Politics in the Midsixties Counterculture." *Reconstructing the Beats*. Ed. Jennie Skerl. New York: Palgrave, 2004.

Johnson, Ronna C., and Nancy M. Grace, eds. *Girls Who Wore Black: Women Writing the Beat Generation*. New Brunswick, NJ: Rutgers UP, 2002.

Jones, Hettie., ed. *Aliens at the Border: The Writing Workshop, Bedford Hills Correctional Facility*. New York: Segue Books, 1997.

———. *All Told*. New York: Hanging Loose, 2003.

———. *Big Star Fallin' Mamma: Five Women in Black Music*. 1976. New York: Viking, 1995.

———. *Drive*. New York: Hanging Loose, 1998.

———. *Having Been Her*. New York: Number Press, 1981.

———. *How I Became Hettie Jones*. New York: Penguin, 1990.

———. *I Hate to Talk About Your Mother: A Novel*. New York: Delacorte, 1980.

———. "This Time It Was Different at the Airport." *Art Against Apartheid: Works for Freedom*. *Ikon Second Series* 5/6 (Winter/Summer 1986): 150–53.

Jones, LeRoi. "The Beat Generation." Correspondence. *Partisan Review* (Summer 1958): 472–73.

———. *Dutchman and The Slave*. New York: Morrow, 1964.

Kandel, Lenore. *The Love Book*. San Francisco: Stolen Paper Review Editions, 1966.

Kerouac, Jack. *The Dharma Bums*. New York: Viking, 1958.

———. *Doctor Sax : Faust Part Three*. New York: Grove, 1959.

———. "Essentials of Spontaneous Prose." *Black Mountain Review* 7 (Autumn 1957): 226–28, 230–37.

———. *On the Road*. 1957. New York: Viking, 1991.

———. "The Origins of the Beat Generation." 1959. *On the Road*. Ed. Scott Donaldson. The Viking Critical Lib. New York: Penguin, 1979. 357–67.

———. *The Subterraneans*. 1958. New York: Grove, 1981.

———. *Visions of Cody*. New York: McGraw-Hill, 1972.

Kinnahan, Linda. *Poetics of the Feminine: Authority and Literary Tradition in William Carlos Williams, Mina Loy, Denise Levertov, and Kathleen Fraser*. Cambridge, UK: Cambridge UP, 1994.

Knight, Brenda. *Women of the Beat Generation: The Writers, Artists and Muses at the Heart of a Revolution*. Berkeley, CA: Conari Press, 1996.

Kovic, Ron. *Born on the Fourth of July*. New York: McGraw-Hill, 1976.

Kristeva, Julia. "Oscillation Between Power and Denial." Interview. Trans. Marilyn A. August. *New French Feminisms*. Ed. Elaine Marks and Isabelle de Courtivron. New York: Schocken, 1981. 165–67.

Kyger, Joanne. *Again: Poems 1989–2000*. Albuquerque: La Alameda Press, 2001.

———. *As Ever: Selected Poems*. New York: Penguin, 2002.

———. *The Japan and India Journals 1960–1964*. Bolinas, CA: Tombouctou Books, 1981. Reprinted as *Strange Big Moon: The Japan and India Journals 1960–1964*. Berkeley, CA: North Atlantic Books, 2000.

———. *Phenomenological*. New York: Institute of Further Studies, 1989.

———. *Places to Go*. Santa Rosa, CA: Black Sparrow Press, 1970.

———. *The Tapestry and the Web*. San Francisco: Four Seasons Foundation, 1965.

———. *The Wonderful Focus of You*. Calair, VT: Z Press, 1979.

Mailer, Norman. "The White Negro." *Dissent* 4 (1957): 276–93.

McNeil, Helen. "The Archaeology of Gender in the Beat Movement." *The Beat Generation Writers*. Ed. A. Robert Lee. London: Pluto, 1996. 178–99.

Meyerowitz, Joanne, ed. *Not June Cleaver: Women and Gender in Postwar America, 1945–1960*. Philadelphia: Temple UP, 1994.

Moody, Anne. *Coming of Age in Mississippi*. New York: Dell, 1968.

Moore, Steven. "Sheri Martinelli: A Modernist Muse." *Gargoyle* 41 (Summer 1998): 28–54.

Pommy Vega, Janine. *Mad Dogs of Trieste: New and Selected Poems*. Santa Rosa, CA: Black Sparrow Press, 2000.

———. *Journal of a Hermit*. Cherry Valley, NY: Cherry Valley Editions, 1974.

———. *Journal of a Hermit &*. Cherry Valley, NY: Cherry Valley Editions, 1979.

———. *Poems to Fernando*. San Francisco: City Lights, 1968.

————. *Tracking the Serpent: Journeys to Four Continents*. San Francisco: City Lights, 1997.

————, ed. *Voices Under the Harvest Moon: An Anthology of Writing from Eastern Correctional Facility*. New York: Segue Books, 1999.

Peabody, Richard, ed. *A Different Beat: Writings by Women of the Beat Generation*. London: High Risk, 1997.

Perry, Charles. *The Haight-Ashbury: A History*. New York: Vintage, 1985.

Schafer, Benjamin G., ed. *The Herbert Huncke Reader*. New York: Morrow, 1997.

Shulman, Alix Kates. *Burning Questions*. 1978. New York: Thunder's Mouth, 1990.

Vickery, Ann. *Leaving Lines of Gender: A Feminist Genealogy of Language Writing*. Middletown, CT: Wesleyan UP, 2000.

Waldman, Anne. *The Beat Book: Writings from the Beat Generation*. Boulder, CO: Shambhala Press, 1996.

————. *Fast Speaking Woman: Chants and Essays*. 1975. Rev. ed. San Francisco: City Lights, 1996.

————. *Giant Night*. New York: Angel Hair Books, 1968.

————. *Helping the Dreamer: New and Selected Poems 1966–1988*. Minneapolis: Coffee House, 1989.

————. *Iovis: All Is Full of Jove*. 2 vols. Minneapolis: Coffee House, 1993, 1997.

————. *Journals and Dreams: Poems*. New York: Stonehill, 1976.

————. *Kill or Cure*. New York: Penguin, 1994.

————. *Marriage: A Sentence*. New York: Penguin, 2000.

————. "My Life a List." Waldman and Webb. Vol. 2. 293–322.

————. *Vow to Poetry: Essays, Interviews, and Manifestos*. Minneapolis: Coffee House, 2001.

Waldman, Anne, and Andrew Schelling, eds. *Disembodied Poetics: Annals of the Jack Kerouac School*. Albuquerque: U of New Mexico P, 1994.

Waldman, Anne, and Lewis Warsh, eds. *The Angel Hair Anthology*. New York: Granary Books, 2001.

Waldman, Anne, and Marilyn Webb, eds. *Talking Poetics from Naropa Institute*. Vols. 1 and 2 of *Annals of the Jack Kerouac School of Disembodied Poetics*. Boulder, CO: Shambhala Press, 1978 and 1979.

weiss, ruth, writer and dir. *The Brink*. 1961 16mm film. 1986 videocassette. San Francisco, CA.

————. *DESERT JOURNAL*. Boston: Good Gay Poets, 1977.

————. *full circle*. Wien, Aus.: Edition Exil, 2002.

————. *GALLERY OF WOMEN*. San Francisco: Adler Press, 1959.

————. *A NEW VIEW OF MATTER*. Prague, The Czech Republic: Mata Press, 1999.

————. *SINGLE OUT*. Mill Valley, CA: D'Aurora Press, 1978.

Janet Wolff. *Feminine Sentences: Essays on Women and Culture*. Cambridge, UK: Polity, 1990.

Index

289